AN ELEMENTARY
INTRODUCTION TO THE
Wolfram
Language

SECOND EDITION

AN ELEMENTARY INTRODUCTION TO THE
Wolfram Language

STEPHEN WOLFRAM

Wolfram Media, Inc.
wolfram-media.com

ISBN 978-1-944183-05-9 (paperback)
ISBN 978-1-944183-02-8 (ebook)

Library of Congress Cataloging-in-Publication Data

Wolfram, Stephen, author.

An elementary introduction to the Wolfram Language / Stephen Wolfram.

Second edition. | Champaign, IL, USA : Wolfram Media, Inc., [2017] | Includes index.

LCCN 2017005534 (print) | LCCN 2017006971 (ebook) | ISBN 9781944183059 (pbk. : alk. paper) |
    ISBN 9781944183028 (ebook)

LCSH: Wolfram language (Computer program language) | Mathematica (Computer file)

LCC QA76.73.W65 W65 2017 (print) | LCC QA76.73.W65 (ebook) | DDC 510/.285536--dc23

LC record available at http://lccn.loc.gov/2017005534

Trademarks: Wolfram, Wolfram Language, Wolfram|Alpha, Wolfram Cloud, Wolfram Programming Lab,
Mathematica, Wolfram Workbench, Wolfram Knowledgebase, Wolfram Notebook, Wolfram Community,
Wolfram Data Drop, Wolfram Demonstrations Project, Wolfram Challenges and Tweet-a-Program.

This book was written and produced using Wolfram Desktop and the Wolfram Language.

Printed by Friesens, Manitoba, Canada. ∞ Acid-free paper.
Second edition. First printing.

Table of Contents

Preface

I've been explaining what's now the Wolfram Language to people for more than 30 years, and I finally decided it was time to take what I'd learned and write a minimal introduction that people could read on their own. This book is the result of that effort.

When we first launched Mathematica—the precursor of the Wolfram Language— in 1988, I published a book that provided both a tutorial introduction and reference guide to the system. The book was very popular and I think contributed substantially to the early success of Mathematica. Over the next decade or so, *The Mathematica Book*, as it came to be known, went through five editions, and steadily grew until it was nearly 1500 pages long.

My goal in *The Mathematica Book* was to systematically cover all aspects of the system. But when we released a huge new version in 2007, it became clear that this was simply no longer possible in a single book. Our online documentation had mean- while steadily grown, and in 2007, with the introduction of a vast number of new examples, it reached the point where a printed version would have been well over 10,000 pages in length.

In 2009 Wolfram|Alpha arrived, with its natural language interface specifically built for use without explanation or documentation. But then, emerging from Mathematica and Wolfram|Alpha, came the Wolfram Language, and there was once again a need for both explanation and documentation.

I believe that the online documentation for the Wolfram Language—which in printed form would exceed 50,000 pages—does very well at explaining the specifics of how to use all the many capabilities of the system. But particularly for newcomers there's also a need to understand the principles of the language—that I've worked so hard over the years to keep coherent and consistent.

The Wolfram Language is unique among programming languages, and different in many ways. But some time ago, I wrote a Fast Introduction for Programmers (wolfr.am/fifp) that in about 30 pages gives modern programmers at least a basic grounding in the principles of the Wolfram Language.

But what about people who don't already know programming? The Wolfram Language provides a unique opportunity not only to introduce anyone to programming, but to get them quickly to the very frontiers of what can be done with computation today.

That this is possible is a consequence of all the effort we've put into creating the technology of the Wolfram Language over the course of nearly three decades. My goal has been to build a language where anyone can specify as simply as possible what they want to do, then inside, all the details are automatically taken care of to get it done.

For the quick question-answering of Wolfram|Alpha, it's enough just to say in plain English what you want. But if you're going to do more systematic tasks, you need a way to explain them precisely. And that's what the Wolfram Language is for.

So how should people learn the Wolfram Language? One approach is immersion: Be in an environment where the Wolfram Language is used. Explore programs that run, and learn from them as examples. In my observation, this can work very well so long as there is at least occasionally someone around to explain principles and help with issues when they come up.

But what about learning the Wolfram Language entirely on one's own? Here I think what's needed is a systematic introduction that progressively builds from one concept to another, answering every obvious question as it goes. And that's what I'm trying to do in this book.

Learning the Wolfram Language is a bit like learning a human language. There's a mixture of vocabulary and principles, that have to be learned hand in hand. The Wolfram Language is immensely more systematic than human languages—with nothing like irregular verbs to memorize—but still has the same kind of progression towards fluency that comes with more and more practice.

I wondered how to write this book. And eventually I decided to base it loosely on Latin textbooks, of the kind I used when I was a kid. Unlike living languages, Latin cannot be learned by immersion, and so there is no choice but to build step by step, as I do in this book.

In some ways learning programming is a bit like learning mathematics. Both have a certain precision: things are either right or wrong. But with the Wolfram Language, programming is much more concrete: at every step you can see what is happening, and whether what you're doing is right. There are no hidden concepts that have to be explained abstractly from outside and cannot explicitly be seen.

Still, there've been two millennia of development in the teaching of mathematics, that have progressively optimized the sequence of presenting arithmetic, algebra and so on. The problem of teaching the Wolfram Language is something completely new, where everything has to be figured out from scratch. Existing programming education isn't much help, because so much of it is about just the kinds of lower-level structure that have been automated away in the Wolfram Language.

I view this book as an experiment: an attempt to provide a particular path through learning the Wolfram Language. I am not trying to cover everything in the language, not least because that would take at least 50,000 pages. Instead, I am trying to explain the principles of the language through a limited number of specific examples.

I've chosen the examples to be interesting and useful in practice. But the bigger point is that through the examples, I cover most of the core principles of the language. And knowing these principles, you'll be ready to go to specific documentation to understand any particular aspect of what the language can do.

Needless to say, the Wolfram Language has many sophisticated capabilities. Some of them—like identifying objects in images—are sophisticated on the inside, but easy to explain. But others—like computing Gröbner bases—are also sophisticated to explain, and may require significant outside knowledge of mathematics or computer science.

My goal is to make this book completely self-contained, and to assume nothing beyond everyday common knowledge. I have avoided any explicit use of mathematics beyond basic arithmetic, though those who know advanced mathematics may notice many connections between concepts of mathematics and concepts in the book.

This is certainly not the only elementary introduction to the Wolfram Language that could be written, and I hope there will be many more. It follows a specific—and in many ways arbitrary—path through the vast capabilities of the language, highlighting certain features but not even mentioning many other equally deserving ones.

Still, I hope that the power and beauty of the language that I have nurtured for more than half my life will shine through, and that many students and other people, with many diverse backgrounds, can use this book to get started with the Wolfram Language and get involved with the kind of computational thinking that is quickly becoming a defining feature of our times.

Stephen Wolfram

What Is the Wolfram Language?

The Wolfram Language is a *computer language*. It gives you a way to communicate with computers, in particular so you can tell them what to do.

There are many computer languages, such as C++, Java, Python and JavaScript. The Wolfram Language is unique in that it's *knowledge based*. That means that it already knows a lot—so you have to tell it much less to get it to do things you want.

In this book, you'll see how to use the Wolfram Language to do a great many things. You'll learn how to think computationally about what you want to do, and how to communicate it to a computer using the Wolfram Language.

Why can't you just say what you want using plain English? That's what you do in Wolfram|Alpha. And it works very well for asking short questions. But if you want to do something more complex, it quickly becomes impractical to describe everything just in plain English. And that's where the Wolfram Language comes in.

It's designed to make it as easy as possible to describe what you want, making use of huge amounts of knowledge that are built into the language. And the crucial thing is that when you use the Wolfram Language to ask for something, the computer immediately knows what you mean, and then can actually do what you want.

I view the Wolfram Language as an optimized tool for turning ideas into reality. You start with an idea of something you want to do. You formulate the idea in computational terms, then you express it in the Wolfram Language. Then it's up to the Wolfram Language to do it as automatically as possible.

You can make things that are visual, textual, interactive or whatever. You can do analyses or figure things out. You can create apps and programs and websites. You can take a very wide variety of ideas and implement them—on your computer, on the web, on a phone, on tiny embedded devices and more.

I started building what's now the Wolfram Language more than 30 years ago. Along the way, particularly in the form of Mathematica, the Wolfram Language has been extremely widely used in the world's research organizations and universities— and a remarkable range of inventions and discoveries have been made with it.

Today the Wolfram Language has emerged as something else: a new kind of general computer language, which redefines what's practical to do with computers. Among the early users of today's Wolfram Language are many of the world's leading innovators and technology organizations. And there are large and important systems—like Wolfram|Alpha—that are written in the Wolfram Language.

But the very knowledge and automation that makes the Wolfram Language so powerful also makes it accessible to anyone. You don't have to know about the workings of computers, or about technical or mathematical ideas; that's the job of the Wolfram Language. All you need to do is to know the Wolfram Language, so you can tell your computer what you want.

As you work through this book, you'll learn the principles of the Wolfram Language. You'll learn how to use the Wolfram Language to write programs, and you'll see some of the computational thinking it's based on. But most of all, you'll learn a set of powerful skills for turning your ideas into reality. Nobody knows yet all the things that the Wolfram Language will make possible. It's going to be exciting to see—and what you learn in this book will let you become a part of that future.

Practicalities of Using the Wolfram Language

The best way to learn the Wolfram Language is to use it. Wolfram Programming Lab is specifically set up for easy access in learning the language, though you can also use other interactive Wolfram Language environments.

In any of these environments, you enter input in the Wolfram Language, and the system immediately computes output from it. You can do this on desktop, web or mobile. On desktop and web, you typically type shift return to say you've finished your input; on mobile you typically press a ❀ button. Your sequence of inputs and outputs—together with any text you may add—all exists in a Wolfram Notebook.

In[1]:= **2 + 2** shift return ⟵—— Input

Out[1]= **4** ⟵—— Output

Within the Wolfram Notebook you'll see a variety of aids to help you enter Wolfram Language input.

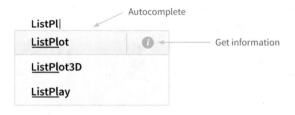

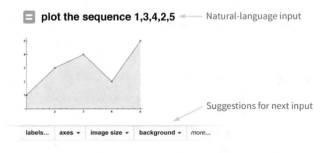

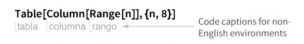

Wolfram Notebooks, with their interactive sequences of inputs and outputs, are an ideal way to learn, explore and write programs in the Wolfram Language. But the Wolfram Language can also operate without its own interactive interface, in a whole variety of software-engineering configurations. Inside, though, the language is still doing the same computations as in the interactive configuration we discuss in this book.

Q&A

Do I need to know programming to read this book?

Absolutely not. This book is a self-contained introduction to programming.

What age group is this book suitable for?

Experience suggests that anything above about age 11 is appropriate. I've tried to choose examples that will be relevant and engaging to all age groups, very much including adults.

How much math do I need to know to read this book?

Nothing beyond basic arithmetic. This is a book about programming in the Wolfram Language, not about math.

Do I need to use a computer while reading this book?

You could read it without one, but it will be much better to try things out interactively with a Wolfram Language session, for example in Wolfram Programming Lab.

Where can I run the Wolfram Language?

It runs natively on desktop computers: Mac, Windows, Linux (including Raspberry Pi). It also runs in the cloud through a web browser, and on mobile devices.

Do I have to read this book sequentially?

It will be a lot better that way. I've constructed the book so it progressively builds up a broader and broader base of concepts. If you jump around, you'll probably need to backtrack a lot.

Why are the topics in this book so different from other programming books?

Because the Wolfram Language is a different and higher-level kind of language, that automates away many of the details that programming books about other languages concentrate on.

Is the Wolfram Language an educational language?

It's certainly used for education (and Mathematica is ubiquitous at universities). But it's also very widely used in industry. It's good for education because it's powerful and easy to learn.

Will learning the Wolfram Language help in learning other languages?

Definitely. Knowing the Wolfram Language you'll understand higher-level concepts, which you'll then see played out in lower-level ways in other languages.

The Wolfram Language seems too easy; is it really programming?

Definitely. And because it automates away the drudgery you might associate with programming, you'll be able to go much further, and understand much more.

Can this book be used for a course?

Absolutely! Check out the book website (wolfr.am/eiwl) for supplementary material.

Can sections of the book be omitted for a course?

The book is written to provide a sequential presentation of material, so the content may require some patching if sections in the middle are dropped.

What version of the Wolfram Language does this book assume I will use?

Anything 11.1 and above. Note that even some fairly simple examples (e.g. Table[x, 5]) won't work in versions earlier than 10.3. If you're running the Wolfram Language in the Wolfram Cloud you'll always be using the latest version, but if you're running on a desktop system you may explicitly have to upgrade.

Is the code in the book "production grade"?

Usually, yes. Occasionally there is code that is slightly more complicated than it needs to be, because the concepts necessary to make it simpler haven't been introduced by that point in the book.

Other Resources

This Book Online

Complete text, with full runnable examples and automatically graded exercises
wolfr.am/eiwl

Wolfram Language Home Page

Broad collection of resources about the Wolfram Language
wolfram.com/language

Wolfram Documentation Center

Documentation on all functions in the Wolfram Language, with extensive examples
reference.wolfram.com/language

Wolfram Programming Lab

Online and desktop access to the Wolfram Language, with educational Explorations
wolfram.com/programming-lab

Wolfram U

Extensive online course material, including a free course based on this book
wolfram-u.com

Fast Introduction for Programmers

Short Wolfram Language tutorial for people with programming experience
wolfram.com/language/fast-introduction-for-programmers

Wolfram Challenges

Dynamic collection of online Wolfram Language programming challenges
challenges.wolfram.com

Wolfram Tweet-a-Program

Many examples of Wolfram Language programs less than 140 characters long
wolfram.com/language/tweet-a-program

Wolfram Demonstrations Project

11,000+ interactive Demonstrations written in the Wolfram Language
demonstrations.wolfram.com

Wolfram Community

Online community for learning and discussing Wolfram technology
community.wolfram.com

Wolfram Home Page

The home page of Wolfram Research, the company behind the Wolfram Language
wolfram.com

Stephen Wolfram's Page

The home page for the author of this book
stephenwolfram.com

1 | Starting Out: Elementary Arithmetic

As a first example of how the Wolfram Language operates, let's look at elementary arithmetic.

Add numbers:

In[1]:= **2 + 2**

Out[1]= 4

In[2]:= **1234 + 5678**

Out[2]= 6912

Multiply numbers:

In[3]:= **1234 ∗ 5678**

Out[3]= 7 006 652

Vocabulary

2 + 2	addition
5 − 2	subtraction
2 ∗ 3	multiplication (2 3 also works)
6 / 2	division
3 ^ 2	raising to a power (e.g. squaring)

Exercises

1.1   Compute 1+2+3.

1.2   Add the numbers 1, 2, 3, 4, 5.

1.3   Multiply the numbers 1, 2, 3, 4, 5.

1.4   Compute 5 squared (i.e. 5×5 or 5 raised to the power 2).

1.5   Compute 3 raised to the fourth power.

1.6   Compute 10 raised to the power 12 (a trillion).

1.7   Compute 3 raised to the power 7×8.

1.8   Add parentheses to 4 − 2 ∗ 3 + 4 to make 14.

1.9   Compute twenty-nine thousand multiplied by seventy-three.

Q&A

In 2+2, etc. how do I tell the Wolfram Language that I've finished my input?

On a computer, press shift   return . On a mobile device, press the ✳ button. See Practicalities of Using the Wolfram Language for more details.

Why is multiplication indicated by *?

Because the * ("star", typically typed as shift   8) looks like a multiplication sign. In the Wolfram Language, you can also just put a space between numbers you want to multiply; the Wolfram Language will then automatically insert a × multiplication sign.

What does "raised to the power" (^) mean?

6^3 means 6×6×6 (i.e. 6 multiplied by itself 3 times); 10^5 means 10×10×10×10×10; etc.

How big can numbers get in the Wolfram Language?

As big as you want—so long as they fit in your computer's memory.

What is the order of operations in the Wolfram Language?

The same as in ordinary math: powers, multiplication, addition. So 4*5^2+7 means (4*(5^2))+7. You can use parentheses just like in math. (In math, people sometimes use […] as well as (…). In the Wolfram Language […] means something different.)

When I do division, how do I avoid getting fractions in my answer?

If you put in numbers with decimal points, you'll get out numbers with decimal points. You can also use N, as we discuss in Section 23.

What are the little spaces between digits in results like 7 006 652?

They're there to help you read the number when it's displayed; they're not part of the number.

How do I enter a big number?

Just type the digits, without putting any commas, spaces or other separators (e.g. 1234123511415223).

What happens if I compute 1/0?

Try it! You'll get a symbolic representation of infinity, on which the Wolfram Language can then do further computations.

More to Explore

Getting Started in Wolfram Programming Lab (wolfr.am/eiwl-1-more)

2 | Introducing Functions

When you type 2 + 2, the Wolfram Language understands it as Plus[2, 2]. Plus is a *function*. There are more than 5000 functions built into the Wolfram Language. Arithmetic uses just a very few of these.

Compute 3+4 using the function Plus:

In[1]:= **Plus[3, 4]**

Out[1]= 7

Compute 1+2+3 using Plus:

In[2]:= **Plus[1, 2, 3]**

Out[2]= 6

The function Times does multiplication:

In[3]:= **Times[2, 3]**

Out[3]= 6

You can put functions inside other functions:

In[4]:= **Times[2, Plus[2, 3]]**

Out[4]= 10

All functions in the Wolfram Language use square brackets, and have names that start with capital letters.

The function Max finds the maximum, or largest, of a collection of numbers.

The maximum of these numbers is 7:

In[5]:= **Max[2, 7, 3]**

Out[5]= 7

The function RandomInteger picks a random integer (whole number) between 0 and whatever size you say.

Pick a random whole number between 0 and 100:

In[6]:= **RandomInteger[100]**

Out[6]= 71

Each time you ask, you get another random number:

In[7]:= **RandomInteger[100]**

Out[7]= 1

Vocabulary

Plus[2, 2]	$2 + 2$	addition
Subtract[5, 2]	$5 - 2$	subtraction
Times[2, 3]	$2 * 3$	multiplication (2 3 also works)
Divide[6, 2]	$6 / 2$	division
Power[3, 2]	$3 \wedge 2$	raising to a power
Max[3, 4]		maximum (largest)
Min[3, 4]		minimum (smallest)
RandomInteger[10]		random whole number

Exercises

2.1   Compute 7+6+5 using the function **Plus**.

2.2   Compute 2×(3+4) using **Times** and **Plus**.

2.3   Use **Max** to find the larger of 6×8 and 5×9.

2.4   Use **RandomInteger** to generate a random number between 0 and 1000.

2.5   Use **Plus** and **RandomInteger** to generate a number between 10 and 20.

Q&A

Do I have to type the capital letters in Plus, RandomInteger, etc.?

Yes. In the Wolfram Language, plus is not the same as Plus. The capital letter in Plus signifies that you're talking about the built-in ("official") plus function.

Do I have to type square brackets [...] when I use functions?

Yes. Square brackets [...] are for functions; parentheses (...) are for grouping, as in 2*(3+4), not for functions.

How does one read Plus[2, 3] out loud?

Usually "plus of 2 and 3"; sometimes "plus of 2 comma 3". "[" can be read as "open bracket"; "]" as "close bracket".

Why use Plus[2, 3] instead of 2 + 3?

For Plus, it's not necessary. But for the vast majority of functions—like Max or RandomInteger—there's no special form like +, so you have to give their names.

Can I mix Plus[...] and +?

Yes. Things like Plus[4 + 5, 2 + 3] or, for that matter, Plus[4, 5] * 5 are just fine.

What does it mean if the Wolfram Language colors some of my input red?

It means you've typed something that the Wolfram Language can't understand. See Section 47 for more information. Start by checking that your open and close brackets are matched.

Tech Notes

- *Expressions* in the Wolfram Language (see **Section 33**) consist of nested trees of functions.

- **Plus** can add any number of numbers, but **Subtract** only subtracts one number from another (to avoid ambiguities between (2−3)−4 and 2−(3−4)).

- The notion of a function is considerably more general in the Wolfram Language than in either traditional mathematics or computer science. For example, $f[\mathit{anything}]$ is considered a function, whether it evaluates to something definite or remains in symbolic form.

More to Explore

Mathematical Functions in the Wolfram Language (wolfr.am/eiwl-2-more)

3 | First Look at Lists

Lists are a basic way to collect things together in the Wolfram Language. {1, 2, 3} is a list of numbers. On their own, lists don't *do* anything; they're just a way to store things. So if you give a list as input, it'll just come back unchanged:

In[1]:= **{1, 2, 3, 4, a, b, c}**

Out[1]= {1, 2, 3, 4, a, b, c}

ListPlot is a function that makes a plot of a list of numbers.

Plot the list of numbers {1, 1, 2, 2, 3, 4, 4}:

In[2]:= **ListPlot[{1, 1, 2, 2, 3, 4, 4}]**

Plot the list of numbers {10, 9, 8, 7, 3, 2, 1}:

In[3]:= **ListPlot[{10, 9, 8, 7, 3, 2, 1}]**

Range is a function that makes a list of numbers.

Generate a list of numbers up to 10:

In[4]:= **Range[10]**

Out[4]= {1, 2, 3, 4, 5, 6, 7, 8, 9, 10}

Generate a list of numbers, then plot it:

In[5]:= **ListPlot[Range[20]]**

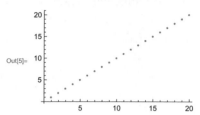

Out[5]=

Reverse reverses the elements in a list.

Reverse the elements in a list:

In[6]:= **Reverse[{1, 2, 3, 4}]**

Out[6]= {4, 3, 2, 1}

Reverse what **Range** has generated:

In[7]:= **Reverse[Range[10]]**

Out[7]= {10, 9, 8, 7, 6, 5, 4, 3, 2, 1}

Plot the reversed list:

In[8]:= **ListPlot[Reverse[Range[10]]]**

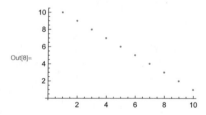

Out[8]=

Join joins lists together, making a single list as the result.

Join lists together:

In[9]:= **Join[{1, 2, 3}, {4, 5}, {6, 7}]**

Out[9]= {1, 2, 3, 4, 5, 6, 7}

In[10]:= **Join[{1, 2, 3}, {1, 2, 3, 4, 5}]**

Out[10]= {1, 2, 3, 1, 2, 3, 4, 5}

Join two lists made by Range:

In[11]:= **Join[Range[3], Range[5]]**

Out[11]= {1, 2, 3, 1, 2, 3, 4, 5}

Plot three lists joined together:

In[12]:= **ListPlot[Join[Range[20], Range[20], Range[30]]]**

Out[12]=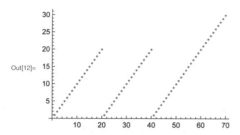

Reverse the list in the middle:

In[13]:= **ListPlot[Join[Range[20], Reverse[Range[20]], Range[30]]]**

Out[13]=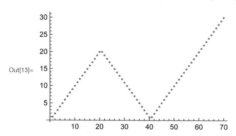

Vocabulary

{1, 2, 3, 4}	list of elements
ListPlot[{1, 2, 3, 4}]	plot a list of numbers
Range[10]	range of numbers
Reverse[{1, 2, 3}]	reverse a list
Join[{4, 5, 6}, {2, 3, 2}]	join lists together

Exercises

3.1   Use **Range** to create the list {1, 2, 3, 4}.

3.2   Make a list of numbers up to 100.

3.3   Use **Range** and **Reverse** to create {4, 3, 2, 1}.

3.4   Make a list of numbers from 1 to 50 in reverse order.

3.5   Use **Range**, **Reverse** and **Join** to create {1, 2, 3, 4, 4, 3, 2, 1}.

3.6   Construct and plot the list 1, 2, 3, 4, ... , 99, 100, 99, 98, ... , 3, 2, 1.

3.7   Use **Range** and **RandomInteger** to make a list with a random length up to 10.

3.8 Find a simpler form for Reverse[Reverse[Range[10]]].

3.9 Find a simpler form for Join[{1, 2}, Join[{3, 4}, {5}]].

3.10 Find a simpler form for Join[Range[10], Join[Range[10], Range[5]]].

3.11 Find a simpler form for Reverse[Join[Range[20], Reverse[Range[20]]]].

Q&A

How does one read {1, 2, 3} out loud?

Usually "list 1 2 3". "{" and "}" are called "braces" or "curly brackets". "{" is "open brace" and "}" is "close brace".

Is a list a function?

Yes. {1, 2, 3} is List[1, 2, 3]. But unlike, say, Plus, the function List doesn't actually compute anything; it just comes back unchanged.

What is ListPlot plotting?

The values of successive list elements. The *x* value of each point gives the position in the list; the *y* value gives the value of that element.

How long can lists be?

As long as you want, until your computer runs out of memory.

Tech Notes

- Range[*m*, *n*] generates numbers from *m* to *n*. Range[*m*, *n*, *s*] generates numbers from *m* to *n* in steps of *s*.

- Many computer languages have constructs like lists (often called "arrays"). But usually they only allow lists of explicit things, like numbers; you can't have a list like {a, b, c} where you haven't said what a, b and c are. You can in the Wolfram Language, though, because the Wolfram Language is *symbolic*.

- {a, b, c} is a list of elements in a definite order; {b, c, a} is a different list.

- Like in math, you can make theorems about Wolfram Language functions. For example, Reverse[Reverse[x]] is equal to x.

More to Explore

Guide to Lists in the Wolfram Language (wolfr.am/eiwl-3-more)

4 | Displaying Lists

ListPlot is one way to display, or *visualize*, a list of numbers. There are lots of others. Different ones tend to emphasize different features of a list.

ListLinePlot plots a list, joining up values:

In[1]:= **ListLinePlot[{1, 3, 5, 4, 1, 2, 1, 4}]**

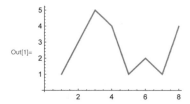

When values jump around, it's usually harder to understand if you don't join them up:

In[2]:= **ListPlot[{1, 3, 5, 4, 1, 2, 1, 4}]**

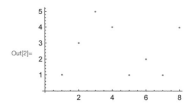

Making a bar chart can be useful too:

In[3]:= **BarChart[{1, 3, 5, 4, 1, 2, 1, 4}]**

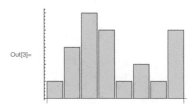

So long as the list isn't too long, a pie chart can be useful:

In[4]:= **PieChart[{1, 3, 5, 4}]**

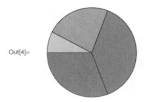

If you just want to know which numbers appear, you can plot them on a number line:

In[5]:= **NumberLinePlot[{1, 7, 11, 25}]**

Out[5]=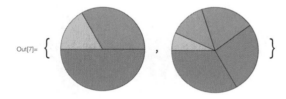

Sometimes you don't want a plot at all; you just want to put the elements of a list in a column:

In[6]:= **Column[{100, 350, 502, 400}]**

Out[6]=
100
350
502
400

Lists can contain anything, including graphics. So you can combine plots by putting them in lists.

Make a list of two pie charts:

In[7]:= **{PieChart[Range[3]], PieChart[Range[5]]}**

Out[7]=
{ 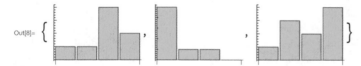 }

Show three bar charts together:

In[8]:= **{BarChart[{1, 1, 4, 2}], BarChart[{5, 1, 1, 0}], BarChart[{1, 3, 2, 4}]}**

Out[8]=
{ , , }

Vocabulary

ListLinePlot[{1, 2, 5}]	values joined by a line
BarChart[{1, 2, 5}]	bar chart (values give bar heights)
PieChart[{1, 2, 5}]	pie chart (values give wedge sizes)
NumberLinePlot[{1, 2, 5}]	numbers arranged on a line
Column[{1, 2, 5}]	elements displayed in a column

Exercises

4.1   Make a bar chart of {1, 1, 2, 3, 5}.

4.2   Make a pie chart of numbers from 1 to 10.

4.3   Make a bar chart of numbers counting down from 20 to 1.

4.4   Display numbers from 1 to 5 in a column.

4.5   Make a number line plot of the squares {1, 4, 9, 16, 25}.

4.6   Make a pie chart with 10 identical segments, each of size 1.

4.7   Make a column of pie charts with 1, 2 and 3 identical segments.

Q&A

How do pie charts work in the Wolfram Language?

As in any pie chart, the wedges have relative sizes determined by the relative sizes of numbers in the list. In the Wolfram Language, the wedge for the first number starts at the 9 o'clock position, and then subsequent wedges read clockwise. The colors of the wedges are chosen in a definite sequence.

How is the vertical scale determined on plots?

It's set up to automatically include all points except distant outliers. Later on (**Section 20**), we'll talk about the PlotRange option, which lets you specify the exact range of the plot.

Tech Note

- Particularly if you're familiar with other computer languages, you may be surprised that a list of plots, for example, can appear as the output of a computation. This is made possible by the crucial fact that the Wolfram Language is *symbolic*. By the way, plots can appear in input as well.

More to Explore

Data Visualization in the Wolfram Language (wolfr.am/eiwl-4-more)

Charting and Information Visualization in the Wolfram Language (wolfr.am/eiwl-4-more2)

5 | Operations on Lists

There are thousands of functions in the Wolfram Language that work with lists.

You can do arithmetic with lists:

In[1]:= **{1, 2, 3} + 10**

Out[1]= {11, 12, 13}

In[2]:= **{1, 1, 2} * {1, 2, 3}**

Out[2]= {1, 2, 6}

Compute the first 10 squares:

In[3]:= **Range[10] ^ 2**

Out[3]= {1, 4, 9, 16, 25, 36, 49, 64, 81, 100}

Plot the first 20 squares:

In[4]:= **ListPlot[Range[20] ^ 2]**

Out[4]=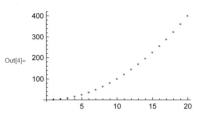

Sort sorts a list into order:

In[5]:= **Sort[{4, 2, 1, 3, 6}]**

Out[5]= {1, 2, 3, 4, 6}

Length finds how long a list is:

In[6]:= **Length[{5, 3, 4, 5, 3, 4, 5}]**

Out[6]= 7

Total gives the total from adding up a list:

In[7]:= **Total[{1, 1, 2, 2}]**

Out[7]= 6

Find the total of the numbers from 1 to 10:

In[8]:= **Total[Range[10]]**

Out[8]= 55

Count counts the number of times something appears in a list.

Count the number of times a appears in the list:

In[9]:= **Count[{a, b, a, a, c, b, a}, a]**

Out[9]= 4

It's often useful to be able to get individual elements of a list. First gives the first element; Last gives the last element. Part gives the element at a particular position.

Pick out the first element of a list:

In[10]:= **First[{7, 6, 5}]**

Out[10]= 7

Pick out the last element:

In[11]:= **Last[{7, 6, 5}]**

Out[11]= 5

Pick out element number 2:

In[12]:= **Part[{7, 6, 5}, 2]**

Out[12]= 6

Picking out the first element in a list you've sorted is the same as finding the minimum element:

In[13]:= **First[Sort[{6, 7, 1, 2, 4, 5}]]**

Out[13]= 1

In[14]:= **Min[{6, 7, 1, 2, 4, 5}]**

Out[14]= 1

If you have a number, like 5671, you can make a list of its digits using IntegerDigits[5671].

Break a number into a list of digits:

In[15]:= **IntegerDigits[1988]**

Out[15]= {1, 9, 8, 8}

Find the last digit:

In[16]:= **Last[IntegerDigits[1988]]**

Out[16]= 8

Take lets you take a specified number of elements from the beginning of a list.

Take the first 3 elements from a list:

In[17]:= **Take[{101, 203, 401, 602, 332, 412}, 3]**

Out[17]= {101, 203, 401}

Take the first 10 digits of 2 to the power 100:

In[18]:= **Take[IntegerDigits[2 ^ 100], 10]**

Out[18]= {1, 2, 6, 7, 6, 5, 0, 6, 0, 0}

Drop drops elements from the beginning of a list.

In[19]:= **Drop[{101, 203, 401, 602, 332, 412}, 3]**

Out[19]= {602, 332, 412}

Vocabulary

{2, 3, 4} + {5, 6, 2}	arithmetic on lists
Sort[{5, 7, 1}]	sort a list into order
Length[{3, 3}]	length of a list (number of elements)
Total[{1, 1, 2}]	total of all elements in a list
Count[{3, 2, 3}, 3]	count occurrences of an element
First[{2, 3}]	first element in a list
Last[{6, 7, 8}]	last element in a list
Part[{3, 1, 4}, 2]	particular part of a list, also written as {3, 1, 4}[[2]]
Take[{6, 4, 3, 1}, 2]	take elements from the beginning of a list
Drop[{6, 4, 3, 1}, 2]	drop elements from the beginning of a list
IntegerDigits[1234]	list of digits in a number

Exercises

5.1   Make a list of the first 10 squares, in reverse order.

5.2   Find the total of the first 10 squares.

5.3   Make a plot of the first 10 squares, starting at 1.

5.4   Use Sort, Join and Range to create {1, 1, 2, 2, 3, 3, 4, 4}.

5.5   Use Range and + to make a list of numbers from 10 to 20, inclusive.

5.6   Make a combined list of the first 5 squares and cubes (numbers raised to the power 3), sorted into order.

5.7   Find the number of digits in 2^128.

5.8   Find the first digit of 2^32.

5.9   Find the first 10 digits in 2^100.

5.10   Find the largest digit that appears in 2^20.

5.11   Find how many zeros appear in the digits of 2^1000.

5.12   Use Part, Sort and IntegerDigits to find the second-smallest digit in 2^20.

5.13   Make a line plot of the sequence of digits that appear in 2^128.

5.14   Use Take and Drop to get the sequence 11 through 20 from Range[100].

Q&A

Can one add lists of different lengths?

No. {1, 2} + {1, 2, 3} won't work. {1, 2, 0} + {1, 2, 3} would be fine, if that's what you mean.

Can there be a list with nothing in it?

Yes. {} is a list of length 0, with no elements. It's usually called the *null list* or the *empty list*.

Tech Notes

- IntegerDigits[5671] gives digits in base 10. IntegerDigits[5671, 2] gives digits in base 2. You can use any base you want. FromDigits[{5, 6, 7, 1}] reconstructs a number from its list of digits.

- Rest[*list*] gives all the elements of *list* after the first one. Most[*list*] gives all elements other than the last one.

More to Explore

Guide to List Manipulation in the Wolfram Language (wolfr.am/eiwl-5-more)

6 | Making Tables

We've seen a few ways to make lists in the Wolfram Language. You can just type them in. You can use Range. And you can use functions like IntegerDigits. One of the most common and flexible ways to make lists is with the function Table.

In its very simplest form, Table makes a list with a single element repeated some specified number of times.

Make a list that consists of 5 repeated 10 times:

In[1]:= **Table[5, 10]**

Out[1]= {5, 5, 5, 5, 5, 5, 5, 5, 5, 5}

This makes a list with x repeated 10 times:

In[2]:= **Table[x, 10]**

Out[2]= {x, x, x, x, x, x, x, x, x, x}

You can repeat lists too:

In[3]:= **Table[{1, 2}, 10]**

Out[3]= {{1, 2}, {1, 2}, {1, 2}, {1, 2}, {1, 2}, {1, 2}, {1, 2}, {1, 2}, {1, 2}, {1, 2}}

Or, actually, anything; here's a list of 3 identical pie charts:

In[4]:= **Table[PieChart[{1, 1, 1}], 3]**

Out[4]=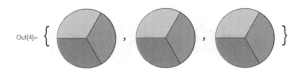

But what if we want to make a table where the elements aren't identical? We can do that by introducing a *variable*, and then *iterating* over that variable.

Iterate over n to make a list where n goes up to 5:

In[5]:= **Table[a[n], {n, 5}]**

Out[5]= {a[1], a[2], a[3], a[4], a[5]}

Here's how this works. To make the first element of the list, n is taken to be 1, so a[n] is a[1]. To make the second element, n is taken to be 2, so a[n] is a[2], and so on. n is called a variable because it's varying as we make the different elements of the list.

Make a table that gives the value of n + 1 when n goes from 1 to 10:

In[6]:= **Table[n + 1, {n, 10}]**

Out[6]= {2, 3, 4, 5, 6, 7, 8, 9, 10, 11}

Make a table of the first 10 squares:

In[7]:= **Table[n^2, {n, 10}]**

Out[7]= {1, 4, 9, 16, 25, 36, 49, 64, 81, 100}

With Table, you can make tables of anything.

Here's a table of successively longer lists produced by Range:

In[8]:= **Table[Range[n], {n, 5}]**

Out[8]= {{1}, {1, 2}, {1, 2, 3}, {1, 2, 3, 4}, {1, 2, 3, 4, 5}}

Here each of the lists produced is shown as a column:

In[9]:= **Table[Column[Range[n]], {n, 8}]**

Out[9]= $\left\{1, \begin{matrix}1\\2\end{matrix}, \begin{matrix}1\\2\\3\end{matrix}, \begin{matrix}1\\2\\3\\4\end{matrix}, \begin{matrix}1\\2\\3\\4\\5\end{matrix}, \begin{matrix}1\\2\\3\\4\\5\\6\end{matrix}, \begin{matrix}1\\2\\3\\4\\5\\6\\7\end{matrix}, \begin{matrix}1\\2\\3\\4\\5\\6\\7\\8\end{matrix}\right\}$

Here's a table of plots of successively longer lists of values:

In[10]:= **Table[ListPlot[Range[10*n]], {n, 3}]**

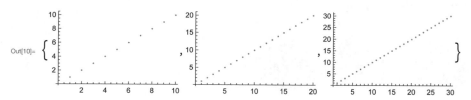

Here are pie charts with successively more segments:

In[11]:= **Table[PieChart[Table[1, n]], {n, 5}]**

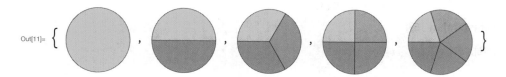

So far we've always used n as our variable. That's a pretty common choice. But we can actually use any (lowercase) letter we want, or any combination of letters. All that matters is that wherever the variable appears, its name is the same.

expt is a perfectly good variable name:

In[12]:= **Table[2 ^ expt, {expt, 10}]**

Out[12]= {2, 4, 8, 16, 32, 64, 128, 256, 512, 1024}

Here we're using x as the variable name, and it happens to appear several times:

In[13]:= **Table[{x, x + 1, x ^ 2}, {x, 5}]**

Out[13]= {{1, 2, 1}, {2, 3, 4}, {3, 4, 9}, {4, 5, 16}, {5, 6, 25}}

In Table[f[n], {n, 5}], n takes on values $1, 2, 3, 4, 5$. Table[f[n], {n, 3, 5}] says to start at 3 instead: $3, 4, 5$.

This generates a table with n going from 1 to 10:

In[14]:= **Table[f[n], {n, 10}]**

Out[14]= {f[1], f[2], f[3], f[4], f[5], f[6], f[7], f[8], f[9], f[10]}

This generates a table with n going from 4 to 10:

In[15]:= **Table[f[n], {n, 4, 10}]**

Out[15]= {f[4], f[5], f[6], f[7], f[8], f[9], f[10]}

This makes n go from 4 to 10 in steps of 2:

In[16]:= **Table[f[n], {n, 4, 10, 2}]**

Out[16]= {f[4], f[6], f[8], f[10]}

The Wolfram Language emphasizes consistency, so for example Range is set up to deal with starting points and steps just like Table.

Generate the range of numbers 4 to 10:

In[17]:= **Range[4, 10]**

Out[17]= {4, 5, 6, 7, 8, 9, 10}

Generate the range of numbers 4 to 10 going in steps of 2:

In[18]:= **Range[4, 10, 2]**

Out[18]= {4, 6, 8, 10}

Go from 0 to 1 in steps of 0.1:

In[19]:= **Range[0, 1, 0.1]**

Out[19]= {0., 0.1, 0.2, 0.3, 0.4, 0.5, 0.6, 0.7, 0.8, 0.9, 1.}

There are usually many ways to do the same thing in the Wolfram Language. For example, here's how Table and Range can produce identical plots.

Generate a table and plot it:

In[20]:= **ListPlot[Table[x − x^2, {x, 0, 1, .02}]]**

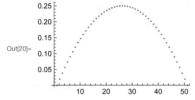

Out[20]=

Get the same result by doing arithmetic with the range of values:

In[21]:= **ListPlot[Range[0, 1, .02] − Range[0, 1, .02]^2]**

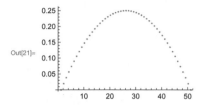

Out[21]=

Table always separately computes each entry in the list it generates—and you can see this if you use RandomInteger in Table.

This generates 20 independent random integers with size up to 10:

In[22]:= **Table[RandomInteger[10], 20]**

Out[22]= {3, 1, 4, 3, 6, 7, 6, 10, 9, 2, 1, 4, 5, 8, 3, 8, 3, 8, 3, 0}

RandomInteger can actually also generate the list directly.

This again generates 20 random integers with size up to 10:

In[23]:= **RandomInteger[10, 20]**

Out[23]= {3, 0, 3, 1, 9, 6, 0, 8, 5, 2, 7, 8, 0, 10, 4, 4, 9, 5, 7, 1}

Vocabulary

Table[x, 5]	list of 5 copies of x
Table[f[n], {n, 10}]	list of values of f[n] with n going up to 10
Table[f[n], {n, 2, 10}]	list of values with n going from 2 to 10
Table[f[n], {n, 2, 10, 4}]	list of values with n going from 2 to 10 in steps of 4
Range[5, 10]	list of numbers from 5 to 10
Range[10, 20, 2]	list of numbers from 10 to 20 in steps of 2
RandomInteger[10, 20]	list of 20 random integers up to 10

Exercises

6.1   Make a list in which the number 1000 is repeated 5 times.

6.2   Make a table of the values of n^3 for n from 10 to 20.

6.3   Make a number line plot of the first 20 squares.

6.4   Make a list of the even numbers (2, 4, 6, …) up to 20.

6.5   Use Table to get the same result as Range[10].

6.6   Make a bar chart of the first 10 squares.

6.7   Make a table of lists of digits for the first 10 squares.

6.8   Make a list line plot of the length of the sequence of digits for each of the first 100 squares.

6.9   Make a table of the first digit of the first 20 squares.

6.10   Make a list line plot of the first digits of the first 100 squares.

Q&A

What does the {…} (list) in Table[n^2, {n, 5}] mean?
A list is always a way of collecting things together. Here what it's collecting is the variable n and its range 5. In the Wolfram Language, this kind of use of a list is called an *iterator specification*.

Why is the {…} (list) in Table[n^2, {n, 5}] needed?
So one can easily generalize to multidimensional arrays, like Table[x^2-y^2, {x, 5}, {y, 5}].

What are the constraints on the names of variables?
They can be any sequence of letters or numbers, but they can't start with a number, and—to avoid possible confusion with built-in Wolfram Language functions—they shouldn't start with a capital letter.

Why do you have to name a variable if the name never matters?
Good question! In Section 26, we'll see how to avoid having named variables. It's very elegant, but it's a little more abstract than what we're doing with Table here.

Can Range deal with negative numbers?
Yes. Range[-2, 2] gives {-2, -1, 0, 1, 2}. Range[2, -2] gives {}, but Range[2, -2, -1] gives {2, 1, 0, -1, -2}.

Tech Notes

- If you specify steps that don't fit evenly in the range you give, Range and Table just go as far as the steps take them, potentially stopping before the upper limit. (So Range[1, 6, 2] gives {1, 3, 5}, stopping at 5, not 6.)

- Using forms like Table[x, 20] requires at least Version 10.2 of the Wolfram Language. In earlier versions, this had to be specified as Table[x, {20}].

More to Explore

The Table Function in the Wolfram Language (wolfr.am/eiwl-6-more)

7 | Colors and Styles

The Wolfram Language doesn't just handle things like numbers. It also for example handles things like colors. It lets you refer to common colors by their names.

Red represents the color red:

In[1]:= **Red**

Out[1]= ■

Make a list of colors:

In[2]:= **{Red, Green, Blue, Purple, Orange, Black}**

Out[2]= {■, ■, ■, ■, ■, ■}

You can do operations on colors. ColorNegate "negates" a color, giving the complementary color. Blend blends a list of colors together.

Negating the color yellow gives blue:

In[3]:= **ColorNegate[Yellow]**

Out[3]= ■

Here's the result of blending yellow, pink and green:

In[4]:= **Blend[{Yellow, Pink, Green}]**

Out[4]= ■

You can specify a color by saying how much red, green and blue it contains. The function RGBColor lets you do that, giving the amount of each color, from 0 to 1.

This gives maximum red, with no green or blue:

In[5]:= **RGBColor[1, 0, 0]**

Out[5]= ■

Maximum red and green gives yellow:

In[6]:= **RGBColor[1, 1, 0]**

Out[6]= ■

This gives a table of colors with maximum red and varying levels of green:

In[7]:= **Table[RGBColor[1, g, 0], {g, 0, 1, 0.05}]**

Out[7]= {■, ■}

It's often convenient to specify colors not directly in terms of red, green and blue, but for example instead in terms of *hue*. The function Hue lets you do this.

A hue of 0.5 corresponds to cyan:

In[8]:= **Hue[0.5]**

Out[8]= ■

Here's a table of colors with hues from 0 to 1:

In[9]:= **Table[Hue[x], {x, 0, 1, 0.05}]**

Out[9]= {■, ■, ■, □, ■, ■, ■, ■, ■, ■, ■, ■, ■, ■, ■, ■, ■, ■, ■, ■, ■}

Sometimes you may want to just pick a random color. RandomColor lets you do this. When you say RandomInteger[10], you're asking to generate a random integer up to 10. But for a random color you don't have to specify a range, so you can just write RandomColor[]—not giving any explicit input to the function.

Generate a random color:

In[10]:= **RandomColor[]**

Out[10]= ■

Make a table of 30 random colors:

In[11]:= **Table[RandomColor[], 30]**

Out[11]= {■, ■, ■, ■, ■, ■, ■, □, ■, ■, ■, ■, ■, ■, □, ■, ■, ■, ■, ■, ■, ■, ■, ■, ■, ■, ■, ■, ■, ■}

Blending together lots of random colors usually gives something muddy:

In[12]:= **Blend[Table[RandomColor[], 20]]**

Out[12]= ■

You can use colors in all sorts of places. For example, you can style output with colors.

This gives the number 1000, styled in red:

In[13]:= **Style[1000, Red]**

Out[13]= 1000

Here are 30 random integers, styled in random colors:

In[14]:= **Table[Style[RandomInteger[1000], RandomColor[]], 30]**

Out[14]= {423, 803, 10, 432, 139, 188, 34, 981, 154, 340, 533, 52, 313, 555, 930, 332, 582, 67, 385, 564, 943, 987, 179, 391, 661, 606, 52, 577, 721, 507}

Another form of styling is size. You can specify a font size in Style.

Show x styled in 30-point type:

In[15]:= **Style[x, 30]**

Out[15]= X

This styles the number 100 in a sequence of different sizes:

In[16]:= **Table[Style[100, n], {n, 30}]**

Out[16]= { , ., .., ..., 100, 100, 100, 100, 100, 100, 100, 100, 100, 100, 100, 100, 100, 100, 100, 100, 100, 100, 100, 100, 100, 100, 100, 100, 100, 100}

You can combine color and size styling; here's x in 25 random colors and sizes:

In[17]:= **Table[Style[x, RandomColor[], RandomInteger[30]], 25]**

Out[17]= {X, X, , x, X, x, X, ., x, x, X, , x, ., X, , x, x, x, X, , X, X, x, }

Vocabulary

Red, Green, Blue, Yellow, Orange, Pink, Purple, …	colors
RGBColor[0.4, 0.7, 0.3]	red, green, blue color
Hue[0.8]	color specified by hue
RandomColor[]	randomly chosen color
ColorNegate[Red]	negate a color (complement)
Blend[{Red, Blue}]	blend a list of colors
Style[x, Red]	style with a color
Style[x, 20]	style with a size
Style[x, 20, Red]	style with a size and color

Exercises

7.1   Make a list of red, yellow and green.

7.2   Make a red, yellow, green column ("traffic light").

7.3   Compute the negation of the color orange.

7.4   Make a list of colors with hues varying from 0 to 1 in steps of 0.02.

7.5   Make a list of colors with maximum red and blue, but with green varying from 0 to 1 in steps of 0.05.

7.6   Blend the colors pink and yellow.

7.7   Make a list of colors obtained by blending yellow with hues from 0 to 1 in steps of 0.05.

7.8   Make a list of numbers from 0 to 1 in steps of 0.1, each with a hue equal to its value.

7.9   Make a purple color swatch of size 100.

7.10   Make a list of red swatches with sizes from 10 to 100 in steps of 10.

7.11   Display the number 999 in red at size 100.

7.12   Make a list of the first 10 squares, in which each value is styled at its size.

7.13   Use Part and RandomInteger to make a length-100 list in which each element is randomly Red, Yellow or Green.

7.14   Use Part to make a list of the first 50 digits of 2^1000, in which each digit has a size equal to 3 times its value.

Q&A

What named colors does the Wolfram Language have?

Red, Green, Blue, Black, White, Gray, Yellow, Brown, Orange, Pink, Purple, LightRed, etc. In Section 16 we'll see how to use ctrl = to enter any color name in plain English.

Why can colors be specified by red, green, blue values?

Basically because that's how we humans perceive colors: there are three kinds of cells in our eyes that are roughly sensitive respectively to red, green and blue components of light. (Some other organisms work differently.)

What does color negation do?

It generates *complementary colors*, defined by computing 1–*value* (one minus the value) for each RGB component. If you negate the "display (emitted light) primaries" red, green, blue, you get the "print (reflected light) primaries" cyan, magenta, yellow.

What is hue?

It's a way of specifying what are often called *pure colors*, independent of their tint, shade, saturation or brightness. Colors of different hues are often arranged around a *color wheel*. The RGB values for a particular hue are determined by a mathematical formula.

Are there other ways to specify colors than RGB?

Yes. A common one (implemented by Hue) is to use the combination of hue, saturation and brightness. LABColor and XYZColor are other examples. GrayLevel represents shades of gray, with GrayLevel[0] being black and GrayLevel[1] being white.

Tech Notes

- The little squares of color used to display a color are usually called *swatches*.

- You can specify named HTML colors by using for example RGBColor["maroon"], as well as hex colors by using for example RGBColor["#00ff00"].

- ChromaticityPlot and ChromaticityPlot3D plot lists of colors in color space.

- You can set lots of other style attributes in the Wolfram Language, like Bold, Italic and FontFamily.

More to Explore

Color in the Wolfram Language (wolfr.am/eiwl-7-more)

8 | Basic Graphics Objects

In the Wolfram Language, Circle[ ] represents a circle. To display the circle as graphics, use the function Graphics. Later, we'll see how to specify the position and size of a circle. But for now, we're just going to deal with a basic circle, which doesn't need any additional input.

Make graphics of a circle:

In[1]:= **Graphics[Circle[ ]]**

Out[1]=

Disk represents a filled-in disk:

In[2]:= **Graphics[Disk[ ]]**

Out[2]=

RegularPolygon gives a regular polygon with however many sides you specify.

Here's a pentagon (5-sided regular polygon):

In[3]:= **Graphics[RegularPolygon[5]]**

Out[3]=

Make a table of graphics of regular polygons with between 5 and 10 sides:

In[4]:= **Table[Graphics[RegularPolygon[n]], {n, 5, 10}]**

Out[4]=

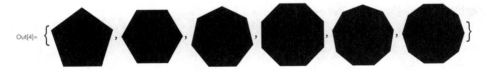

Style works inside Graphics, so you can use it to give colors.

Here's an orange pentagon:

In[5]:= **Graphics[Style[RegularPolygon[5], Orange]]**

Out[5]=

The Wolfram Language works in 3D as well as 2D, with constructs such as Sphere, Cylinder and Cone. When you have 3D graphics, you can rotate them around interactively to see different angles.

Display a sphere in 3D:

In[6]:= **Graphics3D[Sphere[ ]]**

Out[6]=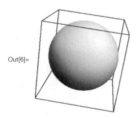

A list of a cone and a cylinder:

In[7]:= **{Graphics3D[Cone[ ]], Graphics3D[Cylinder[ ]]}**

Out[7]= { 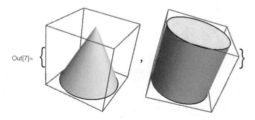 }

A yellow sphere:

In[8]:= **Graphics3D[Style[Sphere[ ], Yellow]]**

Out[8]=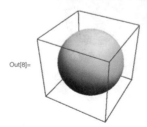

Vocabulary

Circle[ ]	specify a circle
Disk[ ]	specify a filled-in disk
RegularPolygon[*n*]	specify a regular polygon with *n* sides
Graphics[*object*]	display an object as graphics
Sphere[ ], Cylinder[ ], Cone[ ], ...	specify 3D geometric shapes
Graphics3D[*object*]	display an object as 3D graphics

Exercises

8.1   Use RegularPolygon to draw a triangle.

8.2   Make graphics of a red circle.

8.3   Make a red octagon.

8.4   Make a list whose elements are disks with hues varying from 0 to 1 in steps of 0.1.

8.5   Make a column of a red and a green triangle.

8.6   Make a list giving the regular polygons with 5 through 10 sides, with each polygon being colored pink.

8.7   Make a graphic of a purple cylinder.

8.8   Make a list of polygons with 8, 7, 6, ... , 3 sides, and colored with RandomColor, then show them all overlaid with the triangle on top (hint: apply Graphics to the list).

Q&A

How can I make graphics with several objects?

Section 14 will explain. To do so requires understanding *coordinates*.

Why use Circle[ ], not just Circle?

For consistency. As we'll see in Section 14, Circle[ ] is actually short for Circle[{0, 0}, 1], which means a circle of radius 1 and center coordinates {0, 0}.

Why isn't the yellow sphere pure yellow?

Because the Wolfram Language displays it like an actual 3D object, with lighting. If it were pure yellow, you wouldn't see any 3D depth, and it would just look like a 2D disk.

Tech Note

- Another way to specify styles for graphics is to give "directives" in a list, e.g. {Yellow, Disk[], Black, Circle[]}.

More to Explore

Guide to Graphics in the Wolfram Language (wolfr.am/eiwl-8-more)

9 | Interactive Manipulation

So far, we've been using the Wolfram Language in a question-answer way: we type input, and the language responds with output. But the language also lets you set up user interfaces where one can continually manipulate a variable. The function Manipulate works a lot like Table, except that instead of producing a list of results, it gives a slider to interactively choose the value you want.

The slider lets you pick values of n between 1 and 5 (in steps of 1):

In[1]:= **Manipulate[Table[Orange, n], {n, 1, 5, 1}]**

Here's the whole sequence of possible results:

In[2]:= **Table[Table[Orange, n], {n, 1, 5, 1}]**

Out[2]= {{■}, {■, ■}, {■, ■, ■}, {■, ■, ■, ■}, {■, ■, ■, ■, ■}}

Here's a similar interface for displaying a column of powers of a number:

In[3]:= **Manipulate[Column[{n, n^2, n^3}], {n, 1, 10, 1}]**

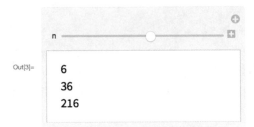

And here's the list of possible results in this case:

In[4]:= **Table[Column[{n, n^2, n^3}], {n, 1, 10, 1}]**

Out[4]= $\left\{\begin{matrix} 1 & 2 & 3 & 4 & 5 & 6 & 7 & 8 & 9 & 10 \\ 1, & 4, & 9 & , 16, & 25 & , 36 & , 49 & , 64 & , 81 & , 100 \\ 1 & 8 & 27 & 64 & 125 & 216 & 343 & 512 & 729 & 1000 \end{matrix}\right\}$

Unlike Table, Manipulate isn't limited to a fixed set of possible values. If you simply omit the step size in Manipulate, it'll assume you want any possible value in the range, not limited to whole numbers.

Without the step size, Manipulate allows any value:

In[5]:= **Manipulate[Column[{n, n^2, n^3}], {n, 1, 10}]**

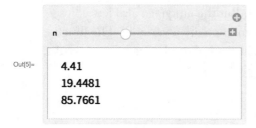

Out[5]=

4.41

19.4481

85.7661

It's very common to have graphics that you want to adjust interactively.

A bar chart that changes as you move the slider:

In[6]:= **Manipulate[BarChart[{1, a, 4, 2 * a, 4, 3 * a, 1}], {a, 0, 5}]**

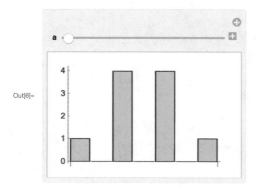

Out[6]=

A pie chart of the same list:

In[7]:= **Manipulate[PieChart[{1, a, 4, 2 * a, 4, 3 * a, 1}], {a, 0, 5}]**

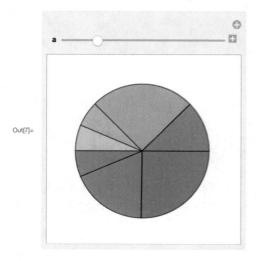

Out[7]=

Manipulate lets you set up any number of controls. You just give the information for each variable in turn, one after another.

Build an interface to vary the number of sides, and the hue, of a polygon:

In[8]:= **Manipulate[Graphics[Style[RegularPolygon[n], Hue[h]]], {n, 5, 20, 1}, {h, 0, 1}]**

Out[8]=

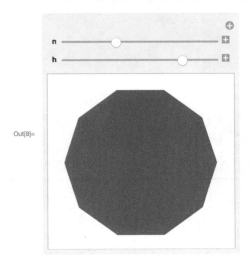

There are many ways to specify controls for Manipulate. If you give a list of possible values, you'll get a *chooser* or *menu*.

Build an interface that lets you choose between three colors:

In[9]:= **Manipulate[Graphics[Style[RegularPolygon[5], color]], {color, {Red, Yellow, Blue}}]**

Out[9]=

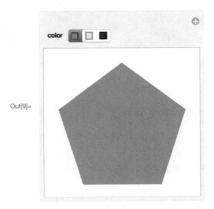

If there are more choices, like for size here, Manipulate sets up a drop-down menu:

In[10]:= **Manipulate[Style[value, color, size], {value, 1, 20, 1},**
{color, {Black, Red, Purple}}, {size, Range[12, 96, 12]}]

Out[10]=

Vocabulary

Manipulate[anything, {n, 0, 10, 1}**]**	manipulate anything with n varying in steps of 1
Manipulate[anything, {x, 0, 10}**]**	manipulate anything with x varying continuously

---

Exercises

9.1 Make a Manipulate to show Range[n] with n varying from 0 to 100.

9.2 Make a Manipulate to plot the whole numbers up to n, where n can range from 5 to 50.

9.3 Make a Manipulate to show a column of between 1 and 10 copies of x.

9.4 Make a Manipulate to show a disk with a hue varying from 0 to 1.

9.5 Make a Manipulate to show a disk with red, green and blue color components varying from 0 to 1.

9.6 Make a Manipulate to show digit sequences of 4-digit integers (between 1000 and 9999).

9.7 Make a Manipulate to create a list of between 5 and 50 equally spaced hues.

9.8 Make a Manipulate that shows a list of a variable number of hexagons (between 1 and 10), and with variable hues.

9.9 Make a Manipulate that lets you show a regular polygon with between 5 and 20 sides, in red, yellow or blue.

9.10 Make a Manipulate that shows a pie chart with a number of equal segments varying from 1 to 10.

9.11 Make a Manipulate that gives a bar chart of the 3 digits in integers from 100 to 999.

9.12 Make a Manipulate that shows n random colors, where n can range from 1 to 50.

9.13 Make a Manipulate to display a column of integer powers with bases from 1 to 25 and exponents from 1 to 10.

9.14 Make a Manipulate of a number line of values of x^n for integer x from 1 to 10, with n varying from 0 to 5.

9.15 Make a Manipulate to show a sphere that can vary in color from green to red.

Q&A

Does Manipulate work the same on web, mobile and desktop?

Ultimately yes. But it can be significantly slower on the web and on some mobile systems, because every time you move a slider it has to communicate over the internet with a server to find out what to do. On desktop and some mobile systems, everything is happening right there, inside your computer or other device—so it's very fast.

Can I make a standalone app out of a Manipulate?

Yes. To make a web app, for example, you just need to use CloudDeploy. We'll talk about this in Section 36.

Can I use random numbers in Manipulate?

Yes, but unless you "seed" them with SeedRandom, the random numbers will be different every time you move a slider.

Tech Notes

- Manipulate supports pretty much all standard user interface control types (checkboxes, menus, input fields, color pickers, etc.).

- Sliders in Manipulate often provide a ⊞ button which opens out to additional controls—including animation, single stepping and numerical value display.

- Many controls are rendered differently on mouse and touch devices, and some controls only work on one or the other.

- If you're running natively on your computer, devices like gamepads should immediately work with Manipulate. You can specify which controls should be hooked to what. ControllerInformation[ ] gives information on all your controllers.

More to Explore

The Wolfram Demonstrations Project (wolfr.am/eiwl-9-more): **more than 11,000 interactive Demonstrations created with Manipulate** (wolfr.am/eiwl-9-more2)

10 | Images

Many functions in the Wolfram Language work on *images*. It's easy to get an image into the Wolfram Language, for example by copying or dragging it from the web or from a photo collection. You can also just capture an image directly from your camera using the function CurrentImage.

Get the current image from your computer's camera (here, me working on this book):

In[1]:= **CurrentImage[ ]**

Out[1]=

You can apply functions to images just like you apply functions to numbers or lists or anything else. The function ColorNegate that we saw in connection with colors also works on images, giving a "negative image".

Negate the colors in the image (making me look pretty weird):

In[2]:= **ColorNegate[**  **]**

Out[2]=

Blur the image:

In[3]:= **Blur[**  **]**

Out[3]=

The number says how much to blur the image:

In[4]:= **Blur[**  **, 10]**

Out[4]=

You can make a table of the results of different amounts of blurring:

In[5]:= **Table[Blur[**  **, n], {n, 0, 15, 5}]**

Out[5]=

ImageCollage puts images together:

In[6]:= **ImageCollage[Table[Blur[**  **, n], {n, 0, 15, 5}]]**

Out[6]=

There's lots of analysis one can do on images. For example, DominantColors finds a list of the most important colors in an image.

In[7]:= **DominantColors[**  **]**

Out[7]= {■, ■, ■, ■}

Binarize makes an image black and white:

In[8]:= **Binarize[**  **]**

Out[8]=

Not surprisingly, the dominant colors in the result are black and white:

In[9]:= **DominantColors[Binarize[**  **]]**

Out[9]= {□, ■}

Another type of analysis is *edge detection*: finding where in the image there are sharp changes in color. The result looks a bit like a sketch derived from the original image.

Pick out edges in the original image:

In[10]:= **EdgeDetect[**  **]**

Out[10]=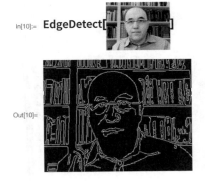

"Add" the original image to the result of the edge detection:

In[11]:= **ImageAdd[**  **]**

Out[11]=

It's often convenient to do image processing interactively, creating interfaces using Manipulate. For example, Binarize lets you specify a threshold for what will be turned black as opposed to white. And often the best way to find the right threshold is just to interactively experiment with it.

Make an interface to adjust the threshold for binarizing an image:

In[12]:= **Manipulate[Binarize[**  **, t], {t, 0, 1}]**

Out[12]=

Vocabulary

CurrentImage[ ]	capture the current image from your computer, etc.
ColorNegate[**]**	negate the colors in an image
Binarize[**]**	convert an image to black and white
Blur[**, 5]**	blur an image
EdgeDetect[**]**	detect the edges in an image
DominantColors[**]**	get a list of dominant colors in an image
ImageCollage[{ **,** **,** **}]**	put together images in a collage
ImageAdd[**,** **]**	add color values of two images

Exercises

10.1 Color negate the result of edge detecting an image. (Use **CurrentImage[ ]** or any other image.)

10.2 Use **Manipulate** to make an interface for blurring an image from 0 to 20.

10.3 Make a table of the results from edge detecting an image with blurring from 1 to 10.

10.4 Make an image collage of an image together with the results of blurring, edge detecting and binarizing it.

10.5 Add an image to a binarized version of it.

10.6 Create a **Manipulate** to display edges of an image as it gets blurred from 0 to 20.

10.7 Image operations work on **Graphics** and **Graphics3D**. Edge detect a picture of a sphere.

10.8 Make a **Manipulate** to make an interface for blurring a purple pentagon from 0 to 20.

10.9 Create a collage of 9 images of disks, each with a random color.

10.10 Use **ImageCollage** to make a combined image of spheres with hues from 0 to 1 in steps of 0.2.

10.11 Make a table of blurring a disk by an amount from 0 to 30 in steps of 5.

10.12 Use **ImageAdd** to add an image to an image of a disk.

10.13 Use **ImageAdd** to add an image to an image of a red octagon.

10.14 Add an image to the color negated version of the edge detected image.

Q&A

What if I don't have a camera on my computer, or can't use it?

Instead of CurrentImage[], just get a test image using for example ExampleData[{"TestImage", "Mandrill"}].

What does the number in Blur mean?

It's the range of pixels that get blurred together.

How does Binarize decide what's black and what's white?

If you don't tell it a threshold, it will pick one based on analyzing the distribution of colors in the image.

Tech Notes

- The very powerful fact that images can appear directly in Wolfram Language code is another consequence of the fact that the Wolfram Language is symbolic.

- A convenient way to get collections of images, say related to crocodiles, is to use WikipediaData["crocodiles", "ImageList"].

- Assuming you've got an appropriate version of the Wolfram Language, WebImageSearch["colorful birds", "Thumbnails"] will get images by searching the web (see Section 44).

- CurrentImage works in modern browsers and on mobile devices as well as on desktop computers.

- Many arithmetic operations just work directly pixel-by-pixel on images (e.g. Sqrt[▢] or ▢-EdgeDetect[▢]), so you don't explicitly have to use ImageAdd, ImageMultiply, etc.

More to Explore

Guide to Image Computation in the Wolfram Language (wolfr.am/eiwl-10-more)

11 | Strings and Text

Another thing the Wolfram Language lets you compute with is text. You enter text as a *string*, indicated by quotes (").

Enter a string:

In[1]:= **"This is a string."**

Out[1]= This is a string.

Just like when you enter a number, a string on its own comes back unchanged—except that the quotes aren't visible when the string is displayed. There are many functions that work on strings. Like StringLength, which gives the length of a string.

StringLength counts the number of characters in a string:

In[2]:= **StringLength["hello"]**

Out[2]= 5

StringReverse reverses the characters in a string:

In[3]:= **StringReverse["hello"]**

Out[3]= olleh

ToUpperCase makes all the characters in a string uppercase (capital letters):

In[4]:= **ToUpperCase["I'm coding in the Wolfram Language!"]**

Out[4]= I'M CODING IN THE WOLFRAM LANGUAGE!

StringTake takes a certain number of characters from the beginning of a string:

In[5]:= **StringTake["this is about strings", 10]**

Out[5]= this is ab

If you take 10 characters, you get a string of length 10:

In[6]:= **StringLength[StringTake["this is about strings", 10]]**

Out[6]= 10

StringJoin joins strings (don't forget spaces if you want to separate words):

In[7]:= **StringJoin["Hello", " ", "there!", " How are you?"]**

Out[7]= Hello there! How are you?

You can make lists of strings, then apply functions to them.

A list of strings:

In[8]:= **{"apple", "banana", "strawberry"}**

Out[8]= {apple, banana, strawberry}

Get the first two characters from each string:

In[9]:= **StringTake[{"apple", "banana", "strawberry"}, 2]**

Out[9]= {ap, ba, st}

StringJoin joins the strings in a list:

In[10]:= **StringJoin[{"apple", "banana", "strawberry"}]**

Out[10]= applebananastrawberry

Sometimes it's useful to turn strings into lists of their constituent characters. Each character is actually a string itself, of length 1.

Characters breaks a string into a list of its characters:

In[11]:= **Characters["a string is made of characters"]**

Out[11]= {a, , s, t, r, i, n, g, , i, s, , m, a, d, e, , o, f, , c, h, a, r, a, c, t, e, r, s}

Once you've broken a string into a list of characters, you can use all the usual list functions on it.

Sort the characters in a string:

In[12]:= **Sort[Characters["a string of characters"]]**

Out[12]= { , , , a, a, a, c, c, e, f, g, h, i, n, o, r, r, r, s, s, t, t}

The invisible elements at the beginning of the list are space characters. If you want to see strings in the form you'd input them, complete with "...", use InputForm.

InputForm shows strings as you would input them, including quotes:

In[13]:= **InputForm[Sort[Characters["a string of characters"]]]**

Out[13]= {" ", " ", " ", "a", "a", "a", "c", "c", "e", "f", "g", "h", "i", "n", "o", "r", "r", "r", "s", "s", "t", "t"}

Functions like StringJoin and Characters work on strings of any kind; it doesn't matter if they're meaningful text or not. There are other functions, like TextWords, that specifically work on meaningful text, written, say, in English.

TextWords gives a list of the words in a string of text:

In[14]:= **TextWords["This is a sentence. Sentences are made of words."]**

Out[14]= {This, is, a, sentence, Sentences, are, made, of, words}

This gives the length of each word:

In[15]:= **StringLength[TextWords["This is a sentence. Sentences are made of words."]]**

Out[15]= {4, 2, 1, 8, 9, 3, 4, 2, 5}

TextSentences breaks a text string into a list of sentences:

In[16]:= **TextSentences["This is a sentence. Sentences are made of words."]**

Out[16]= {This is a sentence., Sentences are made of words.}

There are lots of ways to get text into the Wolfram Language. One example is the WikipediaData function, which gets the current text of Wikipedia articles.

Get the first 100 characters of the Wikipedia article about "computers":

In[17]:= **StringTake[WikipediaData["computers"], 100]**

Out[17]= A computer is a general–purpose device
 that can be programmed to carry out a set of arithmetic or lo

A convenient way to get a sense of what's in a piece of text is to create a word cloud. The function WordCloud does this.

Create a word cloud for the Wikipedia article on "computers":

In[18]:= **WordCloud[WikipediaData["computers"]]**

Out[18]=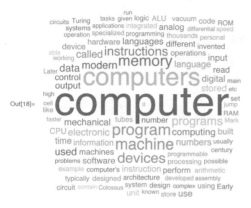

Not surprisingly, "computer" and "computers" are the most common words in the article.

The Wolfram Language has lots of built-in knowledge about words that appear in English and other languages. WordList gives lists of words.

Get the first 20 words from a list of common English words:

In[19]:= **Take[WordList[ ], 20]**

Out[19]= {a, aah, aardvark, aback, abacus, abaft, abalone,
 abandon, abandoned, abandonment, abase, abasement, abash,
 abashed, abashment, abate, abatement, abattoir, abbe, abbess}

Make a word cloud from the first letters of all the words:

In[20]:= **WordCloud[StringTake[WordList[ ], 1]]**

Out[20]=

Strings don't have to contain text. In a juxtaposition of ancient and modern, we can for example generate Roman numerals as strings.

Generate the Roman numeral string for 1988:

In[21]:= **RomanNumeral[1988]**

Out[21]= MCMLXXXVIII

Make a table of the Roman numerals for numbers up to 20:

In[22]:= **Table[RomanNumeral[n], {n, 20}]**

Out[22]= {I, II, III, IV, V, VI, VII, VIII, IX, X, XI, XII, XIII, XIV, XV, XVI, XVII, XVIII, XIX, XX}

As with everything, we can do computations on these strings. For example, we can plot the lengths of successive Roman numerals.

Plot the lengths of the Roman numerals for numbers up to 100:

In[23]:= **ListLinePlot[Table[StringLength[RomanNumeral[n]], {n, 100}]]**

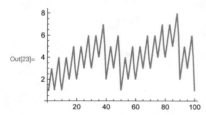

IntegerName gives the English name of an integer.

Generate a string giving the name of the integer 56:

In[24]:= **IntegerName[56]**

Out[24]= fifty-six

Here's a plot of the lengths of integer names in English:

In[25]:= **ListLinePlot[Table[StringLength[IntegerName[n]], {n, 100}]]**

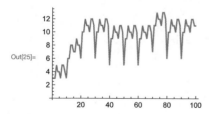

There are various ways to turn letters into numbers (and vice versa).

Alphabet gives the alphabet:

In[26]:= **Alphabet[]**

Out[26]= {a, b, c, d, e, f, g, h, i, j, k, l, m, n, o, p, q, r, s, t, u, v, w, x, y, z}

LetterNumber tells you where in the alphabet a letter appears:

In[27]:= **LetterNumber[{"a", "b", "x", "y", "z"}]**

Out[27]= {1, 2, 24, 25, 26}

FromLetterNumber does the opposite:

In[28]:= **FromLetterNumber[{10, 11, 12, 13, 14, 15}]**

Out[28]= { j, k, l, m, n, o}

Alphabet knows about non-English alphabets too:

In[29]:= **Alphabet["Russian"]**

Out[29]= {а, б, в, г, д, е, ё, ж, з, и, й, к, л, м, н, о, п, р, с, т, у, ф, х, ц, ч, ш, щ, ъ, ы, ь, э, ю, я}

Transliterate converts to (approximately) equivalent English letters:

In[30]:= **Transliterate[Alphabet["Russian"]]**

Out[30]= {a, b, v, g, d, e, e, z, z, i, j, k, l, m, n, o, p, r, s, t, u, f, h, c, c, s, s, ″, y, ′, e, u, a}

This transliterates the word "wolfram" into the Russian alphabet:

In[31]:= **Transliterate["wolfram", "Russian"]**

Out[31]= уолфрам

If you want to, you can also turn text into images, which you can then manipulate using image processing. The function Rasterize makes a *raster*, or *bitmap*, of something.

Generate an image of a piece of text:

In[32]:= **Rasterize[Style["ABC", 100]]**

Out[32]=

Do image processing on it:

In[33]:= **EdgeDetect[Rasterize[Style["ABC", 100]]]**

Out[33]=

Vocabulary

"_string_**"**	a string
StringLength["_string_"**]**	length of a string
StringReverse["_string_"**]**	reverse a string
StringTake["_string_"**, 4]**	take characters at the beginning of a string
StringJoin["_string_"**, **"_string_"**]**	join strings together
StringJoin[{"_string_"**, **"_string_"**}]**	join a list of strings
ToUpperCase["_string_"**]**	convert characters to uppercase
Characters["_string_"**]**	convert a string to a list of characters
TextWords["_string_"**]**	list of words from a string
TextSentences["_string_"**]**	list of sentences
WikipediaData["_topic_"**]**	Wikipedia article about a topic
WordCloud["_text_"**]**	word cloud based on word frequencies
WordList[ ]	list of common words in English
Alphabet[ ]	list of letters of the alphabet
LetterNumber["_c_"**]**	where a letter appears in the alphabet
FromLetterNumber[_n_**]**	letter appearing at a position in the alphabet
Transliterate["_text_"**]**	transliterate text in any language into English
Transliterate["_text_"**, **"_alphabet_"**]**	transliterate text into other alphabets
RomanNumeral[_n_**]**	convert a number to its Roman numeral string
IntegerName[_n_**]**	convert a number to its English name string
InputForm["_string_"**]**	show a string with quotes
Rasterize["_string_"**]**	make a bitmap image

Exercises

11.1   Join two copies of the string "Hello".

11.2   Make a single string of the whole alphabet, in uppercase.

11.3   Generate a string of the alphabet in reverse order.

11.4   Join 100 copies of the string "AGCT".

11.5   Use **StringTake**, **StringJoin** and **Alphabet** to get "abcdef".

11.6   Create a column with increasing numbers of letters from the string **"this is about strings"**.

11.7   Make a bar chart of the lengths of the words in "A long time ago, in a galaxy far, far away".

11.8   Find the string length of the Wikipedia article for "computer".

11.9   Find how many words are in the Wikipedia article for "computer".

11.10 Find the first sentence in the Wikipedia article about "strings".

11.11 Make a string from the first letters of all sentences in the Wikipedia article about computers.

11.12 Find the maximum word length among English words from **WordList[ ]**.

11.13 Count the number of words in **WordList[ ]** that start with "q".

11.14 Make a line plot of the lengths of the first 1000 words from **WordList[ ]**.

11.15 Use **StringJoin** and **Characters** to make a word cloud of all letters in the words from **WordList[ ]**.

11.16 Use **StringReverse** to make a word cloud of the last letters in the words from **WordList[ ]**.

11.17 Find the Roman numerals for the year 1959.

11.18 Find the maximum string length of any Roman-numeral year from 1 to 2020.

11.19 Make a word cloud from the first characters of the Roman numerals up to 100.

11.20 Use **Length** to find the length of the Russian alphabet.

11.21 Generate the uppercase Greek alphabet.

11.22 Make a bar chart of the letter numbers in "wolfram".

11.23 Use **FromLetterNumber** to make a string of 1000 random letters.

11.24 Make a list of 100 random 5-letter strings.

11.25 Transliterate "wolfram" into Greek.

11.26 Get the Arabic alphabet and transliterate it into English.

11.27 Make a white-on-black size-200 letter "A".

11.28 Use **Manipulate** to make an interactive selector of size-100 characters from the alphabet, controlled by a slider.

11.29 Use **Manipulate** to make an interactive selector of black-on-white outlines of rasterized size-100 characters from the alphabet, controlled by a menu.

11.30 Use **Manipulate** to create a "vision simulator" that blurs a size-200 letter "A" by an amount from 0 to 50.

Q&A

What is the difference between "x" and x?

"x" is a string; x is a Wolfram Language symbol, just like Plus or Max, that can be defined to actually do computations. We'll talk much more about symbols later.

How do I enter characters that aren't on my keyboard?

You can use whatever methods your computer provides, or you can do it directly with the Wolfram Language using constructs such as \[Alpha].

How do I put quotes (") inside a string?

Use \" (and if you want to put \" literally in the string, use \\\"). (You'll use a lot of backslashes if you want to put \\\" in: \\\\\\\".)

How are the colors of elements in word clouds determined?

By default it's random within a certain color palette. You can specify it if you want to.

How come the word cloud shows "s" as the most common letter?

Because it is the most common *first* letter for common words in English. If you look at all letters, the most common is "e".

What about letters that aren't English? How are they numbered?

LetterNumber["α", "Greek"] gives numbering in the Greek alphabet. All characters are assigned a *character code*. You can find it using ToCharacterCode.

What alphabets does the Wolfram Language know about?

Basically all the ones that are used today. Try "Greek" or "Arabic", or the name of a language. Note that when a language uses accented characters, it's sometimes tricky to decide what's "in" the alphabet, and what's just derived from it.

Can I translate words instead of just transliterating their letters?

Yes. Use WordTranslation. See Section 35.

Can I get lists of common words in languages other than English?

Yes. Use WordList[Language → "Spanish"], etc.

Tech Notes

- RandomWord[10] gives 10 random words. How many of them do you know?

- StringTake["*string*", -2] takes 2 characters from the end of the string.

- Every character, whether "a", "α" or "狼" is represented by a Unicode character code, found with ToCharacterCode. You can explore "Unicode space" with FromCharacterCode.

- If you get a different result from WikipediaData, that's because Wikipedia has been changed.

- WordCloud automatically removes "uninteresting" words in text, like "the", "and", etc.

- If you can't figure out the name of an alphabet or language, use ctrl = (as described in Section 16) to give it in natural language form.

More to Explore

Guide to String Manipulation in the Wolfram Language (wolfr.am/eiwl-11-more)

12 | Sound

In the Wolfram Language, sound works a lot like graphics, except that instead of having things like circles, one has sound notes. Press the play ▶ button to actually play sounds. If you don't say otherwise, the Wolfram Language will make the notes sound as if they were played on a piano.

Generate a middle C note:

In[1]:= **Sound[SoundNote["C"]]**

Out[1]=

You can specify a sequence of notes by giving them in a list.

Play three notes in sequence:

In[2]:= **Sound[{SoundNote["C"], SoundNote["C"], SoundNote["G"]}]**

Out[2]=

Instead of giving names of notes, you can give a number to specify their pitch. Middle C is 0. Each semitone above middle C goes up by 1. Middle G is 7 semitones above middle C, so it's specified by the number 7. (An octave is 12 semitones.)

Specify the notes by numbers:

In[3]:= **Sound[{SoundNote[0], SoundNote[0], SoundNote[7]}]**

Out[3]=

Use Table to generate a sequence of 5 notes:

In[4]:= **Sound[Table[SoundNote[n], {n, 5}]]**

Out[4]=

If you don't say otherwise, each note lasts 1 second. Use SoundNote[*pitch, length*] to get a different length.

Play each note for 0.1 seconds:

In[5]:= **Sound[Table[SoundNote[n, 0.1], {n, 5}]]**

Out[5]=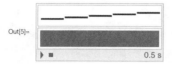

In addition to piano, SoundNote can handle a long list of possible instruments. The name of each instrument is a string.

Play notes on a simulated violin:

In[6]:= **Sound[Table[SoundNote[n, 0.1, "Violin"], {n, 5}]]**

Out[6]=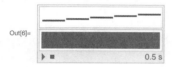

It's easy to make "random music"—different every time you generate it.

Play a sequence of 20 notes with random pitches:

In[7]:= **Sound[Table[SoundNote[RandomInteger[12], 0.1, "Violin"], 20]]**

Out[7]=

Vocabulary

Sound[{...}]	create a sound from notes
SoundNote["C"]	a named note
SoundNote[5]	a note with a numbered pitch
SoundNote[5, 0.1]	a note played for a specified time
SoundNote[5, 0.1, "Guitar"]	a note played on a certain instrument

Exercises

12.1   Generate the sequence of notes with pitches 0, 4 and 7.

12.2   Generate 2 seconds of playing middle A on a cello.

12.3   Generate a "riff" of notes from pitch 0 to pitch 48 in steps of 1, with each note lasting 0.05 seconds.

12.4   Generate a sequence of notes going from pitch 12 down to 0 in steps of 1.

12.5   Generate a sequence of 5 notes starting with middle C, then successively going up by an octave at a time.

12.6   Generate a sequence of 10 notes on a trumpet with random pitches from 0 to 12 and duration 0.2 seconds.

12.7   Generate a sequence of 10 notes with random pitches up to 12 and random durations up to 10 tenths of a second.

12.8   Generate 0.1-second notes with pitches given by the digits of $2^{\wedge}31$.

12.9   Create a sound from the letters in CABBAGE, each playing for 0.3 seconds sounding like a guitar.

12.10 Generate 0.1-second notes with pitches given by the letter numbers of the characters in "wolfram".

Q&A

How do I know which instruments are available?

Look at the list under "Details and Options" in the SoundNote reference page, or just start typing and see the completions you're offered. You can also use instrument numbers, from 1 to 128. All the standard MIDI instruments are there, including percussion.

How do I play notes below middle C?

Just use negative numbers, like SoundNote[-10].

What are sharp and flat notes called?

E♯ (E sharp), Ab (A flat), etc. They also have numbers (e.g. E# is 5). The # and b can be typed as ordinary keyboard characters (though special ♯ and ♭ characters are available too).

How do I make a chord?

Put note names in a list, as in SoundNote[{"C", "G"}].

How do I make a rest?

For a 0.2-second rest, use SoundNote[None, 0.2].

How do I get a sound to play immediately, without having to press the play button?

Use EmitSound, as in EmitSound [Sound[SoundNote["C"]]], etc.

Why do I need quotes in the name of a note like "C"?

Because the name is a Wolfram Language string. If you typed just C, it would be interpreted as a function named C, which isn't what you want.

Can I record audio and manipulate it?

Yes. Use AudioCapture, then use functions like AudioPlot, Spectrogram, AudioPitchShift, etc.

Tech Notes

- **SoundNote** corresponds to MIDI sound. The Wolfram Language also supports "sampled sound", for example using functions like **ListPlay**, as well as an **Audio** construct that represents all aspects of an audio signal.
- To get spoken output, use **Speak**. To make a beep, use **Beep**.

More to Explore

Guide to Sound Generation in the Wolfram Language (wolfr.am/eiwl-12-more)

13 | Arrays, or Lists of Lists

We've seen how Table can be used to make lists. Now let's see how Table can be used to create higher-dimensional arrays of values.

Make a list of 4 copies of x:

In[1]:= **Table[x, 4]**

Out[1]= {x, x, x, x}

Make a list of 4 copies of a list that contains 5 copies of x:

In[2]:= **Table[x, 4, 5]**

Out[2]= {{x, x, x, x, x}, {x, x, x, x, x}, {x, x, x, x, x}, {x, x, x, x, x}}

Use Grid to display the result in a grid:

In[3]:= **Grid[Table[x, 4, 5]]**

Out[3]=
```
x  x  x  x  x
x  x  x  x  x
x  x  x  x  x
x  x  x  x  x
```

You can use Table with two variables to make a 2D array. The first variable corresponds to the row; the second to the column.

Make an array of colors: red going down, blue going across:

In[4]:= **Grid[Table[RGBColor[r, 0, b], {r, 0, 1, .2}, {b, 0, 1, .2}]]**

Out[4]=

Show every array element as its row number:

In[5]:= **Grid[Table[i, {i, 4}, {j, 5}]]**

Out[5]=
```
1  1  1  1  1
2  2  2  2  2
3  3  3  3  3
4  4  4  4  4
```

Show every array element as its column number:

In[6]:= **Grid[Table[j, {i, 4}, {j, 5}]]**

Out[6]=
```
1  2  3  4  5
1  2  3  4  5
1  2  3  4  5
1  2  3  4  5
```

Generate an array in which each element is the sum of its row and column number:

In[7]:= **Grid[Table[i + j, {i, 5}, {j, 5}]]**

Out[7]=
```
2  3  4  5  6
3  4  5  6  7
4  5  6  7  8
5  6  7  8  9
6  7  8  9  10
```

Generate a multiplication table:

In[8]:= **Grid[Table[i * j, {i, 5}, {j, 5}]]**

Out[8]=
```
1   2   3   4   5
2   4   6   8   10
3   6   9   12  15
4   8   12  16  20
5   10  15  20  25
```

ArrayPlot lets you visualize values in an array. Larger values are shown darker.

Visualize a multiplication table:

In[9]:= **ArrayPlot[Table[i * j, {i, 5}, {j, 5}]]**

Out[9]=

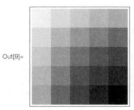

Generate and plot an array of random values:

In[10]:= **ArrayPlot[Table[RandomInteger[10], 30, 30]]**

Out[10]=

ArrayPlot also lets you put colors as values:

In[11]:= **ArrayPlot[Table[RandomColor[], 30, 30]]**

Out[11]=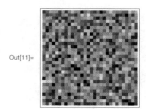

Images are ultimately arrays of pixels. Color images make each pixel have red, green and blue values. Black-and-white images have pixels with values 0 (black) or 1 (white). You can get the actual pixel values using ImageData.

Find the value of pixels in an image of a "W":

In[12]:= **ImageData[Binarize[Rasterize["W"]]]**

Out[12]= {{1, 1, 1, 1, 1, 1, 1, 1, 1, 1, 1, 1, 1}, {1, 1, 1, 1, 1, 1, 1, 1, 1, 1, 1, 1, 1},
{1, 1, 1, 1, 1, 1, 1, 1, 1, 1, 1, 1, 1}, {1, 1, 1, 1, 1, 1, 1, 1, 1, 1, 1, 1, 1}, {1, 1, 1, 1, 1, 1, 1, 1, 1, 1, 1, 1, 1},
{0, 0, 1, 1, 1, 0, 0, 1, 1, 1, 0, 0, 0}, {1, 0, 1, 1, 1, 0, 0, 1, 1, 1, 0, 0, 1}, {1, 0, 1, 1, 1, 0, 0, 1, 1, 1, 0, 0, 1},
{1, 0, 1, 1, 0, 0, 0, 0, 1, 1, 0, 0, 1}, {1, 0, 0, 1, 0, 1, 1, 0, 1, 0, 0, 0, 1}, {1, 0, 0, 1, 0, 1, 1, 0, 1, 0, 1, 0, 1},
{1, 1, 0, 1, 0, 1, 1, 0, 1, 0, 1, 0, 1}, {1, 1, 0, 0, 0, 1, 1, 0, 0, 0, 1, 0, 1}, {1, 1, 0, 0, 1, 1, 1, 1, 0, 0, 1, 0, 1},
{1, 1, 0, 0, 1, 1, 1, 1, 0, 0, 1, 0, 1}, {1, 1, 1, 1, 1, 1, 1, 1, 1, 1, 1, 1, 1}, {1, 1, 1, 1, 1, 1, 1, 1, 1, 1, 1, 1, 1},
{1, 1, 1, 1, 1, 1, 1, 1, 1, 1, 1, 1, 1}, {1, 1, 1, 1, 1, 1, 1, 1, 1, 1, 1, 1, 1}}

Use ArrayPlot to visualize the array of values:

In[13]:= **ArrayPlot[ImageData[Binarize[Rasterize["W"]]]]**

Out[13]=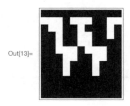

The image is of very low resolution, because that's how Rasterize made it in this case. It's also white-on-black instead of black-on-white. That's because in an image 0 is black and 1 is white (like in RGBColor), while ArrayPlot's default is to make larger values darker.

You can do arithmetic with arrays, just like lists. That means it's easy to swap 0 and 1 in this array: Just subtract everything from 1, so every 0 becomes 1 – 0 = 1, and every 1 becomes 1 – 1 = 0.

Find pixel values, then do arithmetic to swap 0 and 1 in the array:

In[14]:= **1 – ImageData[Binarize[Rasterize["W"]]]**

Out[14]= {{0, 0, 0, 0, 0, 0, 0, 0, 0, 0, 0, 0}, {1, 1, 1, 0, 1, 1, 1, 0, 0, 1, 1}, {0, 1, 1, 0, 0, 1, 0, 0, 0, 1, 0},
{0, 0, 1, 0, 0, 1, 1, 0, 0, 1, 0}, {0, 0, 1, 0, 0, 1, 1, 0, 0, 0, 0}, {0, 0, 1, 1, 1, 0, 1, 1, 1, 0, 0},
{0, 0, 0, 1, 1, 0, 0, 1, 1, 0, 0}, {0, 0, 0, 1, 0, 0, 0, 1, 0, 0, 0}, {0, 0, 0, 1, 0, 0, 0, 1, 0, 0, 0},
{0, 0, 0, 0, 0, 0, 0, 0, 0, 0, 0}, {0, 0, 0, 0, 0, 0, 0, 0, 0, 0, 0}, {0, 0, 0, 0, 0, 0, 0, 0, 0, 0, 0}}

The result is black-on-white:

In[15]:= **ArrayPlot[1 – ImageData[Binarize[Rasterize["W"]]]]**

Out[15]=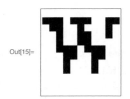

Vocabulary

Table[*x*, 4, 5]	make a 2D array of values
Grid[*array*]	lay out values from an array in a grid
ArrayPlot[*array*]	visualize the values in an array
ImageData[*image*]	get the array of pixel values from an image

---

Exercises

13.1 Make a 12×12 multiplication table.

13.2 Make a 5×5 multiplication table for Roman numerals.

13.3 Make a 10×10 grid of random colors.

13.4 Make a 10×10 grid of randomly colored random integers between 0 and 10.

13.5 Make a grid of all possible strings consisting of pairs of letters of the alphabet ("aa", "ab", etc.).

13.6 Visualize {1, 4, 3, 5, 2} with a pie chart, number line, line plot and bar chart. Place these in a 2×2 grid.

13.7 Make an array plot of hue values x ∗ y, where x and y each run from 0 to 1 in steps of 0.05.

13.8 Make an array plot of hue values x/y, where x and y each run from 1 to 50 in steps of 1.

13.9 Make an array plot of the lengths of Roman numeral strings in a multiplication table up to 100×100.

Q&A

Can the limits of one variable in a table depend on another?

Yes, later ones can depend on earlier ones. Table[x, {i, 4}, {j, i}] makes a "ragged" triangular array.

Can I make tables that are lists of lists of lists?

Yes, you can make tables of any dimension. Image3D gives a way to visualize 3D arrays.

Why does 0 correspond to black, and 1 to white, in images?

0 means zero intensity of light, i.e. black. 1 means maximum intensity, i.e. white.

How do I get the original image back from the output of ImageData?

Just apply the function Image to it.

Tech Notes

- Arrays in the Wolfram Language are just lists in which each element is itself a list. The Wolfram Language also allows much more general structures, that mix lists and other things.

- Lists in the Wolfram Language correspond to mathematical *vectors*; lists of equal-length lists correspond to *matrices*.

- If most of the entries in an array are 0 (or some other fixed value), you can use SparseArray to construct an array just by giving the positions and values of nonzero elements.

14 | Coordinates and Graphics

We've used ListPlot and ListLinePlot to plot lists of values, where each value appears after the one before. But by giving lists containing *pairs of coordinates* instead of single values, we can use these functions to plot points at arbitrary positions.

Plot a list of values where each value appears after the one before:

In[1]:= **ListPlot[{4, 3, 2, 1, 1, 1, 1, 2, 3, 4}]**

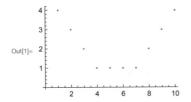

Plot a sequence of arbitrary points specified by {x, y} coordinates:

In[2]:= **ListLinePlot[{{1, 1}, {1, 5}, {6, 4}, {6, 2}, {2, 3}, {5, 5}}]**

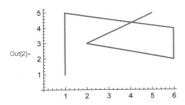

The position of each point here is specified by {x, y} coordinates. Following the standard convention in mathematics, the x value says how far across horizontally the point should be; the y value says how far up vertically it should be.

Generate a sequence of random {x, y} coordinates:

In[3]:= **Table[RandomInteger[20], 10, 2]**

Out[3]= {{19, 8}, {11, 20}, {14, 15}, {5, 8}, {6, 4}, {16, 14}, {1, 17}, {10, 7}, {5, 6}, {17, 2}}

Another way to get random coordinates:

In[4]:= **RandomInteger[20, {10, 2}]**

Out[4]= {{2, 2}, {20, 18}, {16, 2}, {13, 13}, {6, 15}, {11, 18}, {10, 20}, {17, 20}, {8, 14}, {2, 10}}

Plot 100 points at random coordinates:

In[5]:= **ListPlot[Table[RandomInteger[1000], 100, 2]]**

Out[5]=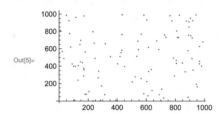

We can use coordinates to construct graphics. Earlier we saw how to make graphics of one circle. To make graphics of more than one circle we have to say where each circle is, which we can do by giving the coordinates of their centers.

Place circles by giving the coordinates of their centers:

In[6]:= **Graphics[{Circle[{1, 1}], Circle[{1, 2}], Circle[{3, 1}]}]**

Out[6]=

If we apply color styles it's easier to see which circle is which:

In[7]:= **Graphics[{Style[Circle[{1, 1}], Red], Style[Circle[{1, 2}], Green], Style[Circle[{3, 1}], Blue]}]**

Out[7]=

Make a graphic with 100 randomly placed circles, each with center coordinates up to 50:

In[8]:= **Graphics[Table[Circle[RandomInteger[50, 2]], 100]]**

Out[8]=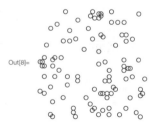

A 2D array of circles, arranged so that they just touch:

In[9]:= **Graphics[Table[Circle[{x, y}], {x, 0, 10, 2}, {y, 0, 10, 2}]]**

Out[9]=

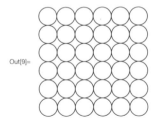

Circle [{x, y}] means a circle centered at position {x, y}. If you don't say otherwise, the circle is given radius 1. You can make a circle of any radius using Circle [{x, y}, r].

Use different radii for different circles:

In[10]:= **Graphics[{Circle[{1, 1}, 0.5], Circle[{1, 2}, 1.2], Circle[{3, 1}, 0.8]}]**

Out[10]=

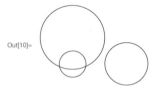

Make 10 concentric circles:

In[11]:= **Graphics[Table[Circle[{0, 0}, r], {r, 10}]]**

Out[11]=

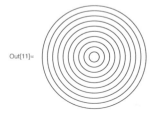

Draw larger circles with centers that shift progressively to the right:

In[12]:= **Graphics[Table[Circle[{x, 0}, x], {x, 10}]]**

Out[12]=

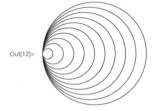

Pick both positions and radii at random:

In[13]:= **Graphics[Table[Circle[RandomInteger[50, 2], RandomInteger[10]], 100]]**

Out[13]=

RegularPolygon works much the same as Circle and Disk, except that in addition to giving the position of the center and the size, you also have to specify how many sides the polygon should have.

Make graphics of a size-1 regular pentagon and a size-0.5 regular heptagon:

In[14]:= **Graphics[{RegularPolygon[{1, 1}, 1, 5], RegularPolygon[{3, 1}, 0.5, 7]}]**

Out[14]=

You can mix different kinds of graphics objects:

In[15]:= **Graphics[{RegularPolygon[{1, 1}, 1, 5],**
         Circle[{1, 1}, 1], RegularPolygon[{3, 1}, .5, 7], Disk[{2, 2}, .5]}]

Out[15]=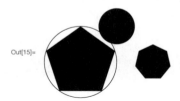

To make arbitrary graphics, you need the basic *graphics primitives* Point, Line and Polygon. Point[{x, y}] represents a point at coordinate position {x, y}. To get multiple points, you can either give a list of Point[{x, y}]s, or you can give a list of coordinate positions inside a single Point.

Graphics of three points at specified positions:

In[16]:= **Graphics[{Point[{0, 0}], Point[{2, 0}], Point[{1, 1.5}]}]**

Out[16]=

An alternative form, where all the coordinate positions are collected in a single list:

In[17]:= **Graphics[Point[{{0, 0}, {2, 0}, {1, 1.5}}]]**

Out[17]=

Make a line joining the positions:

In[18]:= **Graphics[Line[{{0, 0}, {2, 0}, {1, 1.5}}]]**

Out[18]=

Make a polygon with corners at the positions you give:

In[19]:= **Graphics[Polygon[{{0, 0}, {2, 0}, {1, 1.5}}]]**

Out[19]=

RegularPolygon makes a regular polygon in which all sides and angles are the same. Polygon lets you make any polygon, even strange ones that fold over themselves.

A polygon with 20 corners at random coordinates below 100; the polygon folds over itself:

In[20]:= **Graphics[Polygon[Table[RandomInteger[100], 20, 2]]]**

Out[20]=

The things we've done so far here immediately generalize to 3D. Instead of having two coordinates $\{x, y\}$ we have three: $\{x, y, z\}$. In the Wolfram Language, x by default goes across the screen, y goes "into" the screen, and z goes up the screen.

Two spheres stacked on top of each other:

In[21]:= **Graphics3D[{Sphere[{0, 0, 0}], Sphere[{0, 0, 2}]}]**

Out[21]=

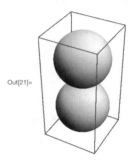

A 3D array of spheres (radius 1/2 makes them just touch):

In[22]:= **Graphics3D[Table[Sphere[{x, y, z}, 1/2], {x, 5}, {y, 5}, {z, 5}]]**

Out[22]=

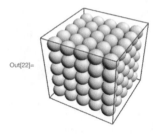

A 3D array of points:

In[23]:= **Graphics3D[Table[Point[{x, y, z}], {x, 10}, {y, 10}, {z, 10}]]**

Out[23]=

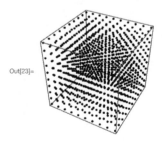

50 spheres at random 3D positions, with each coordinate running up to 10:

In[24]:= **Graphics3D[Table[Sphere[RandomInteger[10, 3]], 50]]**

Out[24]=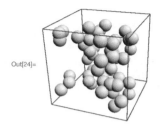

If you don't say otherwise, 3D objects like spheres are drawn solid, so you can't see through them. But just like you can specify what color something is, you can also specify its *opacity*. Opacity 1 means completely opaque, so you can't see through it at all; opacity 0 means completely transparent.

Specify opacity 0.5 for all spheres:

In[25]:= **Graphics3D[Table[Style[Sphere[RandomInteger[10, 3]], Opacity[0.5]], 50]]**

Out[25]=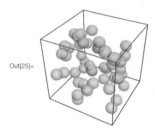

You can use Manipulate to make graphics—in 2D or 3D—that can be manipulated.

Manipulate the position and opacity of the second sphere:

In[26]:= **Manipulate[**
    Graphics3D[{Sphere[{0, 0, 0}], Style[Sphere[{x, 0, 0}], Opacity[o]]}], {x, 1, 3}, {o, 0.5, 1}]

Out[26]=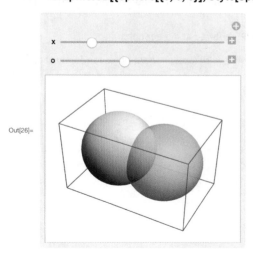

Vocabulary

Point[{x, y}]	a point at coordinates {x, y}
Line[{{1, 1}, {2, 4}, {1, 2}}]	a line connecting specified coordinates
Circle[{x, y}]	a circle with center at {x, y}
Circle[{x, y}, r]	a circle with center at {x, y} and radius r
RegularPolygon[{x, y}, s, n]	a regular polygon with center {x, y} and n sides each s long
Polygon[{{1, 1}, {2, 4}, {1, 2}}]	a polygon with the specified corners
Sphere[{x, y, z}]	a sphere with center at {x, y, z}
Sphere[{x, y, z}, r]	a sphere with center at {x, y, z} and radius r
Opacity[*level*]	specify an opacity level (0: transparent; 1: solid)

Exercises

14.1   Make graphics of 5 concentric circles centered at {0, 0} with radii 1, 2, ... , 5.

14.2   Make 10 concentric circles with random colors.

14.3   Make graphics of a 10×10 grid of circles with radius 1 centered at integer points {x, y}.

14.4   Make a 10×10 grid of points with coordinates at integer positions up to 10.

14.5   Make a **Manipulate** with between 1 and 20 concentric circles.

14.6   Place 50 spheres with random colors at random integer coordinates up to 10.

14.7   Make a 10×10×10 array of spheres with RGB components ranging from 0 to 1. The spheres should be centered at integer coordinates, and should just touch each other.

14.8   Make a **Manipulate** with t varying between −2 and +2 that contains circles of radius x centered at {t ∗ x, 0} with x going from 1 to 10.

14.9   Make a 5×5 array of regular hexagons with size 1/2, centered at integer points.

14.10   Make a line in 3D that goes through 50 random points with integer coordinates randomly chosen up to 50.

Q&A

What determines the range of coordinates shown?

By default it's picked automatically, but you can set it explicitly using the PlotRange option, as discussed in Section 20.

How can I put axes on graphics?

Use the option (see Section 20) Axes → True.

How do I change the appearance of the edges of a polygon or disk?

Use EdgeForm inside Style.

What other graphics constructs are there?

Quite a few. Examples include Text (for placing text inside graphics), Arrow (for putting arrowheads on lines, etc.), Inset (for putting graphics inside graphics) and FilledCurve.

How do I get rid of the box around 3D graphics?

Use the option (see Section 20) Boxed → False.

Tech Notes

- The random circles here are drawn at integer coordinates. You can use RandomReal to place them at arbitrary coordinates.

- Instead of using Style, you can give directives for graphics in a list, like {Red, Disk[ ]}. A particular directive will affect every graphics object that appears after it in the list.

- In 2D graphics, objects are drawn in whatever order you give them, so later ones can cover up earlier ones.

- You can apply geometric transformations to graphics objects using functions like Translate, Scale and Rotate.

- Polygons that fold over themselves (say, to make a bowtie shape) are displayed using an even-odd rule.

- 3D graphics can include Cuboid, Tetrahedron and polyhedra specified by PolyhedronData, as well as shapes defined by arbitrary meshes of points in 3D space.

More to Explore

Guide to Graphics in the Wolfram Language (wolfr.am/eiwl-14-more)

15 | The Scope of the Wolfram Language

In the past 14 sections, we've seen many things the Wolfram Language can do. But what we've seen is only the very beginning. We've discussed around 85 built-in functions—but altogether the language has more than 5000.

You can go to the Documentation Center to start exploring all these functions.

The front page of the Wolfram Language Documentation Center:

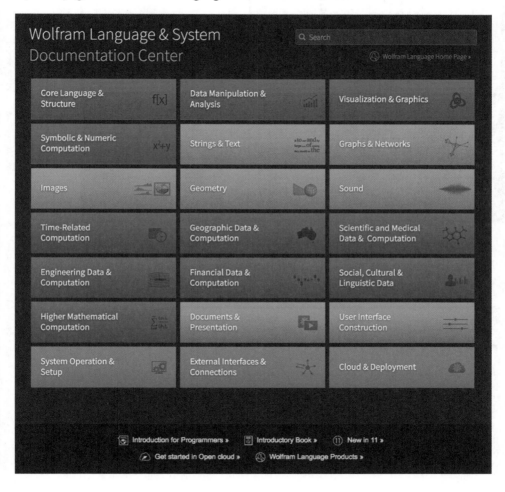

Let's pick Geometry as an example.

Open the Geometry tile:

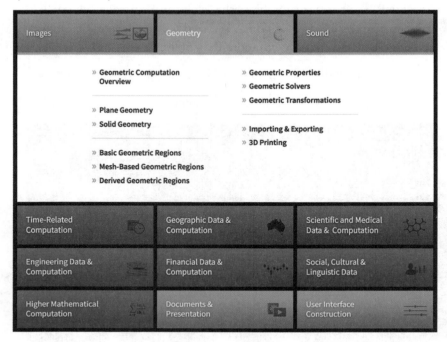

The Documentation Center has *guide pages* with overviews of functions related to particular topics.

The guide page for Plane Geometry:

Now you can visit the *function page* for a particular function, say Parallelogram.

The function page for Parallelogram:

There's a summary at the top, then lots of examples of how the Parallelogram function can be used, as well as a section to open to get more details.

Run the first example from the Parallelogram function page:

In[1]:= **Graphics[Parallelogram[ ]]**

Out[1]=

Whenever you start typing the name of a function, you'll see an autocomplete menu. Click the  to see the function page for a particular function.

Select from the autocomplete menu to pick a function:

When the name is complete you'll see:

Parallelogram|

Press the ≫ to see:

Parallelogram

$\text{Parallelogram}\left[p, \left\{v_1, v_2\right\}\right]$

represents a parallelogram with origin p and directions v_1 and v_2.

All the functions in the Wolfram Language follow the same principles—so for example the Parallelogram function works very much like the RegularPolygon function that we already discussed.

Q&A

How do I get to the Documentation Center?

It depends where you're running the Wolfram Language. If you're using the web or mobile, click the 📖 icon. On the desktop, go to the Help menu.

How do I try examples in the documentation?

Often you can just run them right inside the documentation. Alternatively, copy them to your working notebook and run them there.

How long does it take to learn the whole Wolfram Language?

As in learning a human language, it takes some time to become fluent, and to know the principles of the language. One can go on learning specific vocabulary almost indefinitely.

How much of the Wolfram Language does one need to know to use it in practice?

One needs to know its principles, as they are covered, for example, in this book. As with a human language, one can have a comparatively small working vocabulary, not least because there are usually many ways to express a given thing. It's easy to expand vocabulary in any particular case just by looking at documentation.

How can I read Wolfram Language code if I'm not fluent in English?

It'll help if you switch on *code captions*—which give short descriptions for every function name that appears, and are available for many languages.

Tech Note

- There's computable data about the structure of the Wolfram Language right in the Wolfram Language, accessible from WolframLanguageData.

More to Explore

The Wolfram Language Home Page (wolfr.am/eiwl-15-more)

Wolfram Language Documentation Center (wolfr.am/eiwl-15-more2)

16 | Real-World Data

A central feature of the Wolfram Language is that it's got immense amounts of real-world data built in. It's got data on countries and animals and movies, and lots more. It gets all this from the Wolfram Knowledgebase, which is being updated all the time—and is what powers Wolfram|Alpha and services based on it.

But how can you talk about a country in the Wolfram Language? The easiest way is just to use plain English. You can tell the Wolfram Language you're going to be giving it plain English by pressing ⌃ = (hold down the Control key and press the = key), or on a touch device, by pressing the ⊟ button.

Enter the plain English "united states":

⊟ united states

As soon as you press return (or click away), the Wolfram Language will try to interpret what you typed. Assuming it succeeds, it'll display a little yellow box that represents a *Wolfram Language entity*. In this case, it's the entity corresponding to the United States.

United States (country) ✓

Press the check mark to confirm that's what you want:

United States (country)

Now you can ask for lots of *properties* of this entity. Like you could ask for the US flag.

Ask for the flag property of the United States:

In[1]:= **United States** (country) **["Flag"]**

The result you get is something you can go on doing computation with—like in this case image processing.

Color-negate the US flag:

In[2]:= ColorNegate[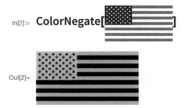]

Out[2]=

If all you want to do is to get the US flag, you can just ask for it in English.

In[3]:=

Out[3]=

EntityValue is a more flexible way to ask for the values of properties.

Use EntityValue to get the US flag:

In[4]:= **EntityValue[US , "Flag"]**

Out[4]=

EntityValue also works with lists of entities.

Get flags for a list of countries:

In[5]:= **EntityValue[{ US , brazil , china }, "Flag"]**

Out[5]=

The Wolfram Language has deep knowledge about countries, as about many other things.

Find out how many radio stations there are in the list of countries:

In[6]:= **EntityValue[{ US , brazil , china }, "RadioStations"]**

Out[6]= {13 769, 1822, 673}

Make a pie chart of the results:

In[7]:= **PieChart[EntityValue[{ US , brazil , china }, "RadioStations"]]**

Out[7]=

Find countries that border Switzerland:

In[8]:= 🔲 switzerland ["BorderingCountries"]

Out[8]= { Austria , France , Germany , Italy , Liechtenstein }

Find their flags:

In[9]:= **EntityValue[** Switzerland (country) **["BorderingCountries"], "Flag"]**

Out[9]=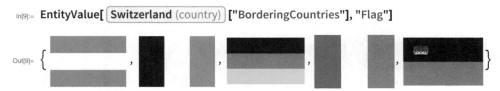

Sometimes you'll want to talk about a class of entities—like, say, planets.

Ask for planets, and get the class of entities corresponding to planets:

In[10]:= 🔲 planets

Out[10]= ▦ planets

Classes of entities are indicated by ▦. You can get a list of all entities in a class using EntityList.

Get the list of planets:

In[11]:= **EntityList[**🔲 planets **]**

Out[11]= { Mercury , Venus , Earth , Mars , Jupiter , Saturn , Uranus , Neptune }

Get images of all of the planets:

In[12]:= **EntityValue[**🔲 planets **, "Image"]**

Out[12]=

EntityValue can actually handle entity classes directly, so you don't need to use EntityList with it.

Get the radius of each of the planets, and make a bar chart of them:

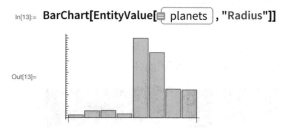

It's very convenient to use plain English to describe things. But a downside is that it can be ambiguous. If you say "mercury", do you mean the planet Mercury or the chemical element mercury or something else called "mercury"? When you use ctrl =, it'll always make an initial choice. But if you press the ··· you can change to another choice. Press the check mark ✓ to accept a choice.

To see how the Wolfram Language internally represents entities you can use InputForm.

Show the internal form of the entity that represents the United States:

In[14]:= **InputForm[⊟ USA]**

Out[14]= Entity["Country", "UnitedStates"]

Show the internal form for New York City:

In[15]:= **InputForm[⊟ nyc]**

Out[15]= Entity["City", {"NewYork", "NewYork", "UnitedStates"}]

There are millions of entities in the Wolfram Language, each with a definite internal form. In principle you could enter any entity using its internal form. But unless you're using the same entity over and over again, it's much more practical just to use ctrl = and enter a name for the entity in plain English.

There are thousands of different types of entities in the Wolfram Language, covering all sorts of areas of knowledge. To find out about them, check out the Wolfram Language documentation, or the Wolfram|Alpha examples pages. Each type of entity then has a list of properties—often hundreds of them. One way to find this list is to use EntityProperties.

Possible properties for amusement parks:

In[16]:= **EntityProperties["AmusementPark"]**

Out[16]= { administrative division , type , area , city , closing date ,

country , image , latitude , longitude , name , number of rides ,

opening date , owner , coordinates , slogan , rides , status }

In practice, though, a good approach is to ask in plain English for a property of some entity, then to look at the interpretation that's found, and re-use the property from it.

Ask for the height of the Eiffel Tower:

▤ height of the eiffel tower

In[17]:= ▤ eiffel tower ["Height"]

Out[17]= 1062.99 ft

Re-use the "Height" property, applied to the Great Pyramid:

In[18]:= ▤ pyramid of giza ["Height"]

Out[18]= 456.037 ft

Different types of entities have different properties. One common property for many types of entities is "Image".

Get images of various entities:

In[19]:= ▤ koala ["Image"]

Out[19]=

In[20]:= ▤ eiffel tower ["Image"]

Out[20]=

In[21]:= 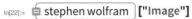 **["Image"]**

Out[21]=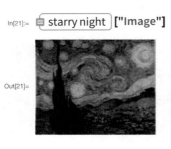

In[22]:= 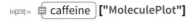 **["Image"]**

Out[22]=

Other types of objects have other properties.

A plot of a caffeine molecule:

In[23]:=  **["MoleculePlot"]**

Out[23]=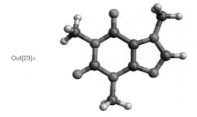

Rotatable 3D graphics of a skull:

In[24]:= 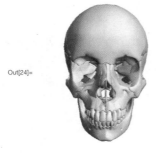 **["Graphics3D"]**

Out[24]=

A net that folds up into our 3D company logo:

In[25]:= 📄 rhombic hexecontahedron ["NetImage"]

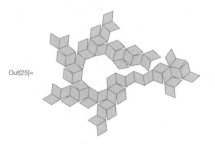

Out[25]=

Vocabulary

ctrl **=**	plain English input
EntityList[*class***]**	entities in a class
EntityValue[*entities***, ***property***]**	value of a property of an entity
EntityProperties[*type***]**	list of properties for an entity type
InputForm[*entity***]**	internal Wolfram Language representation of an entity

---

Exercises

16.1   Find the flag of Switzerland.

16.2   Get an image of an elephant.

16.3   Use the "Mass" property to generate a list of the masses of the planets.

16.4   Make a bar chart of the masses of the planets.

16.5   Make an image collage of images of the planets.

16.6   Edge detect the flag of China.

16.7   Find the height of the Empire State Building.

16.8   Compute the height of the Empire State Building divided by the height of the Great Pyramid.

16.9   Compute the elevation of Mount Everest divided by the height of the Empire State Building.

16.10   Find the dominant colors in the painting *The Starry Night*.

16.11   Find the dominant colors in an image collage of the flag images of all countries in Europe.

16.12   Make a pie chart of the GDP of countries in Europe.

16.13   Add an image of a koala to an image of the Australian flag.

Where does the Wolfram Language get its real-world data?

It's all from the central Wolfram Knowledgebase. We've been building this knowledgebase for many years, carefully curating data from thousands of primary sources.

Is the data in the Wolfram Language regularly updated?

Yes. We put a lot of effort into keeping it all up to date. And in fact there's new data flowing in every second—about market prices, weather, earthquakes, aircraft positions and lots more.

How accurate is the data in the Wolfram Language?

We go to a lot of trouble to make it as accurate as possible, and we check it extensively. But ultimately we often have to rely on what governments and other outside organizations report.

What is the relation to Wolfram|Alpha?

Wolfram|Alpha uses the same knowledgebase as the Wolfram Language.

How should I refer to a particular entity?

However you want to. The Wolfram Language is set up to understand all common ways to refer to entities. ("New York City", "NYC", "the big apple", etc., all work.)

How can I find all properties and values for a given entity?

Use *entity*["Dataset"] or *entity*["PropertyAssociation"].

What does it mean if EntityValue gives Missing[…]?

It means the value you've asked for isn't known, or at least isn't in the Wolfram Knowledgebase. Use DeleteMissing to delete Missing[…] elements in a list.

Can I set up my own entities, and put in my own data about them?

Yes, using EntityStore.

Tech Notes

- The Wolfram Knowledgebase is stored in the cloud, so even if you're using a desktop version of the Wolfram Language, you'll need to connect to the network to start getting real-world data.

- The Wolfram Knowledgebase contains many trillions of specific facts and values, stored in a Wolfram Language symbolic framework, with a variety of underlying database technologies.

- The Wolfram Knowledgebase has been systematically built and curated from large numbers of primary sources of data. It doesn't come from web searching.

- Real-world data often involves *units*, which we'll discuss in the next section.

- Instead of using natural language, you can access the Wolfram Knowledgebase through specific functions like CountryData and MovieData. Sometimes this may be faster.

- If you want to find the original source of a particular piece of data, you can look at documentation (e.g. for CountryData, etc.), or you can ask for the data in Wolfram|Alpha and follow source links.

- Sometimes you want to talk about a special instance of an entity, like a country in a particular year, or a certain amount of a substance. You can do this using EntityInstance.

- RandomEntity finds random entities of a given type.

- There's a symmetry between entities and properties. *entity*[*property*] gives the same result as *property*[*entity*]. To get values of several properties, use *entity*[{p_1, p_2, …}]; to get values for several entities, use *property*[{e_1, e_2, …}]. (Note that for *property*[*entity*] you need the full property object, as obtained from ctrl = , not just the name of the property as a string.)

More to Explore

Major Areas Covered by the Wolfram Knowledgebase (wolfr.am/eiwl-16-more)

Geographic Data and Computation (wolfr.am/eiwl-16-more2)

Scientific and Medical Data and Computation (wolfr.am/eiwl-16-more3)

Engineering Data and Computation (wolfr.am/eiwl-16-more4)

Social, Cultural and Linguistic Data (wolfr.am/eiwl-16-more5)

17 | Units

As soon as you're dealing with real-world quantities, it's inevitable that you'll run into *units*. In the Wolfram Language, you can enter quantities with units using ctrl = .

Enter a quantity of time in units of hours:

2.6 hours

2.6 h ✓

Press the check mark to accept the interpretation:

2.6 h

You can use InputForm to see how the Wolfram Language internally represents this.

Show the internal form of a quantity:

In[1]:= **InputForm[** 2.6 hours **]**

Out[1]= **Quantity[2.6, "Hours"]**

You can always enter quantities directly like this, or you can use ctrl = , either for the whole thing, or just for the units.

The Wolfram Language knows about all the 10,000 or so common kinds of units. UnitConvert converts between them.

Convert from hours to minutes:

In[2]:= **UnitConvert[** 2.6 h , **"Minutes"]**

Out[2]= **156. min**

You can do arithmetic with quantities even if they have different units.

Add a length in feet to one in centimeters:

In[3]:= 7.5 ft + 14 cm

Out[3]= **242.6 cm**

Divide one length by another:

In[4]:= 7.5 ft / 14 cm

Out[4]= **16.3286**

You can compute with money too.

Use dollars in a computation:

In[5]:= 7.5 * ⊟ $3 + 2.51 * ⊟ $8

Out[5]= $42.58

Multiply a price per pound by a weight in kilograms:

In[6]:= ⊟ $15/lb * ⊟ 5.6 kg

Out[6]= $185.19

You can convert between currencies. The Wolfram Language always knows the latest conversion rate.

In[7]:= CurrencyConvert[⊟ 100 euros , ⊟ US dollars]

Out[7]= $112.10

There are many places where units show up. Another example is in angles—and this is such a common case that the Wolfram Language lets you handle it in a special way. You can enter an angle like 30 degrees either as 30 Degree, or as 30 °, where the ° can be typed as esc deg esc.

Display a string rotated by 30 degrees:

In[8]:= Rotate["hello", 30 °]

Out[8]= hello

If you leave off the Degree or °, the Wolfram Language will assume you're talking about *radians*, which go from 0 to 2π (about 6.28) around a circle, rather than degrees, which go from 0 to 360.

$\pi/2$ radians is equivalent to 90°:

In[9]:= Rotate["hello", Pi/2]

Out[9]= hello

Make a list of rotations in degrees from 0 to 360:

In[10]:= Table[Rotate[n, n Degree], {n, 0, 360, 30}]

Out[10]= {0, 30, 60, 90, 120, 150, 180, 210, 240, 270, 300, 330, 360}

There's lots to do with angles. For example, AnglePath gives the path you'd follow if you successively turned by a sequence of angles.

Start off horizontal, then turn three times by 80°:

In[11]:= **Graphics[Line[AnglePath[{0 °, 80 °, 80 °, 80 °}]]]**

Out[11]=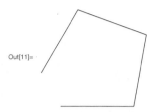

Keep turning by 80° and you'll eventually get back to where you started:

In[12]:= **Graphics[Line[AnglePath[Table[80 °, 20]]]]**

Out[12]=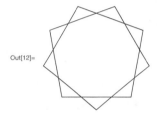

If you keep increasing the angle, you get an interesting pattern:

In[13]:= **Graphics[Line[AnglePath[Table[n ∗ 5 °, {n, 200}]]]]**

Out[13]=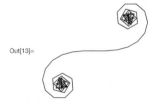

Vocabulary

UnitConvert[*quantity, unit***]**	convert between units
CurrencyConvert[*amount, unit***]**	convert between currencies
30 Degree	angle in degrees
30 °	angle in degrees entered with ⌈esc⌉ deg ⌈esc⌉
Rotate[*expr, angle***]**	rotate on the screen
AnglePath[{*angle₁, angle₂, …***}]**	path derived from a sequence of turns

---

Exercises

17.1 Convert 4.5 lbs (pounds) to kilograms.

17.2 Convert 60.25 mph to kilometers per hour.

17.3 Find the height of the Eiffel Tower in miles.

17.4 Find the height of Mount Everest divided by the height of the Eiffel Tower.

17.5 Find the mass of the Earth divided by the mass of the Moon.

17.6 Convert 2500 Japanese yen to US dollars.

17.7 Find the total of 35 ounces, 1/4 ton, 45 lbs and 9 stone in kilograms.

17.8 Get a list of the distances to each planet using the "DistanceFromEarth" property, and convert all the results to light minutes.

17.9 Rotate the string "hello" by 180°.

17.10 Make a table of a size-100 "A" rotated by 0° through 360° in steps of 30°.

17.11 Make a Manipulate to rotate an image of a cat between 0° and 180°.

17.12 Generate graphics for a path obtained by turning 0°, 1°, 2°, ... , 180°.

17.13 Make graphics of the path obtained by turning a constant angle 100 times, controlling the angle from 0° to 360° with a Manipulate.

17.14 Make graphics of the path obtained by successively turning by the digits of 2^10000 multiplied by 30°.

Q&A

What unit abbreviations does the Wolfram Language understand?

Pretty much any common abbreviation, whether it's miles/hr or mph or mi/h, etc. (If you're wondering if an abbreviation will work, just try it.)

Does the Wolfram Language pick units based on what country I'm in?

Yes. For example, it'll tend to use inches if you're in the US, and centimeters if you're in continental Europe.

Do I have to be connected to the network to use units?

Only to interpret input like 5 kg. If you type Quantity[5, "Kilograms"] you don't need the network—except to deal with units like currencies whose values are always changing.

What can I do if my unit conversion gives me an exact fraction but I want a decimal number?

Use the function N[...] to find a decimal approximation. Or add a decimal point to a number in your input. We'll talk more about this in Section 23.

Why don't I get the same result for the currency conversion example?

Because, without doubt, the conversion rates have changed.

Tech Notes

- The Wolfram Language handles all 160 or so standard currencies (including ones like bitcoin). If necessary, you can use the ISO currency code (USD, UKP, etc.) to specify a currency.

- Degree isn't a function; like Red, Green, etc. it's a *symbol*. We'll talk more about these later.

- AnglePath implements "turtle graphics" familiar from languages like Logo and Scratch.

- AnglePath3D generalizes AnglePath to 3D, allowing for "flying turtles", spacecraft simulations, etc.

More to Explore

Guide to Units in the Wolfram Language (wolfr.am/eiwl-17-more)

18 | Geocomputation

The Wolfram Language has extensive built-in knowledge of geography. For example, it knows where New York City is, and it can compute how far it is from there to Los Angeles.

Compute the distance between the centers of New York and Los Angeles:

In[1]:= **GeoDistance[** new york **,** los angeles **]**

Out[1]= 2432.07 mi

You can also plot locations on a map, using GeoListPlot.

Plot New York and Los Angeles on a map:

In[2]:= **GeoListPlot[{** new york **,** los angeles **}]**

Out[2]=

Plot countries on a map:

In[3]:= **GeoListPlot[{** iceland **,** france **,** italy **}]**

Out[3]=

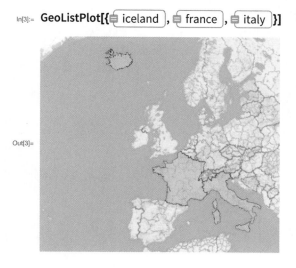

You can do things at a much smaller scale too.

Plot two famous locations in Paris:

In[4]:= **GeoListPlot[{⊟ Eiffel Tower , ⊟ Louvre }]**

Out[4]=

GeoListPlot is the analog for geography of ListPlot. GeoGraphics is the analog of Graphics.

Generate a map of New York City:

In[5]:= **GeoGraphics[⊟ New York City]**

Out[5]=

GeoPath represents a path on the surface of the Earth.

Show the shortest path from New York to Tokyo:

In[6]:= **GeoGraphics[GeoPath[{▤ New York , ▤ Tokyo }]]**

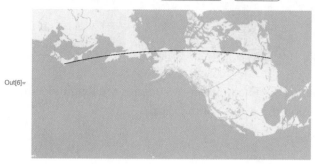

Out[6]=

Styling works just like in other graphics:

In[7]:= **GeoGraphics[Style[GeoPath[{▤ New York , ▤ Tokyo }], Thick, Red]]**

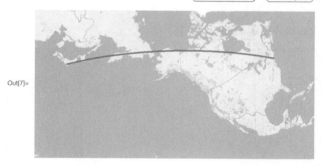

Out[7]=

GeoDisk is the analog of Disk; you specify its center and its radius.

Show a 1-mile-radius disk around the Eiffel Tower:

In[8]:= **GeoGraphics[GeoDisk[▤ eiffel tower , ▤ 1 mile]]**

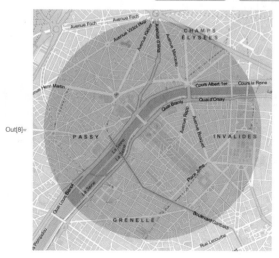

Out[8]=

Generate a table of maps, with disks whose sizes go up as powers of 10:

In[9]:= **Table[GeoGraphics[GeoDisk[⊟ eiffel tower , ⊟ 1 mile *10^n]], {n, 0, 4}]**

Out[9]=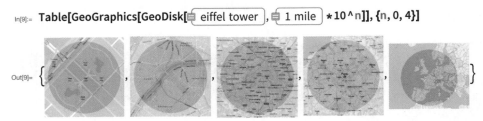

GeoPosition gives a position on the Earth. The numbers it contains are longitude and latitude—the standard coordinates on the surface of the Earth.

Find the geo position of the Eiffel Tower:

In[10]:= **GeoPosition[⊟ eiffel tower]**

Out[10]= GeoPosition[{48.8583, 2.29444}]

Draw a 4000-mile-radius disk around 0 latitude, 0 longitude:

In[11]:= **GeoGraphics[GeoDisk[GeoPosition[{0, 0}], ⊟ 4000 miles]]**

Out[11]=

Notice that the disk isn't quite circular. That's because we have to use a *projection* to draw the surface of the Earth on a flat map. It's one of the many subtleties in doing geocomputation.

GeoNearest finds what's nearest to a given place on the Earth. You tell it what type of thing to look for, and how many you want it to find.

Find the nearest 5 countries to 0 longitude, 0 latitude:

In[12]:= **GeoNearest["Country", GeoPosition[{0, 0}], 5]**

Out[12]= { Ghana , Ivory Coast , Equatorial Guinea , Togo , Benin }

Find the nearest cities instead:

In[13]:= **GeoNearest["City", GeoPosition[{0, 0}], 5]**

Out[13]= { Takoradi , Sekondi , Cape Coast , Elmina , Shama }

It's often nice to know your own geo position. So long as your computer, phone, etc. knows, Here will give you that.

Find where your computer (or phone, etc.) thinks it is:

In[14]:= **Here**

Out[14]= GeoPosition[{40.11, −88.24}]

You can do computations with Here.

Compute how far it is to the Eiffel Tower:

In[15]:= **GeoDistance[Here, ▤ eiffel tower]**

Out[15]= 4245.54 mi

Find the nearest 5 volcanoes to my position:

In[16]:= **GeoNearest["Volcano", Here, 5]**

Out[16]= { Dotsero , Valles Caldera , Carrizozo , Zuni-Bandera , Yellowstone }

Plot volcanoes on a map:

In[17]:= **GeoListPlot[GeoNearest["Volcano", Here, 30]]**

Out[17]=

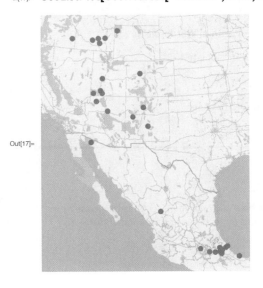

Vocabulary

GeoDistance[$entity_1$, $entity_2$]	geo distance between entities
GeoListPlot[{$entity_1$, $entity_2$, ...}]	plot a list of entities on a map
GeoGraphics[...]	map constructed from primitives
GeoPath[{$entity_1$, $entity_2$}]	path between entities
GeoDisk[$entity$, r]	disk with radius r around an entity
Here	where your computer, phone, etc. thinks it is
GeoPosition[$entity$]	geo position of an entity
GeoNearest["$type$", $location$, n]	nearest n objects of a certain type to a location

Exercises

18.1   Find the distance from New York to London.

18.2   Divide the distance from New York to London by the distance from New York to San Francisco.

18.3   Find the distance from Sydney to Moscow in kilometers.

18.4   Generate a map of the United States.

18.5   Plot on a map Brazil, Russia, India and China.

18.6   Plot on a map the path from New York City to Beijing.

18.7   Plot a disk centered on the Great Pyramid, with radius 10 miles.

18.8   Plot a disk centered on New York with a radius large enough to just reach San Francisco.

18.9   Find the nearest 5 countries to the North Pole (**GeoPosition**["NorthPole"]).

18.10   Find the flags of the 3 countries nearest to latitude 45°, longitude 0°.

18.11   Plot the 25 volcanoes closest to Rome.

18.12   Find the difference in latitude between New York and Los Angeles.

Q&A

Can I get different projections for maps?

Yes. Just use the GeoProjection option. There are more than 300 built-in projections to choose from. The default projection used in any particular case depends on the scale and location of the map.

How detailed are the maps in the Wolfram Language?

They go down to the level of individual streets. Most streets in the world are included.

How does the Wolfram Language find my geo position?

It uses the function FindGeoLocation. On a mobile device, this will normally ask for your GPS position. On a computer, it'll normally try to deduce your location from your internet address—this won't always work correctly. You can always explicitly set your geo location by assigning a value to $GeoLocation.

How can I specify the range of a map?

Use the option GeoRange → *distance* (e.g. GeoRange → 🖥 5 miles) or GeoRange → *place* (e.g. GeoRange → 🖥 Europe), as discussed in Section 20.

Can the Wolfram Language compute driving directions?

Yes. Use TravelDirections. GeoDistance gives the direct shortest path; TravelDistance gives the path following roads, etc. TravelTime gives estimated travel time.

Is the Wolfram Language restricted to maps of the Earth?

No. For example, the moon and Mars also work. Use the option GeoModel → "Moon", etc.

Tech Notes

- You need to be connected to the network to use maps in the Wolfram Language.

- Instead of entering 🖥 nyc , 🖥 LA you can just enter 🖥 nyc, LA and get the same result.

- If you give GeoDistance extended regions (like countries), it'll compute the shortest distance between any points in the regions.

- GeoPosition uses numerical values of longitude and latitude, not 35 Degree, etc.

- GeoPosition normally uses decimal degrees. Use FromDMS to convert from degrees-minutes-seconds.

- To color regions on a map by values, use GeoRegionValuePlot.

- To draw bubbles of different sizes around points on a map (e.g. populations of cities), use GeoBubbleChart.

More to Explore

Guide to Maps & Cartography in the Wolfram Language (wolfr.am/eiwl-18-more)

Guide to Geographic Data & Entities in the Wolfram Language (wolfr.am/eiwl-18-more2)

19 | Dates and Times

In the Wolfram Language, Now gives your current date and time.

Get the current date and time (as of when I wrote this!):

In[1]:= **Now**

Out[1]= 📅 **Fri 17 Mar 2017 13:39:00 GMT−5.**

You can do computations on this, for example adding a week.

Add a week to the current date and time:

In[2]:= **Now +** ▤ 1 week

Out[2]= 📅 **Fri 24 Mar 2017 13:39:00 GMT−5.**

Use ctrl = to enter a date in any standard format.

Enter a date:

In[3]:= ▤ june 23, 1988

Out[3]= 📅 Day: **Thu 23 Jun 1988**

You can do arithmetic with dates, say, subtracting them to find how far apart they are.

Subtract two dates:

In[4]:= **Now −** ▤ june 23, 1988

Out[4]= 10 494. days

Convert the date difference to years:

In[5]:= **UnitConvert[Now −** ▤ june 23, 1988 **, "Years"]**

Out[5]= 28.7507 yr

DayRange is the analog of Range for dates:

Give a list of the days spanning from yesterday to tomorrow:

In[6]:= **DayRange[Yesterday, Tomorrow]**

Out[6]= { 📅 Day: **Thu 16 Mar 2017** , 📅 Day: **Fri 17 Mar 2017** , 📅 Day: **Sat 18 Mar 2017** }

DayName finds the day of the week for a particular date.

Compute the day of the week 45 days from now:

In[7]:= **DayName[Today +** 🗐 **45 days** **]**

Out[7]= Monday

Once you know a date, there are lots of things you can compute. For example, MoonPhase gives the phase of the moon (or, more accurately, the fraction of the Moon that is illuminated when seen from the Earth).

Compute the phase of the moon now:

In[8]:= **MoonPhase[Now]**

Out[8]= 0.7606

Compute the phase of the moon on a certain date:

In[9]:= **MoonPhase[**🗐 **june 23, 1988** **]**

Out[9]= 0.5756

Generate an icon for the phase of the moon:

In[10]:= **MoonPhase[**🗐 **june 23, 1988** **, "Icon"]**

Out[10]=

If you know both the date and a location on Earth, you can work out when the sun will rise and set.

Compute when sunset will be today at my current location:

In[11]:= **Sunset[Here, Today]**

Out[11]= 🗓 Minute: **Fri 17 Mar 2017 19:04 GMT−5.**

Compute the time between successive sunrises:

In[12]:= **Sunrise[Here, Tomorrow] − Sunrise[Here, Today]**

Out[12]= 1438 min

They're about a minute off from being exactly 1 day (24 hours) apart:

In[13]:= **Sunrise[Here, Tomorrow] – Sunrise[Here, Today] –** ⬚ 1 day

Out[13]= −2 min

Time zones are one of many subtleties. LocalTime gives the time in the time zone of a particular location.

Find the local time now in New York City:

In[14]:= **LocalTime[**⬚ New York **]**

Out[14]= 📅 Fri 17 Mar 2017 14:44:22 GMT−4.

Find the local time now in London:

In[15]:= **LocalTime[**⬚ London **]**

Out[15]= 📅 Fri 17 Mar 2017 18:44:29 GMT

Among the many areas where the Wolfram Language has extensive data is weather. The function AirTemperatureData uses this data to give the historical air temperature at a particular time and place.

Find the air temperature here at 6 pm yesterday:

In[16]:= **AirTemperatureData[Here,** ⬚ 6 pm yesterday **]**

Out[16]= 39.92 °F

If you provide a pair of dates, AirTemperatureData computes a *time series* of estimated temperatures between those dates.

Give a time series of air temperature measurements from a week ago until now:

In[17]:= **AirTemperatureData[Here, {**⬚ 1 week ago **, Now}]**

Out[17]= **TimeSeries[** ➕ 📈 Time: **10 Mar 2017** to **17 Mar 2017**
Data points: **247** **]**

DateListPlot is the analog of ListPlot for time series, where each value occurs at a particular date.

Plot the list of air temperature measurements:

In[18]:= **DateListPlot[AirTemperatureData[Here, {⊟ 1 week ago , Now}]]**

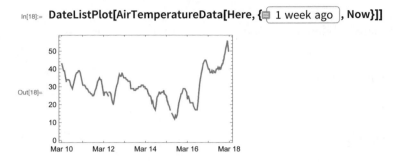

Out[18]=

The plot shows that, not surprisingly, the temperature is higher during the day than at night.

As another example, let's look at data that goes much further back in time. WordFrequencyData tells one how frequently a particular word occurs, say in a sample of books published in a given year. There's a lot of history one can see by looking at how this changes over the years and centuries.

Find the time series of how frequently the word "automobile" occurs:

In[19]:= **WordFrequencyData["automobile", "TimeSeries"]**

Out[19]= **TimeSeries[** ⊞ _⋀ Time: **01 Jan 1706** to **01 Jan 2008** Data points: **158** **]**

Cars started to exist around 1900, but gradually stopped being called "automobiles":

In[20]:= **DateListPlot[WordFrequencyData["automobile", "TimeSeries"]]**

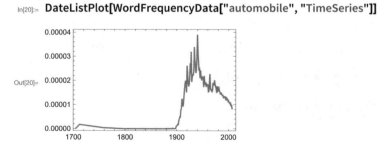

Out[20]=

WordFrequencyData is set up to make it easy to compare frequencies of different words. Let's see how "monarchy" and "democracy" have fared over the years. "Democracy" is definitely more popular now, but "monarchy" was more popular in the 1700s and 1800s.

Compare historical word frequency between "monarchy" and "democracy":

In[21]:= **DateListPlot[WordFrequencyData[{"monarchy", "democracy"}, "TimeSeries"]]**

Out[21]=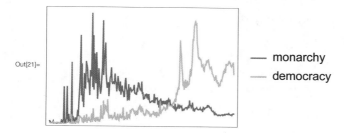

Vocabulary

Now	current date and time
Today	date object for today
Tomorrow	date object for tomorrow
Yesterday	date object for yesterday
DayRange[$date_1$, $date_2$**]**	list of dates from $date_1$ to $date_2$
DayName[$date$**]**	day of the week of $date$
MoonPhase[$date$**]**	moon phase on $date$
Sunrise[$location$, $date$**]**	time of sunrise on $date$ at $location$
Sunset[$location$, $date$**]**	time of sunset on $date$ at $location$
LocalTime[$location$**]**	current time at $location$
AirTemperatureData[$location$, $time$**]**	air temperature at $time$ at $location$
AirTemperatureData[$location$, {$time_1$, $time_2$}**]**	time series of air temperatures from $time_1$ to $time_2$ at $location$
DateListPlot[$timeseries$**]**	plot a time series
WordFrequencyData["$word$", "TimeSeries"**]**	time series of word frequencies

Exercises

19.1   Compute how many days have elapsed since January 1, 1900.

19.2   Compute what day of the week January 1, 2000 was.

19.3   Find the date a hundred thousand days ago.

19.4   Find the local time in Delhi.

19.5   Find the length of daylight today by subtracting today's sunrise from today's sunset.

19.6   Generate an icon for the current phase of the moon.

19.7   Make a list of the numerical phase of the moon for each of the next 10 days.

19.8   Generate a list of icons for the moon phases from today until 10 days from now.

19.9   Compute the time today between sunrise in New York City and in London.

19.10   Find the air temperature at the Eiffel Tower at noon yesterday.

19.11   Plot the temperature at the Eiffel Tower over the past week.

19.12   Find the difference in air temperatures between Los Angeles and New York City now.

19.13   Plot the historical frequency of the word "groovy".

Q&A

How can I get a date as a string?
Use DateString[*date*]. There are many options for the format of the string. For example, DateString[*date*, "DateShort"] uses short day and month names.

How can I extract the month or some other element from a date?
Use DateValue. DateValue[*date*, "Month"] gives the month number, DateValue[*date*, "MonthName"] gives the month name, etc.

How far in the past can dates be in the Wolfram Language?
As far as you want. The Wolfram Language knows about historical calendar systems, and the history of time zones. It also has the data to accurately compute sunrise, etc. going back at least 1000 years.

Why are sunrise and sunset given only to the minute?
Because you can't compute more accurately than that exactly when the sun will actually rise and set without knowing things like air temperature that affect the bending of light in the Earth's atmosphere.

Where does the Wolfram Language get air temperature data from?
The worldwide network of weather stations, located at airports and other places. If you've got your own air temperature measuring device, you can connect it to the Wolfram Language through the Wolfram Data Drop (see Section 43).

What is a time series?
It's a way of specifying the values of something at a series of times. You can enter a time series in the Wolfram Language as TimeSeries [{{ *time*$_1$, *value*$_1$}, {*time*$_2$, *value*$_2$}, ...}]. The Wolfram Language lets you do arithmetic and many other operations with time series.

What does DateListPlot do?
It plots values against times or dates. The values can be given in a TimeSeries [...] or in a list of the form {{*time*$_1$, *value*$_1$}, {*time*$_2$, *value*$_2$}, ...}.

Tech Notes

- The Wolfram Language decides whether to interpret a date like 8/10/15 as month/day/year or day/month/year based on what country you're in. You can pick the other interpretation if you want.

- Monday, etc. are *symbols* with intrinsic meaning, not strings.

- DateObject lets you specify the "granularity" of a date (day, week, month, year, decade, etc.). CurrentDate, NextDate, DateWithinQ, etc. operate on granular dates.

- You can see what's "inside" DateObject[...] using InputForm.

More to Explore

Guide to Dates & Times in the Wolfram Language (wolfr.am/eiwl-19-more)

20 | Options

Many functions in the Wolfram Language have *options* that determine the details of how they work. For example, in making a plot, you can use PlotTheme → "Web" to use a web-oriented visual theme. On a keyboard, the → is automatically formed if you type -> (i.e. – followed by >).

A standard plot, with no options given:

In[1]:= **ListLinePlot[RandomInteger[10, 10]]**

Out[1]=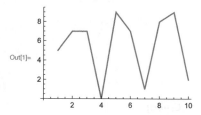

A plot with the PlotTheme option given as "Web":

In[2]:= **ListLinePlot[RandomInteger[10, 10], PlotTheme → "Web"]**

Out[2]=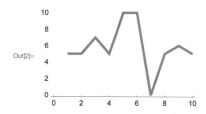

A plot with the PlotTheme option given as "Detailed":

In[3]:= **ListLinePlot[RandomInteger[10, 10], PlotTheme → "Detailed"]**

Out[3]=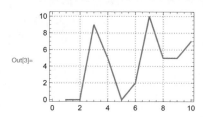

A plot with the PlotTheme option given as "Marketing":

In[4]:= **ListLinePlot[RandomInteger[10, 10], PlotTheme → "Marketing"]**

Out[4]=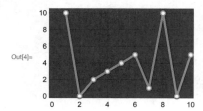

You can add more options. For example, Filling specifies what filling to add to a plot.

Fill the plot to the axis:

In[5]:= **ListLinePlot[RandomInteger[10, 10], PlotTheme → "Web", Filling → Axis]**

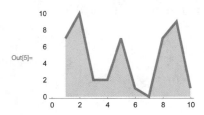

Background lets you specify a background color.

Also include an option for background color:

In[6]:= **ListLinePlot[RandomInteger[10, 10],**
       PlotTheme → "Web", Filling → Axis, Background → LightGreen]

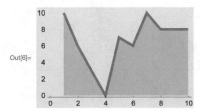

If you don't mention a particular option, the Wolfram Language will use a pre-defined default for that option. Most often that default is Automatic, which means that the language will automatically determine what to do.

One option that's often useful for graphics is PlotRange, which specifies what range of values to include in a plot. With the default PlotRange → Automatic, the system will try to automatically show the "interesting" part of the plot. PlotRange → All shows all values.

With default options all but one "outlier" value are displayed:

In[7]:= **ListLinePlot[{36, 16, 9, 64, 1, 340, 36, 0, 49, 81}]**

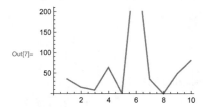

PlotRange → All says to include all points:

In[8]:= **ListLinePlot[{36, 16, 9, 64, 1, 340, 36, 0, 49, 81}, PlotRange → All]**

Out[8]=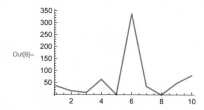

PlotRange → 30 specifies to show values up to 30:

In[9]:= **ListLinePlot[{36, 16, 9, 64, 1, 340, 36, 0, 49, 81}, PlotRange → 30]**

Out[9]=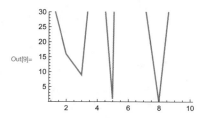

PlotRange → {20, 100} specifies to show values between 20 and 100:

In[10]:= **ListLinePlot[{36, 16, 9, 64, 1, 340, 36, 0, 49, 81}, PlotRange → {20, 100}]**

Out[10]=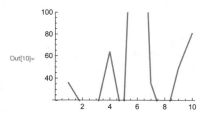

You can specify ranges for all types of graphics. In GeoListPlot and GeoGraphics you can use the option GeoRange to specify what part of the world to include in a plot.

By default, a geo plot of France pretty much includes only France:

In[11]:= **GeoListPlot[]**

Out[11]=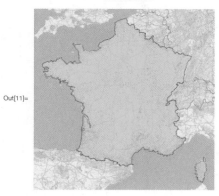

This requests a range that includes all of Europe:

In[12]:= **GeoListPlot[** france **, GeoRange →** europe **]**

Out[12]=

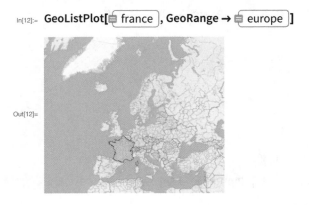

GeoRange → All specifies to use the whole world:

In[13]:= **GeoListPlot[** france **, GeoRange → All]**

Out[13]=

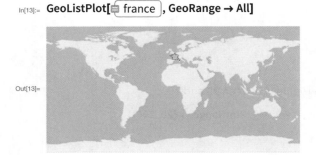

There are many other options for GeoListPlot. For example GeoBackground specifies what kind of background should be used. GeoLabels adds labels. Joined makes the points be joined.

Use a relief map as the background:

In[14]:= **GeoListPlot[** france **, GeoRange →** europe **, GeoBackground → "ReliefMap"]**

Out[14]=

Automatically add labels for geo objects:

In[15]:= **GeoListPlot[{⊟ paris , ⊟ new york , ⊟ sydney }, GeoLabels → Automatic]**

Out[15]=

Say it's **True** that the points should be joined:

In[16]:= **GeoListPlot[{⊟ los angeles , ⊟ chicago , ⊟ new york city }, Joined → True]**

Out[16]=

The function ListLinePlot has 57 different options you can set; GeoListPlot has 54. Some options are common to all graphics functions. For example, AspectRatio determines the overall shape of graphics, specifying the ratio of height to width.

With an aspect ratio of 1/3, the plot is 3 times wider than it is tall:

In[17]:= **ListLinePlot[RandomInteger[10, 10], AspectRatio → 1/3]**

Out[17]=

The option ImageSize specifies the overall size of graphics.

Draw a circle with a "tiny" overall image size:

In[18]:= **Graphics[Circle[], ImageSize → Tiny]**

Out[18]=

Draw circles with specific image sizes between 5 and 50 pixels:

In[19]:= **Table[Graphics[Circle[], ImageSize → n], {n, 5, 50, 5}]**

Out[19]= 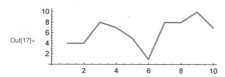 { ∘, ○, ○, ○, ○, ○, ○, ○, ○, ○ }

It's not just Graphics that allows options. Lots of other functions do too. An example is Style, which supports many options.

Set an option to use "Chalkboard" font to style text:

In[20]:= **Style["text in a different font", 20, FontFamily → "Chalkboard"]**

Out[20]= text in a different font

It's quite common for options to describe details of output, for example in WordCloud.

Create a word cloud with random word orientations:

In[21]:= **WordCloud[DeleteStopwords[WikipediaData["computer"]],**
      WordOrientation → "Random"]

Out[21]=

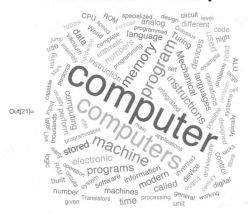

Grid has many options. The Frame option controls whether and how a frame is drawn.

Create a multiplication table with a frame around each entry:

In[22]:= **Grid[Table[i * j, {i, 5}, {j, 5}], Frame → All]**

Out[22]=

1	2	3	4	5
2	4	6	8	10
3	6	9	12	15
4	8	12	16	20
5	10	15	20	25

Like Graphics, Grid has a Background option:

In[23]:= **Grid[Table[i * j, {i, 5}, {j, 5}], Frame → All, Background → LightYellow]**

Out[23]=

1	2	3	4	5
2	4	6	8	10
3	6	9	12	15
4	8	12	16	20
5	10	15	20	25

Vocabulary

PlotTheme	theme for a plot (e.g. "Web", "Detailed", etc.)
Filling	filling to add to a plot (Axis, Bottom, etc.)
PlotRange	range of values to include in a plot (All, etc.)
GeoRange	geo range to include (All, specific country, etc.)
GeoBackground	background map ("ReliefMap", "OutlineMap", etc.)
GeoLabels	labels to add to a map (e.g. Automatic)
Joined	whether to make points be joined (True, False)
Background	background color
AspectRatio	ratio of height to width
ImageSize	size in pixels
Frame	whether to include a frame (True, All, etc.)
FontFamily	family of font to use (e.g. "Helvetica")
WordOrientation	how to orient words in a word cloud

Exercises

20.1 Create a list plot of Range[10] themed for the web.

20.2 Create a list plot of Range[10] with filling to the axis.

20.3 Create a list plot of Range[10] with a yellow background.

20.4 Create a map of the world with Australia highlighted.

20.5 Create a map of the Indian Ocean with Madagascar highlighted.

20.6 Use GeoGraphics to create a map of South America showing topography (relief map).

20.7 Make a map of Europe with France, Finland and Greece highlighted and labeled.

20.8 Make a 12×12 multiplication table as a grid with white type on a black background.

20.9 Make a list of 100 disks with random integer image sizes up to 40.

20.10 Make a list of pictures of regular pentagons with image size 30 and aspect ratios from 1 to 10.

20.11 Make a Manipulate that varies the size of a circle between 5 and 500.

20.12 Create a framed 10×10 grid of random colors.

20.13 Make a line plot of the lengths of Roman numerals up to 100, with a plot range that would be sufficient for all numerals up to 1000.

Q&A

How can I get a list of the options for a function?

Look at the documentation. Or use for example Options[WordCloud]. Also, whenever you start typing the name of an option, you'll see a menu of possible completions.

How do I find out the possible settings for an option?

Look at the documentation for that option. Also, when you type →, you'll typically get a menu of possible common settings.

What is *opt* → *value* internally?

It's Rule[*opt*, *value*]. Rules are used in lots of places in the Wolfram Language. *a* → *b* is usually read aloud as "*a* goes to *b*" or "*a* arrow *b*".

When are values of options given as strings?

Only a small set of standard option settings (such as Automatic, None and All) are not strings. Specialized settings for particular options are normally strings.

Can one reset the default for an option?

Yes, using SetOptions. Though you have to be careful not to forget that you've done it.

Tech Notes

- Many options can be set to be pure functions (see Section 26). It's important to put parentheses in the correct place, as in ColorFunction → (Hue[#/4] &), or you won't get the correct meaning.

- $FontFamilies gives a list of possible settings for FontFamily.

More to Explore

Guide to Graphics Options in the Wolfram Language (wolfr.am/eiwl-20-more)

Guide to Formatting Options in the Wolfram Language (wolfr.am/eiwl-20-more2)

21 | Graphs and Networks

A *graph* is a way of showing connections between things—say, how webpages are linked, or how people form a social network.

Let's start with a very simple graph, in which 1 connects to 2, 2 to 3 and 3 to 4. Each of the connections is represented by → (typed as –>).

A very simple graph of connections:

In[1]:= **Graph[{1 → 2, 2 → 3, 3 → 4}]**

Out[1]= ○————————▶○————————▶○————————▶○

Automatically label all the "vertices":

In[2]:= **Graph[{1 → 2, 2 → 3, 3 → 4}, VertexLabels → All]**

Out[2]=   ○———1———▶○———2———▶○———3———▶○ 4

Let's add one more connection: to connect 4 to 1. Now we have a loop.

Add another connection, forming a loop:

In[3]:= **Graph[{1 → 2, 2 → 3, 3 → 4, 4 → 1}, VertexLabels → All]**

Out[3]=

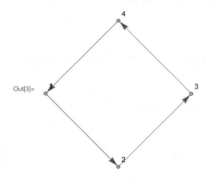

Add two more connections, including one connecting 2 right back to 2:

In[4]:= **Graph[{1 → 2, 2 → 3, 3 → 4, 4 → 1, 3 → 1, 2 → 2}, VertexLabels → All]**

Out[4]=

As we add connections, the Wolfram Language chooses to place the vertices or nodes of the graph differently. All that really matters for the meaning, however, is how the vertices are connected. And if you don't specify otherwise, the Wolfram Language will try to lay the graph out so it's as untangled and easy to understand as possible.

There are options, though, to specify other layouts. Here's an example. It's the same graph as before, with the same connections, but the vertices are laid out differently.

A different layout of the same graph (check by tracing the connections):

In[5]:= **Graph[{1 → 2, 2 → 3, 3 → 4, 4 → 1, 3 → 1, 2 → 2},**
      VertexLabels → All, GraphLayout → "RadialDrawing"]

Out[5]=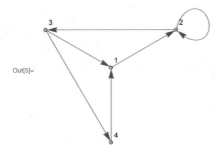

You can do computations on the graph, say finding the shortest path that gets from 4 to 2, always following the arrows.

The shortest path from 4 to 2 on the graph goes through 1:

In[6]:= **FindShortestPath[Graph[{1 → 2, 2 → 3, 3 → 4, 4 → 1, 3 → 1, 2 → 2}], 4, 2]**

Out[6]= {4, 1, 2}

Now let's make another graph. This time let's have 3 nodes, and let's have a connection between every one of them.

Start by making an array of all possible connections between 3 objects:

In[7]:= **Table[i → j, {i, 3}, {j, 3}]**

Out[7]= {{1 → 1, 1 → 2, 1 → 3}, {2 → 1, 2 → 2, 2 → 3}, {3 → 1, 3 → 2, 3 → 3}}

The result here is a list of lists. But what **Graph** needs is just a single list of connections. We can get that by using **Flatten** to "flatten" out the sublists.

Flatten "flattens out" all sublists, wherever they appear:

In[8]:= **Flatten[{{a, b}, 1, 2, 3, {x, y, {z}}}]**

Out[8]= {a, b, 1, 2, 3, x, y, z}

Get a "flattened" list of connections from the array:

In[9]:= **Flatten[Table[i → j, {i, 3}, {j, 3}]]**

Out[9]= {1 → 1, 1 → 2, 1 → 3, 2 → 1, 2 → 2, 2 → 3, 3 → 1, 3 → 2, 3 → 3}

Show the graph of these connections:

In[10]:= **Graph[Flatten[Table[i → j, {i, 3}, {j, 3}]], VertexLabels → All]**

Out[10]=

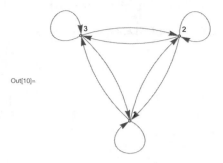

Generate the completely connected graph with 6 nodes:

In[11]:= **Graph[Flatten[Table[i → j, {i, 6}, {j, 6}]]]**

Out[11]=

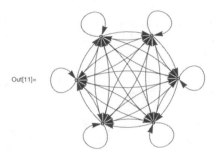

Sometimes the "direction" of a connection doesn't matter, so we can drop the arrows.

The "undirected" version of the graph:

In[12]:= **UndirectedGraph[Flatten[Table[i → j, {i, 6}, {j, 6}]]]**

Out[12]=

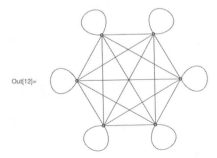

Now let's make a graph with random connections. Here is an example with 20 connections between randomly chosen nodes.

Make a graph with 20 connections between randomly chosen nodes numbered from 0 to 10:

In[13]:= `Graph[Table[RandomInteger[10] → RandomInteger[10], 20], VertexLabels → All]`

Out[13]=

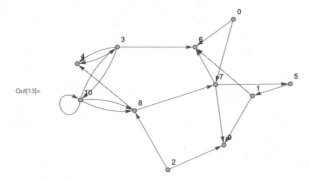

You'll get a different graph if you generate different random numbers. Here are 6 graphs.

Six randomly generated graphs:

In[14]:= `Table[Graph[Table[RandomInteger[10] → RandomInteger[10], 20]], 6]`

Out[14]=

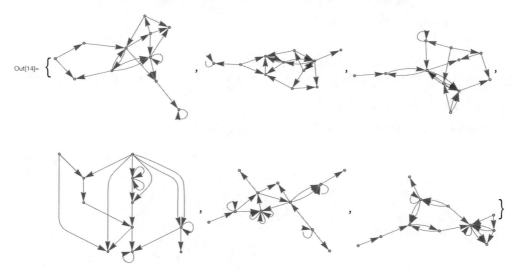

There's lots of analysis that can be done on graphs. One example is to break a graph into "communities"—clumps of nodes that are more connected to each other than to the rest of the graph. Let's do that for a random graph.

Make a plot that collects "communities" of nodes together:

In[15]:= **CommunityGraphPlot[** 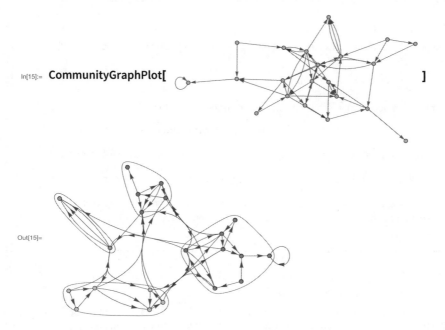 **]**

Out[15]=

The result is a graph with the exact same connections as the original, but with the nodes arranged to illustrate the "community structure" of the graph.

Vocabulary

Graph[{$i \rightarrow j$, ...}]	a graph or network of connections
UndirectedGraph[{$i \rightarrow j$, ...}]	a graph with no directions to connections
VertexLabels	an option for what vertex labels to include (e.g. All)
FindShortestPath[$graph$, a, b]	find the shortest path from one node to another
CommunityGraphPlot[$list$]	display a graph arranged into "communities"
Flatten[$list$]	flatten out sublists in a list

Exercises

21.1 Make a graph consisting of a loop of 3 nodes.

21.2 Make a graph with 4 nodes in which every node is connected.

21.3 Make a table of undirected graphs with between 2 and 10 nodes in which every node is connected.

21.4 Use Table and Flatten to get {1, 2, 1, 2, 1, 2}.

21.5 Make a line plot of the result of concatenating all digits of all integers from 1 to 100 (i.e. ..., 8, 9, 1, 0, 1, 1, 1, 2, ...).

21.6 Make a graph with 50 nodes, in which node i connects to node i + 1.

21.7 Make a graph with 4 nodes, in which each connection connects i to Max [i, j].

21.8 Make a graph in which each connection connects i to j − i, where i and j both range from 1 to 5.

21.9 Generate a graph with 100 nodes, each with a connection going to one randomly chosen node.

21.10 Generate a graph with 100 nodes, each connecting to two randomly chosen nodes.

21.11 For the graph {1 → 2, 2 → 3, 3 → 4, 4 → 1, 3 → 1, 2 → 2}, make a grid giving the shortest paths between every pair of nodes, with the start node as row and end node as column.

Q&A

What's the difference between a "graph" and a "network"?

There's no difference. They're just different words for the same thing, though "graph" tends to be more common in math and other formal areas, and "network" more common in more applied areas.

What are the vertices and edges of a graph?

Vertices are the points, or nodes, of a graph. Edges are the connections. Because graphs have arisen in so many different places, there are quite a few different names used for the same thing.

How is i → j understood?

It's Rule[i, j]. Rules are used in lots of places in the Wolfram Language—such as giving settings for options.

Can I compute my Facebook friend graph?

Yes. Use SocialMediaData ["Facebook", "FriendNetwork"]. Note, though, that only your friends who've opted in through Facebook will be included. (See Section 44.)

How big a graph can the Wolfram Language handle?

It's mostly limited by the amount of memory in your computer. Graphs with tens or hundreds of thousands of nodes are not a problem.

Can I specify properties of nodes and edges?

Yes. You can give Graph lists of nodes and edges that include things like Property[*node*, VertexStyle → Red] or Property[*edge*, EdgeWeight → 20]. You can also give overall options to Graph.

Tech Notes

- Graphs, like strings, images, graphics, etc., are first-class objects in the Wolfram Language.

- You can enter undirected edges in a graph using <->, which displays as ⟷.

- CompleteGraph[n] gives the completely connected graph with n nodes. Among other kinds of special graphs are KaryTree, ButterflyGraph, HypercubeGraph, etc.

- There are lots of ways to make random graphs (random connections, random numbers of connections, scale-free networks, etc.). RandomGraph[{100, 200}] makes a random graph with 100 nodes and 200 edges.

- AdjacencyMatrix[$graph$] gives the adjacency matrix for a graph. AdjacencyGraph[$matrix$] constructs a graph from an adjacency matrix.

- PlanarGraph[$graph$] tries to lay a graph out without any edges crossing—if that's possible.

More to Explore

Guide to Graphs and Networks in the Wolfram Language (wolfr.am/eiwl-21-more)

22 | Machine Learning

So far in this book, when we've wanted the Wolfram Language to do something, we've written code to tell it exactly what to do. But the Wolfram Language is also set up to be able to learn what to do just by looking at examples, using the idea of *machine learning*.

We'll talk about how to train the language yourself. But first let's look at some built-in functions that have already been trained on huge numbers of examples.

LanguageIdentify takes pieces of text, and identifies what human language they're in.

Identify the language each phrase is in:

In[1]:= **LanguageIdentify[{ "thank you", "merci", "dar las gracias", "感謝", "благодарить"}]**

Out[1]= { English , French , Spanish , Chinese , Russian }

The Wolfram Language can also do the considerably more difficult "artificial intelligence" task of identifying what an image is of.

Identify what an image is of:

In[2]:= **ImageIdentify[**  **]**

Out[2]= cheetah

There's a general function Classify, which has been taught various kinds of classification. One example is classifying the "sentiment" of text.

Upbeat text is classified as having positive sentiment:

In[3]:= **Classify["Sentiment", "I'm so excited to be programming"]**

Out[3]= Positive

Downbeat text is classified as having negative sentiment:

In[4]:= **Classify["Sentiment", "math can be really hard"]**

Out[4]= Negative

You can also train Classify yourself. Here's a simple example of classifying handwritten digits as 0 or 1. You give Classify a collection of training examples, followed by a particular handwritten digit. Then it'll tell you whether the digit you give is a 0 or 1.

With training examples, Classify correctly identifies a handwritten 0:

In[5]:= Classify[{◯ → 0, / → 1, ◐ → 0, / → 1, \ → 1, ◑ → 0, ◯ → 0, / → 1, / → 1,
    ◐ → 0, ◑ → 0, ◐ → 0, ▎ → 1, ◑ → 0, / → 1, ◯ → 0, \ → 1, ▎ → 1, / → 1},
    ◐]

Out[5]= 0

To get some sense of how this works—and because it's useful in its own right—let's talk about the function Nearest, that finds what element in a list is nearest to what you supply.

Find what number in the list is nearest to 22:

In[6]:= Nearest[{10, 20, 30, 40, 50, 60, 70, 80}, 22]

Out[6]= {20}

Find the nearest three numbers:

In[7]:= Nearest[{10, 20, 30, 40, 50, 60, 70, 80}, 22, 3]

Out[7]= {20, 30, 10}

Nearest can find nearest colors as well.

Find the 3 colors in the list that are nearest to the color you give:

In[8]:= Nearest[{■, ■, ■, □, ■, ■, ■, ■, ■, ■, ■, ■, ■, ■, ■, ■, ■}, □, 3]

Out[8]= {□, ■, ■}

It also works on words.

Find the 10 words nearest to "good" in the list of words:

In[9]:= Nearest[WordList[ ], "good", 10]

Out[9]= {good, food, goad, god, gold, goo, goody, goof, goon, goop}

There's a notion of nearness for images too. And though it's far from the whole story, this is effectively part of what ImageIdentify is using.

Something that's again related is recognizing text (*optical character recognition* or OCR). Let's make a piece of text that's blurred.

Create an image of the word "hello", then blur it:

In[10]:= **Blur[Rasterize[Style["hello", 30]], 3]**

Out[10]= **hello**

TextRecognize can still recognize the original text string in this.

Recognize text in the image:

In[11]:= **TextRecognize[hello]**

Out[11]= hello

If the text gets too blurred TextRecognize can't tell what it says—and you probably can't either.

Generate a sequence of progressively more blurred pieces of text:

In[12]:= **Table[Blur[Rasterize[Style["hello", 15]], r], {r, 0, 4}]**

Out[12]= {hello, hello, hello, hello, hello}

As the text gets more blurred, TextRecognize makes a mistake, then gives up altogether:

In[13]:= **Table[TextRecognize[Blur[Rasterize[Style["hello", 15]], r]], {r, 0, 4}]**

Out[13]= {hello, hello, hella, , }

Something similar happens if we progressively blur the picture of a cheetah. When the picture is still fairly sharp, ImageIdentify will correctly identify it as a cheetah. But when it gets too blurred ImageIdentify starts thinking it's more likely to be a lion, and eventually the best guess is that it's a picture of a person.

Progressively blur a picture of a cheetah:

In[14]:= **Table[Blur[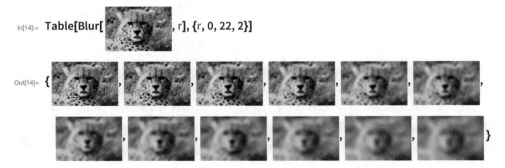, r], {r, 0, 22, 2}]**

Out[14]= {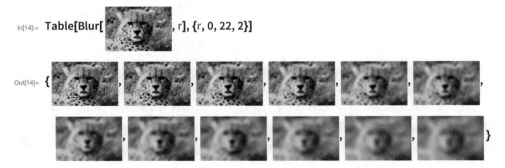}

When the picture gets too blurred, ImageIdentify no longer thinks it's a cheetah:

In[15]:= **Table[ImageIdentify[Blur[** **, r]], {r, 0, 22, 2}]**

Out[15]= { cheetah , cheetah , cheetah , cheetah , lion , red wolf , domestic dog ,
musteline mammal , domestic dog , person , person , person }

ImageIdentify normally just gives what it thinks is the most likely identification. You can tell it, though, to give a list of possible identifications, starting from the most likely. Here are the top 10 possible identifications, in all categories.

ImageIdentify thinks this might be a cheetah, but it's more likely to be a lion, or it could be a dog:

In[16]:= **ImageIdentify[** **, All, 10]**

Out[16]= { lion , red wolf , cheetah , wildcat , domestic dog ,
striped hyena , pine marten , mountain lion , working dog , lynx }

When the image is sufficiently blurred, ImageIdentify can have wild ideas about what it might be:

In[17]:= **ImageIdentify[** **, All, 10]**

Out[17]= { person , domestic dog , edible fruit , hunting dog , cat ,
berry , terrier , wildcat , working dog , soft-finned fish }

In machine learning, one often gives training that explicitly says, for example, "this is a cheetah", "this is a lion". But one also often just wants to automatically pick out categories of things without any specific training.

One way to start doing this is to take a collection of things—say colors—and then to find clusters of similar ones. This can be achieved using FindClusters.

Collect "clusters" of similar colors into separate lists:

In[18]:= **FindClusters[{■, □, ■, ■, ■, ■, ■, ■, ■, □, ■, □, ■, □, □, ■, ■, ■, ■, ■, □, □, ■, ■}]**

Out[18]= {{■, ■, ■, ■, ■, ■, ■, ■, ■}, {□, ■, □, □, ■, ■, □, ■}, {■, ■, ■, ■, ■, ■}, {□, □}}

You can get a different view by connecting each color to the three most similar colors in the list, then making a graph out of the connections. In the particular example here, there end up being three disconnected subgraphs.

Create a graph of connections based on nearness in "color space":

In[19]:= **NearestNeighborGraph[**
{⬛, ⬜, ⬛, ⬛, ⬛, ⬛, ⬛, ⬛, ⬜, ⬜, ⬜, ⬛, ⬛, ⬜, ⬛, ⬛, ⬜, ⬛, ⬜, ⬜, ⬛, ⬛}, 3, **VertexLabels → All]**

Out[19]=

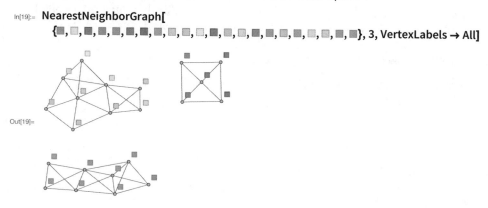

A *dendrogram* is a tree-like plot that lets you see a whole hierarchy of what's near what.

Show nearby colors successively grouped together:

In[20]:= **Dendrogram[{**⬛, ⬜, ⬛, ⬛, ⬛, ⬛, ⬛, ⬛, ⬜, ⬜, ⬜, ⬛, ⬜, ⬜, ⬛, ⬛, ⬜, ⬛, ⬜, ⬜, ⬛, ⬛**}]**

Out[20]=

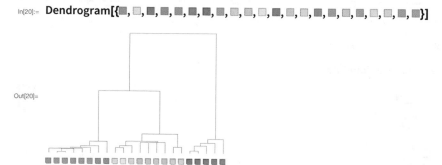

When we compare things—whether they're colors or pictures of animals—we can think of identifying certain *features* that allow us to distinguish them. For colors, a feature might be how light the color is, or how much red it contains. For pictures of animals, a feature might be how furry the animal looks, or how pointy its ears are.

In the Wolfram Language, FeatureSpacePlot takes collections of objects and tries to find what it considers the "best" distinguishing features of them, then uses the values of these to position objects in a plot.

FeatureSpacePlot doesn't explicitly say what features it's using—and actually they're usually quite hard to describe. But what happens in the end is that FeatureSpacePlot arranges things so that objects that have similar features are drawn nearby.

FeatureSpacePlot makes similar colors be placed nearby:

In[21]:= **FeatureSpacePlot[{■, □, ■, ■, ■, ■, ■, ■, ■, ■, ■, □, ■, ■, ■, ■, ■, ■, ■, ■, □, ■, ■}]**

Out[21]=

If one uses, say, 100 colors picked completely at random, then FeatureSpacePlot will again place colors it considers similar nearby.

100 random colors laid out by FeatureSpacePlot:

In[22]:= **FeatureSpacePlot[RandomColor[100]]**

Out[22]=

Let's try the same kind of thing with images of letters.

Make a rasterized image of each letter in the alphabet:

In[23]:= **Table[Rasterize[FromLetterNumber[n]], {n, 26}]**

Out[23]= {a, b, c, d, e, f, g, h, i, j, k, l, m, n, o, p, q, r, s, t, u, v, w, x, y, z}

FeatureSpacePlot will use visual features of these images to lay them out. The result is that letters that look similar—like y and v or e and c—will wind up nearby.

In[24]:= **FeatureSpacePlot[Table[Rasterize[FromLetterNumber[n]], {n, 26}]]**

Out[24]=

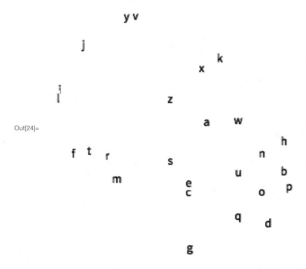

Here's the same thing, but now with pictures of cats, cars and chairs. FeatureSpacePlot immediately separates the different kinds of things.

FeatureSpacePlot places photographs of different kinds of things quite far apart:

In[25]:= **FeatureSpacePlot[{**

Out[25]=

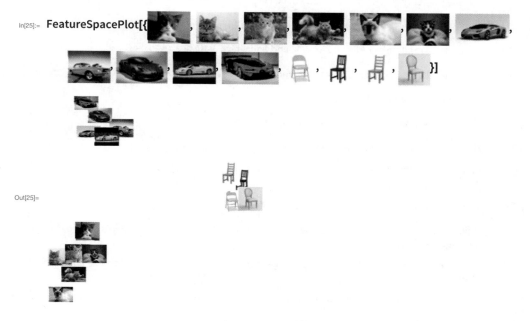

Vocabulary

LanguageIdentify[*text***]**	identify what human language text is in
ImageIdentify[*image***]**	identify what an image is of
TextRecognize[*text***]**	recognize text from an image (OCR)
Classify[*training*, *data***]**	classify data on the basis of training examples
Nearest[*list*, *item***]**	find what element of *list* is nearest to *item*
FindClusters[*list***]**	find clusters of similar items
NearestNeighborGraph[*list*, *n***]**	connect elements of *list* to their *n* nearest neighbors
Dendrogram[*list***]**	make a hierarchical tree of relations between items
FeatureSpacePlot[*list***]**	plot elements of *list* in an inferred "feature space"

Exercises

22.1 Identify what language the word "ajatella" comes from.

22.2 Apply **ImageIdentify** to an image of a tiger, getting the image using ⌃ = .

22.3 Make a table of image identifications for an image of a tiger, blurred by an amount from 1 to 5.

22.4 Classify the sentiment of "I'm so happy to be here".

22.5 Find the 10 words in **WordList[ ]** that are nearest to "happy".

22.6 Generate 20 random numbers up to 1000 and find which 3 are nearest to 100.

22.7 Generate a list of 10 random colors, and find which 5 are closest to **Red**.

22.8 Of the first 100 squares, find the one nearest to 2000.

22.9 Find the 3 European flags nearest to the flag of Brazil.

22.10 Make a graph of the 2 nearest neighbors of each color in **Table[Hue[h], {h, 0, 1, .05}]**.

22.11 Generate a list of 100 random numbers from 0 to 100, and make a graph of the 2 nearest neighbors of each one.

22.12 Collect the flags of Asia into clusters of similar flags.

22.13 Make raster images of the letters of the alphabet at size 20, then make a graph of the 2 nearest neighbors of each one.

22.14 Generate a table of the results of using **TextRecognize** on "hello" rasterized at size 50 and then blurred by between 1 and 10.

22.15 Make a dendrogram for images of the first 10 letters of the alphabet.

22.16 Make a feature space plot for the uppercase letters of the alphabet.

Q&A

How come I'm getting different results from the ones shown here?

Probably because Wolfram Language machine learning functions are continually getting more training—and so their results may change, hopefully always getting better. For TextRecognize, the results can depend in detail on the fonts used, and exactly how they're rendered and rasterized on your computer.

How does ImageIdentify work inside?

It's based on artificial neural networks inspired by the way brains seem to work. It's been trained with millions of example images, from which it's progressively learned to make distinctions. And a bit like in the game of "twenty questions", by using enough of these distinctions it can eventually determine what an image is of.

How many kinds of things can ImageIdentify recognize?

At least 10,000—which is more than a typical human. (There are about 5000 "picturable nouns" in English.)

What makes ImageIdentify give a wrong answer?

A common cause is that what it's asked about isn't close enough to anything it's been trained on. This can happen if something is in an unusual configuration or environment (for example, if a boat is not on a bluish background). ImageIdentify usually tries to find some kind of match, and the mistakes it makes often seem very "humanlike".

Can I ask ImageIdentify the probabilities it assigns to different identifications?

Yes. For example, to find the probabilities for the top 10 identifications in all categories use ImageIdentify[*image*, All, 10, "Probability"].

How many examples does Classify typically need to work well?

If the general area (like everyday images) is one it already knows well, then as few as a hundred. But in areas that are new, it can take many millions of examples to achieve good results.

How does Nearest figure out a distance between colors?

It uses the function ColorDistance, which is based on a model of human color vision.

How does Nearest determine nearby words?

By looking at those at the smallest EditDistance, that is, reached by the smallest number of single-letter insertions, deletions and substitutions.

Can a single graph have several disconnected parts?

Absolutely. An example is the last graph in this section.

What features does FeatureSpacePlot use?

There's no easy answer. When it's given a collection of things, it'll learn features that distinguish them—though it's typically primed by having seen many other things of the same general type (like images).

Tech Notes

- The Wolfram Language stores its latest machine learning classifiers in the cloud—but if you're using a desktop system, they'll automatically be downloaded, and then they'll run locally.

- BarcodeImage and BarcodeRecognize work with bar codes and QR codes instead of pure text.

- ImageIdentify is the core of what the imageidentify.com website does.

- If you just give Classify training examples, it'll produce a ClassifierFunction that can later be applied to many different pieces of data. This is pretty much always how Classify is used in practice.

- You can get a large standard training set of handwritten digits using ResourceData ["MNIST"].

- Classify automatically picks between methods such as *logistic regression*, *naive Bayes*, *random forests* and *support vector machines*, as well as *neural networks*.

- FindClusters does *unsupervised machine learning*, where the computer just looks at data without being told anything about it. Classify does *supervised machine learning*, being given a set of training examples.

- Dendrogram does *hierarchical clustering*, and can be used to reconstruct evolutionary trees in areas like bioinformatics and historical linguistics.

- FeatureSpacePlot does *dimension reduction*, taking data that's represented by many parameters, and finding a good way to "project" these down so they can be plotted in 2D.

- Rasterize /@ Alphabet[ ] is a better way to make a list of rasterized letters, but we won't talk about /@ until Section 25.

- FeatureExtraction lets you get out the feature vectors used by FeatureSpacePlot.

- FeatureNearest is like Nearest except that it learns what should be considered near by looking at the actual data you give. It's what you need to do something like build an image-search function.

- You can build and train your own neural nets in the Wolfram Language using functions like NetChain, NetGraph and NetTrain. NetModel gives access to prebuilt nets.

More to Explore

Guide to Machine Learning in the Wolfram Language (wolfr.am/eiwl-22-more)

23 | More about Numbers

When you do a computation with whole numbers, the Wolfram Language gives you an exact answer. It does the same with exact fractions.

Adding 1/2+1/3 gives an exact answer as a fraction:

In[1]:= **1/2+1/3**

Out[1]= $\dfrac{5}{6}$

Often you'll just want a numerical or decimal approximation. You can get that using the function N (for "numerical").

Get an approximate numerical answer:

In[2]:= **N[1/2+1/3]**

Out[2]= 0.833333

If there's any decimal number in your input, the Wolfram Language will automatically give you an approximate answer.

The presence of a decimal number makes the result be approximate:

In[3]:= **1.8/2+1/3**

Out[3]= 1.23333

It's enough just to have a decimal point at the end of a number:

In[4]:= **1/2.+1/3**

Out[4]= 0.833333

The Wolfram Language can handle numbers of any size, at least so long as they fit in your computer's memory.

Here's 2 raised to the power 1000:

In[5]:= **2 ^ 1000**

Out[5]= 10 715 086 071 862 673 209 484 250 490 600 018 105 614 048 117 055 336 074 437 503 883 703 510 ˙.
511 249 361 224 931 983 788 156 958 581 275 946 729 175 531 468 251 871 452 856 923 140 435 ˙.
984 577 574 698 574 803 934 567 774 824 230 985 421 074 605 062 371 141 877 954 182 153 046 ˙.
474 983 581 941 267 398 767 559 165 543 946 077 062 914 571 196 477 686 542 167 660 429 831 ˙.
652 624 386 837 205 668 069 376

Get a numerical approximation:

In[6]:= **N[2 ^ 1000]**

Out[6]= 1.07151×10^{301}

This approximate form is given in *scientific notation*. If you need to enter scientific notation, you can do it with *^ .

Enter a number in scientific notation:

In[7]:= **2.7*^6**

Out[7]= 2.7×10^6

Commonly used numbers like π (pi) are built into the Wolfram Language.

Get a numerical approximation to π:

In[8]:= **N[Pi]**

Out[8]= 3.14159

The Wolfram Language can compute to *arbitrary precision*, so for example it can find millions of digits of π if you want them.

Compute 250 digits of π:

In[9]:= **N[Pi, 250]**

Out[9]= 3.1415926535897932384626433832795028841971693993751058209749445923078164062862089986280348253421170679821480865132823066470938446095505822317253594081284811174502841027019385211055596446229489549303819644288109756659334461284756482337867831652712019

There are many functions in the Wolfram Language that handle *integers* (whole numbers). There are also many functions that handle *real numbers*—approximate numbers with decimals. An example is RandomReal, which gives random real numbers.

Generate a random real number in the range 0 to 10:

In[10]:= **RandomReal[10]**

Out[10]= 2.08658

Generate 5 random real numbers:

In[11]:= **Table[RandomReal[10], 5]**

Out[11]= {4.15071, 4.81048, 8.82945, 9.84995, 9.08313}

An alternative way to ask for 5 random real numbers:

In[12]:= **RandomReal[10, 5]**

Out[12]= {6.47318, 3.29181, 3.57615, 8.11204, 3.38286}

Random real numbers in the range 20 to 30:

In[13]:= **RandomReal[{20, 30}, 5]**

Out[13]= {24.1202, 20.1288, 20.393, 25.6455, 20.9268}

The Wolfram Language has a huge range of mathematical functions built in, from basic to very sophisticated.

Find the 100th prime number:

In[14]:= **Prime[100]**

Out[14]= 541

Find the millionth prime number:

In[15]:= **Prime[1 000 000]**

Out[15]= 15 485 863

Plot the first 50 primes:

In[16]:= **ListPlot[Table[Prime[n], {n, 50}]]**

Out[16]=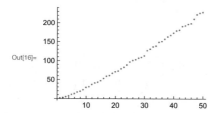

Three functions common in many practical situations are Sqrt (square root), Log10 (logarithm to base 10) and Log (natural logarithm).

The square root of 16 is 4:

In[17]:= **Sqrt[16]**

Out[17]= 4

If you don't ask for a numerical approximation, you'll get an exact formula:

In[18]:= **Sqrt[200]**

Out[18]= $10\sqrt{2}$

N gives a numerical approximation:

In[19]:= **N[Sqrt[200]]**

Out[19]= 14.1421

Logarithms are often useful when you're dealing with numbers that have a wide range of sizes. Let's plot the masses of the planets. With ListPlot one can't tell anything about the planets before Jupiter. But ListLogPlot shows the relative sizes much more clearly.

Make an ordinary ListPlot of the masses of the planets:

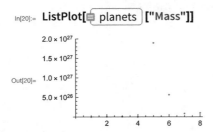

Make a log plot:

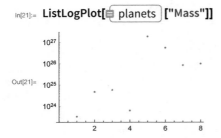

There are a few more functions that show up frequently in general programming. First, there's the almost trivial function Abs, that finds the absolute value, or positive part, of a number.

Abs effectively just drops minus signs:

In[22]:= **{Abs[3], Abs[−3]}**

Out[22]= {3, 3}

Next there's Round, which rounds to the nearest whole number.

Round rounds to the nearest whole number:

In[23]:= **{Round[3.2], Round[3.4], Round[3.6], Round[3.9]}**

Out[23]= {3, 3, 4, 4}

Another function that's very useful is Mod. Let's say you're counting up minutes in an hour. When you reach 60, you'll want to start again from 0. That's what Mod lets you do.

Compute a sequence of numbers mod 60:

In[24]:= **{Mod[50, 60], Mod[55, 60], Mod[60, 60], Mod[65, 60], Mod[70, 60]}**

Out[24]= {50, 55, 0, 5, 10}

Vocabulary

N[*expr***]**	numerical approximation
Pi	the number π (pi)≈3.14
Sqrt[*x***]**	square root
Log10[*x***]**	logarithm to base 10
Log[*x***]**	natural logarithm (ln)
Abs[*x***]**	absolute value (drop minus signs)
Round[*x***]**	round to nearest integer
Prime[*n***]**	nth prime number
Mod[*x, n***]**	modulo ("clock arithmetic")
RandomReal[*max***]**	random real number between 0 and *max*
RandomReal[*max, n***]**	list of n random real numbers
ListLogPlot[*data***]**	plot on a logarithmic scale

Exercises

23.1   Find $\sqrt{2}$ to 500-digit precision.

23.2   Generate 10 random real numbers between 0 and 1.

23.3   Make a plot of 200 points with random real x and y coordinates between 0 and 1.

23.4   Create a random walk using AnglePath and 1000 random real numbers between 0 and 2π.

23.5   Make a table of Mod[n^2, 10] for n from 0 to 30.

23.6   Make a line plot of Mod[n^n, 10] for n from 1 to 100.

23.7   Make a table of the first 10 powers of π, rounded to integers.

23.8   Make a graph by connecting n with Mod[n^2, 100] for n from 0 to 99.

23.9   Generate graphics of 50 circles with random real coordinates 0 to 10, random real radii from 0 to 2, and random colors.

23.10   Make a plot of the nth prime divided by n * log (n), for n from 2 to 1000.

23.11   Make a line plot of the differences between successive primes up to 100.

23.12   Generate a sequence of 20 middle C notes with random durations between 0 and 0.5 seconds.

23.13   Make an array plot of Mod [i, j] for i and j up to 50.

23.14   Make a list for n from 2 to 10 of array plots for x and y up to 50 of x ^ y mod n.

Q&A

What are examples of mathematical functions in the Wolfram Language?

From standard school math, ones like Sin, Cos, ArcTan, Exp, as well as GCD, Factorial, Fibonacci. From physics and engineering and higher math, ones like Gamma ("gamma function"), BesselJ ("Bessel function"), EllipticK ("elliptic integral"), Zeta ("Riemann zeta function"), PrimePi, EulerPhi. From statistics, ones like Erf, NormalDistribution, ChiSquareDistribution. Hundreds of functions altogether.

What is the precision of a number?

It's the total number of decimal digits quoted in the number. N[100/3, 5] gives 33.333, which has 5 digits of precision. The number 100/3 is exact; N[100/3, 5] approximates it to 5-digit precision.

What does the $\because$ at the end of each line in a long number mean?

It's there to show that the number continues onto the next line—like a hyphen in text.

Can I work with numbers in bases other than 10?

Yes. Enter a number in base 16 as 16^^ffa5. Find digits using IntegerDigits [655, 16].

Can the Wolfram Language handle complex numbers?

Of course. The symbol I (capital "i") represents the square root of −1.

Why does N[1.5/7, 100] not give me a 100-digit result?

Because 1.5 is an approximate number with much less than 100-digit precision. N[15/70, 100] will for example give a 100-digit-precision number.

Tech Notes

- The Wolfram Language does "arbitrary-precision computation", meaning that it can keep as many digits in a number as you want.

- When you generate a number with a certain precision using N, the Wolfram Language will automatically keep track of how that precision is affected by computations—so you don't have to do your own numerical analysis of roundoff errors.

- If you type a number like 1.5, it's assumed to be at the native "machine precision" of numbers on your computer (usually about 16 digits, though only 6 are usually displayed). Use 1.5 ` 100 to specify 100-digit precision.

- With exact input (like 4 or 2/3 or Pi), the Wolfram Language always tries to give exact output. But if the input contains an approximate number (like 2.3), or if you use N, it'll use numerical approximation.

- Numerical approximation is often crucial in making large-scale computations feasible.

- PrimeQ tests if a number is prime (see Section 28). FactorInteger finds the factors of an integer.

- RandomReal can give numbers that aren't just uniformly distributed. For example, RandomReal[NormalDistribution[]] gives normally distributed numbers.

- Round rounds to the nearest integer (up or down); Floor always rounds down; Ceiling always rounds up.

- RealDigits is the analog of IntegerDigits for real numbers.

More to Explore

Guide to Numbers in the Wolfram Language (wolfr.am/eiwl-23-more)

Guide to Mathematical Functions in the Wolfram Language (wolfr.am/eiwl-23-more2)

24 | More Forms of Visualization

We've seen how to plot lists of data with ListPlot and ListLinePlot. If you want to plot several sets of data at the same time, you just have to give them in a list.

Plot two sets of data at the same time:

In[1]:= **ListLinePlot[{{1, 3, 4, 3, 1, 2}, {2, 2, 4, 5, 7, 6, 8}}]**

Out[1]=
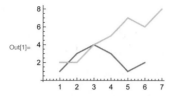

The PlotStyle option lets you specify the style for each set of data:

In[2]:= **ListLinePlot[{{1, 3, 4, 3, 1, 2}, {2, 2, 4, 5, 7, 6, 8}}, PlotStyle → {Red, Dotted}]**

Out[2]=
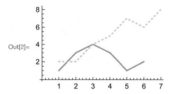

The Mesh option lets you show the actual data points too:

In[3]:= **ListLinePlot[{{1, 3, 4, 3, 1, 2}, {2, 2, 4, 5, 7, 6, 8}}, Mesh → All, MeshStyle → Red]**

Out[3]=
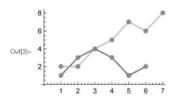

As well as looking at the sequence of values in a list, it's also very common to want to see how often different values occur. You can do this with Histogram.

Here are the lengths of the first 30 common English words:

In[4]:= **StringLength[Take[WordList[ ], 30]]**

Out[4]= {1, 3, 8, 5, 6, 5, 7, 7, 9, 11, 5, 9, 5, 7, 9, 5, 9, 8, 4, 6, 5, 5, 10, 11, 12, 8, 10, 7, 9, 6}

The histogram shows how often each length occurs among the first 200 words:

In[5]:= **Histogram[StringLength[Take[WordList[ ], 200]]]**

Out[5]=
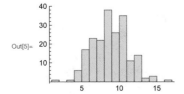

Including all the words gives a smoother result:

In[6]:= **Histogram[StringLength[WordList[ ]]]**

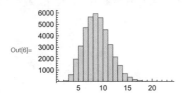

Out[6]=

Sometimes you'll have data you want to visualize in 3D. For example, GeoElevationData can give an array of height values. ListPlot3D makes a 3D plot.

Find an array of height values around Mount Everest, and plot it in 3D:

In[7]:= **ListPlot3D[GeoElevationData[GeoDisk[☰ mount everest , ☰ 2 miles]]]**

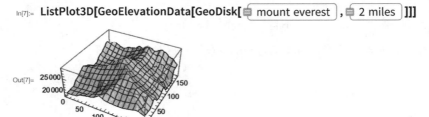

Out[7]=

Show it without a mesh:

In[8]:= **ListPlot3D[**
        GeoElevationData[GeoDisk[☰ mount everest , ☰ 2 miles]], MeshStyle → None]

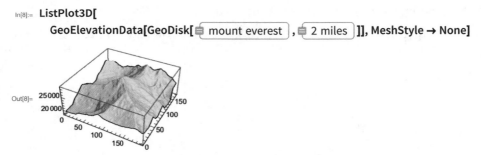

Out[8]=

An alternative visualization is a *contour plot*, in which one's effectively looking from above, and drawing contour lines at evenly spaced heights.

Make a contour plot, in which successive ranges of heights are separated by contour lines:

In[9]:= **ListContourPlot[GeoElevationData[GeoDisk[☰ mount everest , ☰ 2 miles]]]**

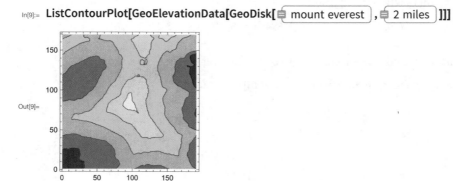

Out[9]=

When one's dealing with large amounts of data, it's often better to use a simpler visualization, such as a *relief plot*, that essentially just colors according to height.

Make a relief plot of the topography 100 miles around Mount Everest:

In[10]:= **ReliefPlot[GeoElevationData[GeoDisk[** ▤ mount everest **,** ▤ 100 miles **]]]**

Out[10]=

Vocabulary

ListLinePlot[{$list_1$**,** $list_2$**, …}]**	plot several lists together
Histogram[*list***]**	make a histogram
ListPlot3D[*array***]**	plot an array of heights in 3D
ListContourPlot[*array***]**	plot contours for an array of heights
ReliefPlot[*array***]**	make a relief plot
GeoElevationData[*region***]**	array of geo elevations for a region
PlotStyle	option for styling each set of data
Mesh	whether to have a mesh of points or lines
MeshStyle	option for styling a mesh

Exercises

24.1 Make a plot with lines joining the squares, the cubes and the 4th powers of integers up to 10.

24.2 Make a plot of the first 20 primes, joined by a line, filled to the axis and with a red dot at each prime.

24.3 Make a 3D plot of the topography for 20 miles around Mount Fuji.

24.4 Make a relief plot of the topography for 100 miles around Mount Fuji.

24.5 Make a 3D plot of heights generated from Mod[i, j] with i and j going up to 100.

24.6 Make a histogram of the differences between successive primes for the first 10000 primes.

24.7 Make a histogram of the first digits of squares of integers up to 10000 (illustrating *Benford's law*).

24.8 Make a histogram of the length of Roman numerals up to 1000.

24.9 Make a histogram of sentence lengths in the Wikipedia article on computers.

24.10 Make a list of histograms of 10000 instances of totals of n random reals up to 100, with n going from 1 to 5 (illustrating the central limit theorem).

24.11 Generate a 3D list plot using the image data from a binarized size-200 letter "W" as heights.

Q&A

What other kinds of visualizations are there?

Lots. Like ListStepPlot and ListStreamPlot, or BubbleChart and BarChart3D, or SmoothHistogram and BoxWhiskerChart, or AngularGauge and VerticalGauge.

How do I combine plots I've generated separately?

Use Show to combine them on common axes. Use GraphicsGrid, etc. (see Section 37) to put them side by side.

How can I specify the bins to use in a histogram?

Histogram[*list*, *n*] uses *n* bins. Histogram[*list*, {*xmin*, *xmax*, *dx*}] uses bins from *xmin* to *xmax* in steps *dx*.

What's the difference between a bar chart and a histogram?

A bar chart is a direct representation of data; a histogram represents the frequency with which data occurs. In a bar chart, the height of each bar gives the value of a single piece of data. In a histogram, the height of each bar gives the total number of pieces of data that occur within the *x* range of the bar.

How can I draw contour lines on a 3D topography plot?

Use MeshFunctions → (#3 &). The (#3 &) is a *pure function* (see Section 26) that uses the third (*z*) coordinate to make a mesh.

How do I label heights in a contour plot?

Use ContourLabels → All.

Tech Notes

- The Wolfram Language makes many automatic choices for visualization functions. You can override these choices using options.

- An alternative to using PlotStyle is to insert Style directly into the data given to functions like ListLinePlot.

- At least over much of the Earth, GeoElevationData has data measurements down to a resolution of about 40 meters.

More to Explore

Guide to Data Visualization in the Wolfram Language (wolfr.am/eiwl-24-more)

25 | Ways to Apply Functions

When you write f[x] it means "apply the function f to x". An alternative way to write the same thing in the Wolfram Language is f@x.

f@x is the same as f[x]:

In[1]:= **f@x**

Out[1]= f[x]

It's often convenient to write out chains of functions using @:

In[2]:= **f@g@h@x**

Out[2]= f[g[h[x]]]

Avoiding the brackets can make code easier to type, and read:

In[3]:= **ColorNegate@EdgeDetect@**

Out[3]=

There's a third way to write f[x] in the Wolfram Language: as an "afterthought", in the form x // f.

Apply f "as an afterthought" to x:

In[4]:= **x // f**

Out[4]= f[x]

You can have a sequence of "afterthoughts":

In[5]:= **x // f // g // h**

Out[5]= h[g[f[x]]]

The functions here read in the order they are applied:

In[6]:= 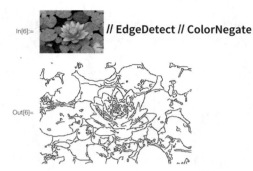 **// EdgeDetect // ColorNegate**

Out[6]=

A particularly common use of // is to apply N (for numerical evaluation) "as an afterthought".

Apply numerical evaluation "as an afterthought":

In[7]:= **2 Pi ^ 3 + 1 // N**

Out[7]= 63.0126

In working with the Wolfram Language, a powerful notation that one ends up using all the time is /@, which means "apply to each element".

Apply f to each element in a list:

In[8]:= **f /@ {1, 2, 3}**

Out[8]= {f[1], f[2], f[3]}

f usually would just get applied to the whole list:

In[9]:= **f[{1, 2, 3}]**

Out[9]= f[{1, 2, 3}]

Framed is a function that displays a frame around something.

Display x framed:

In[10]:= **Framed[x]**

Out[10]= x

Applying Framed to a list just puts a frame around the whole list.

Apply Framed to a whole list:

In[11]:= **Framed[{x, y, z}]**

Out[11]= {x, y, z}

@ does exactly the same thing:

In[12]:= **Framed@{x, y, z}**

Out[12]= $\boxed{\{x, y, z\}}$

Now use **/@** to apply Framed to each element in the list:

In[13]:= **Framed/@{x, y, z}**

Out[13]= $\left\{\boxed{x}, \boxed{y}, \boxed{z}\right\}$

The same thing works with any other function. For example, apply the function Hue separately to each number in a list.

/@ applies Hue separately to each number in the list:

In[14]:= **Hue/@{0.1, 0.2, 0.3, 0.4}**

Out[14]= {■, ■, ■, ■}

Here's what the **/@** is doing:

In[15]:= **{Hue[0.1], Hue[0.2], Hue[0.3], Hue[0.4]}**

Out[15]= {■, ■, ■, ■}

It's the same story with Range, though now the output is a list of lists.

/@ applies Range separately to each number, producing a list of lists:

In[16]:= **Range/@{3, 2, 5, 6, 7}**

Out[16]= {{1, 2, 3}, {1, 2}, {1, 2, 3, 4, 5}, {1, 2, 3, 4, 5, 6}, {1, 2, 3, 4, 5, 6, 7}}

Here's the equivalent, all written out:

In[17]:= **{Range[3], Range[2], Range[5], Range[6], Range[7]}**

Out[17]= {{1, 2, 3}, {1, 2}, {1, 2, 3, 4, 5}, {1, 2, 3, 4, 5, 6}, {1, 2, 3, 4, 5, 6, 7}}

Given a list of lists, **/@** is what one needs to do an operation separately to each sublist.

Apply PieChart separately to each list in a list of lists:

In[18]:= **PieChart/@{{1, 1, 1, 1, 1, 1, 1}, {1, 1, 1, 4, 4, 4}, {1, 2, 1, 2, 1, 2}}**

Out[18]=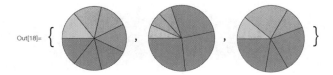

You can use exactly the same idea with lots of other functions.

Apply Length to each element, getting the length of each sublist:

In[19]:= **Length /@ {{a, a}, {a, a, b, c}, {a, a, b, b, b, b}, {a, a, a}, {c, c}}**

Out[19]= {2, 4, 6, 3, 2}

Applying Length to the whole list just gives the total number of sublists:

In[20]:= **Length @ {{a, a}, {a, a, b, c}, {a, a, b, b, b, b}, {a, a, a}, {c, c}}**

Out[20]= 5

Apply Reverse to each element, getting three different reversed lists:

In[21]:= **Reverse /@ {{a, b, c}, {x, y, z}, {1, 2, 3, 4}}**

Out[21]= {{c, b, a}, {z, y, x}, {4, 3, 2, 1}}

Apply Reverse to the whole list, reversing its elements:

In[22]:= **Reverse @ {{a, b, c}, {x, y, z}, {1, 2, 3, 4}}**

Out[22]= {{1, 2, 3, 4}, {x, y, z}, {a, b, c}}

As always, the form with brackets is exactly equivalent:

In[23]:= **Reverse[{{a, b, c}, {x, y, z}, {1, 2, 3, 4}}]**

Out[23]= {{1, 2, 3, 4}, {x, y, z}, {a, b, c}}

Some calculational functions are *listable*, which means they automatically apply themselves to elements in a list.

N is listable, so you don't have to use /@ to get it applied to each element in a list:

In[24]:= **N[{1/3, 1/4, 1/5, 1/6}]**

Out[24]= {0.333333, 0.25, 0.2, 0.166667}

The same is true with Prime:

In[25]:= **Prime[{10, 100, 1000, 10 000}]**

Out[25]= {29, 541, 7919, 104 729}

A function like Graphics definitely isn't listable.

This makes a single graphic with three objects in it:

In[26]:= **Graphics[{Circle[ ], RegularPolygon[7], Style[RegularPolygon[3], Orange]}]**

Out[26]=

This gives three separate graphics, with Graphics applied to each object:

In[27]:= **Graphics /@ {Circle[ ], RegularPolygon[7], Style[RegularPolygon[3], Orange]}**

Out[27]=

When you enter f /@ {1, 2, 3}, the Wolfram Language interprets it as Map[f, {1, 2, 3}]. f /@ x is usually read as "map f over x".

The internal interpretation of f /@ {1, 2, 3}:

In[28]:= **Map[f, {1, 2, 3}]**

Out[28]= {f[1], f[2], f[3]}

Vocabulary

f **@** x	equivalent to $f[x]$
x **//** f	equivalent to $f[x]$
f **/@** {a, b, c}	apply f separately to each element of the list
Map[f, {a, b, c}**]**	alternative form of /@
Framed[$expr$**]**	put a frame around something

Exercises

25.1 Use /@ and Range to reproduce the result of Table[f[n], {n, 5}].

25.2 Use /@ twice to generate Table[f[g[n]], {n, 10}].

25.3 Use // to create a[b[c[d[x]]]].

25.4 Make a list of letters of the alphabet, with a frame around each one.

25.5 Color negate an image of each planet, giving a list of the results.

25.6 Use /@ to draw separate maps of each country in the G5.

25.7 Binarize each flag in Europe, and make an image collage of the result.

25.8 Find a list of the dominant colors in images of the planets, putting the results for each planet in a column.

25.9 Find the total of the letter numbers given by **LetterNumber** for the letters in the word "wolfram".

Q&A

Why not always use f@x instead of f[x]?

f@x is a fine equivalent to f[x], but the equivalent of f[1+1] is f@(1+1), and in that case, f[1+1] is shorter and easier to understand.

Why is /@ called Map?

It comes from math. Given a set {1, 2, 3}, f/@{1, 2, 3} can be thought of as mapping of this set to another one.

How does one say "//" and "/@"?

Typically "slash slash" and "slash at".

When do I need to use parentheses with @, // and /@?

It's determined by the *precedence* or *binding* of different operators. @ binds tighter than +, so f@1+1 means f[1]+1 not f@(1+1) or f[1+1]. // binds looser than +, so 1/2+1/3 // N means (1/2+1/3) // N. In a notebook you can find how things are grouped by repeatedly clicking on your input, and seeing how the selection expands.

Tech Notes

- Quite a few functions are "listable", so they automatically map themselves over lists.

- Range is listable, so Range[{3, 4, 5}] is the same as Range/@{3, 4, 5}.

More to Explore

Guide to Functional Programming in the Wolfram Language (wolfr.am/eiwl-25-more)

26 | Pure Anonymous Functions

After all the examples we've seen of the Wolfram Language, we're now ready to go to a slightly higher level of abstraction, and tackle the very important concept of *pure functions* (also known as *pure anonymous functions*).

Using pure functions will let us unlock a new level of power in the Wolfram Language, and also let us redo some of the things we've done before in a simpler and more elegant way.

Let's start with a simple example. Say we've got a list of images, and we want to apply Blur to each of them. That's easy to do with /@.

Apply Blur to each image in the list:

In[1]:= **Blur /@ {** ◯ **,** ◯ **,** ◯ **}**

Out[1]= **{** ◯ **,** ◯ **,** ◯ **}**

But now let's say we want to include the parameter 5 in Blur. How can we do that? The answer is to use a pure function.

Include a parameter by introducing a pure function:

In[2]:= **Blur[♯, 5] & /@ {** ◯ **,** ◯ **,** ◯ **}**

Out[2]= **{** ◯ **,** ◯ **,** ◯ **}**

The original blur written as a pure function:

In[3]:= **Blur[♯] & /@ {** ◯ **,** ◯ **,** ◯ **}**

Out[3]= **{** ◯ **,** ◯ **,** ◯ **}**

The ♯ is a "slot" into which each element is put. The & says that what comes before it is a pure function.

Here's the equivalent of Blur[♯, 5] & /@ … expanded out:

In[4]:= **{Blur[** ◯ **, 5], Blur[** ◯ **, 5], Blur[** ◯ **, 5]}**

Out[4]= **{** ◯ **,** ◯ **,** ◯ **}**

Let's look at some other examples. Every time, the slot indicates where to put each element when the pure function is applied.

Rotate each string by 90°:

In[5]:= **Rotate[⌗, 90 Degree] &/@{"one", "two", "three"}**

Out[5]=

Take a string and rotate it different amounts:

In[6]:= **Rotate["hello", ⌗] &/@{30 °, 90 °, 180 °, 220 °}**

Out[6]=

Show text in a list of different colors:

In[7]:= **Style["hello", 20, ⌗] &/@{Red, Orange, Blue, Purple}**

Out[7]= {hello, hello, hello, hello}

Make circles different sizes:

In[8]:= **Graphics[Circle[ ], ImageSize → ⌗] &/@{20, 40, 30, 50, 10}**

Out[8]= {◯, ◯, ◯, ◯, ○}

Show framed columns of a color and its negation:

In[9]:= **Framed[Column[{⌗, ColorNegate[⌗]}]] &/@{Red, Green, Blue, Purple, Orange}**

Out[9]= {▣, ▣, ▣, ▣, ▣}

Compute the lengths of three Wikipedia articles:

In[10]:= **StringLength[WikipediaData[⌗]] &/@{"apple", "peach", "pear"}**

Out[10]= {31 045, 24 153, 11 115}

Pair topics with results:

In[11]:= **{⌗, StringLength[WikipediaData[⌗]]} &/@{"apple", "peach", "pear"}**

Out[11]= {{apple, 31 045}, {peach, 24 153}, {pear, 11 115}}

Make a grid of everything:

In[12]:= **Grid[{♯, StringLength[WikipediaData[♯]]} &/@{"apple", "peach", "pear"}]**

Out[12]=
```
apple   31 045
peach   24 153
 pear   11 115
```

This makes a list of digits, then maps a pure function over it:

In[13]:= **Style[♯, Hue[♯/10], 5∗♯] &/@IntegerDigits[2^100]**

Out[13]= $\{,\ _2,\ 6,\ 7, 6,\ _5,,\ 6,,,_2,_2,\ 8,_2,_2,\ 9,_4,,,_4,\ 9, 6, 7,,_3,_2,,\ _5,_3,\ 7, 6\}$

Here's what the pure function would do if mapped over {6, 8, 9}:

In[14]:= **{Style[6, Hue[6/10], 5∗6], Style[8, Hue[8/10], 5∗8], Style[9, Hue[9/10], 5∗9]}**

Out[14]= $\{6, 8, 9\}$

Now that we've seen some examples of pure functions in action, let's look more abstractly at what's going on.

This maps an abstract pure function over a list:

In[15]:= **f[♯, x] &/@{a, b, c, d, e}**

Out[15]= {f[a, x], f[b, x], f[c, x], f[d, x], f[e, x]}

Here's the minimal example:

In[16]:= **f[♯] &/@{a, b, c, d, e}**

Out[16]= {f[a], f[b], f[c], f[d], f[e]}

It's equivalent to:

In[17]:= **f/@{a, b, c, d, e}**

Out[17]= {f[a], f[b], f[c], f[d], f[e]}

We can put slots wherever we want in the pure function, as many times as we want. All the slots will get filled with whatever the pure function is applied to.

Apply a slightly more complicated pure function:

In[18]:= **f[♯, {x, ♯}, {♯, ♯}] &/@{a, b, c}**

Out[18]= {f[a, {x, a}, {a, a}], f[b, {x, b}, {b, b}], f[c, {x, c}, {c, c}]}

It's easier to read in a column:

In[19]:= **f[♯, {x, ♯}, {♯, ♯}] &/@{a, b, c} // Column**

Out[19]=
f[a, {x, a}, {a, a}]
f[b, {x, b}, {b, b}]
f[c, {x, c}, {c, c}]

OK, now we're ready to finally discuss how pure functions really work. When we write f[x], we're applying the function f to x. Often we'll use a specific named function instead of f, say Blur, so we have Blur[x], etc.

But the point is that we can also replace f with a pure function. Then whatever we apply this to will be used to fill the slot in the pure function.

Apply a pure function to x, so the ♯ slot gets filled with x:

In[20]:= **f[♯, a] & [x]**

Out[20]= f[x, a]

An equivalent form, written with @ instead of [...]:

In[21]:= **f[♯, a] & @ x**

Out[21]= f[x, a]

So now we can see what /@ is doing: it's just applying the pure function to each element in the list.

In[22]:= **f[♯, a] &/@{x, y, z}**

Out[22]= {f[x, a], f[y, a], f[z, a]}

The same thing, written out more explicitly:

In[23]:= **{f[♯, a] & @ x, f[♯, a] & @ y, f[♯, a] & @ z}**

Out[23]= {f[x, a], f[y, a], f[z, a]}

Why is this useful? First of all, because it's the foundation for all the things pure functions do with /@. But it's actually also often useful on its own, for example as a way to avoid having to repeat things.

Here's an example of a pure function involving three occurrences of ♯.

Apply a pure function to Blend[{Red, Yellow}]:

In[24]:= **Column[{♯, ColorNegate[♯], ♯}] & [Blend[{Red, Yellow}]]**

Out[24]=
■
■
■

This is what it looks like without the pure function:

In[25]:= **Column[{Blend[{Red, Yellow}], ColorNegate[Blend[{Red, Yellow}]], Blend[{Red, Yellow}]}]**

Out[25]=

In the Wolfram Language, a pure function works just like anything else. On its own, though, it doesn't do anything.

Enter a pure function on its own and it'll come back unchanged:

In[26]:= **f[#, 2] &**

Out[26]= f[#1, 2] &

Give it to the function Map (/@), though, and it'll be used to do a computation.

Map uses the pure function to do a computation:

In[27]:= **Map[f[#, 2] &, {a, b, c, d, e}]**

Out[27]= {f[a, 2], f[b, 2], f[c, 2], f[d, 2], f[e, 2]}

Over the course of the next few sections, we'll see more and more uses of pure functions.

Vocabulary

code &	a pure function
#	slot in a pure function

Exercises

26.1   Use Range and a pure function to create a list of the first 20 squares.

26.2   Make a list of the result of blending yellow, green and blue with red.

26.3   Generate a list of framed columns containing the uppercase and lowercase versions of each letter of the alphabet.

26.4   Make a list of letters of the alphabet, in random colors, with frames having random background colors.

26.5   Make a table of G5 countries, together with their flags, and arrange the result in a fully framed grid.

26.6   Make a list of word clouds for the Wikipedia articles about apple, peach and pear.

26.7   Make a list of histograms of the word lengths in Wikipedia articles on apple, peach and pear.

26.8   Make a list of maps of Central America, highlighting each country in turn.

Q&A

Why are they called "pure functions"?

Because all they do is serve as functions that can be applied to arguments. They're also sometimes called *anonymous functions*, because, unlike say Blur, they're not referred to by a name. Here I'm calling them "pure anonymous functions" to communicate both meanings.

Why does one need the &?

The & (*ampersand*) indicates that what comes before it is the "body" of a pure function, not the name of a function. f/@{1, 2, 3} gives {f[1], f[2], f[3]}, but f &/@{1, 2, 3} gives {f, f, f}.

What is f[#, 1] & interpreted as?

Function[f[#, 1]]. The Function here is sometimes called the "function function".

Tech Notes

- Pure functions are a characteristic feature of *functional programming*. They're often called *lambda expressions*, after their use in mathematical logic in the 1930s. Confusingly, the term "pure function" sometimes just means a function that has no *side effects* (i.e. assigns no values to variables, etc.)

- Table[f[x], {x, {a, b, c }}] actually does the same as f/@{a, b, c}. It's sometimes useful, particularly if one doesn't want to have to explain pure functions.

- Be careful if you have multiple nested &'s in an expression! Sometimes you may have to insert parentheses. And sometimes you may have to use Function with a named variable, as in Function[x, x^2] rather than #^2 &, to avoid conflicts between uses of # in different functions.

- It sometimes makes for good-looking code to write Function[x, x^2] as x ⟼ x^2. The ⟼ can be typed as \[Function] or esc fn esc . A form like x ⟼ x^2 coincides with the standard mathematical notation for "x is mapped to x^2" or "x becomes x^2".

- Options can often be pure functions. It's important to put parentheses around the whole pure function, as in ColorFunction → (Hue[#/4] &), or it won't be interpreted as you expect.

More to Explore

Guide to Functional Programming in the Wolfram Language (wolfr.am/eiwl-26-more)

27 | Applying Functions Repeatedly

f[x] applies f to x. f[f[x]] applies f to f[x], or effectively nests the application of f. It's common to want to repeat or nest a function.

This makes a list of the results of nesting f up to 4 times:

In[1]:= **NestList[f, x, 4]**

Out[1]= {x, f[x], f[f[x]], f[f[f[x]]], f[f[f[f[x]]]]}

Using Framed as the function makes it a little more obvious what's going on:

In[2]:= **NestList[Framed, x, 5]**

Out[2]=

If you want to see a list of the results of successive nestings, use NestList. If you only want to see the final result, use Nest.

This gives the final result of 5 levels of nesting:

In[3]:= **Nest[Framed, x, 5]**

Out[3]=

Nestedly apply EdgeDetect to an image, first finding edges, then edges of edges and so on.

Nestedly do edge detection on an image:

In[4]:= **NestList[EdgeDetect,** ⬤ **, 6]**

Out[4]=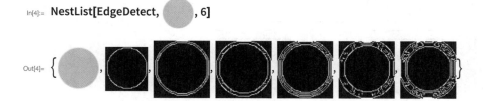

Use a pure function to both edge-detect and color-negate at each step:

In[5]:= **NestList[ColorNegate[EdgeDetect[#]] &,** ⬤ **, 6]**

Out[5]=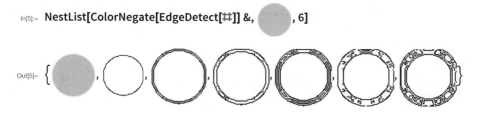

Start with red, and nestedly blend with yellow, getting more and more yellow.

Add another yellow into the blend at each step:

In[6]:= **NestList[Blend[{♯, Yellow}] &, Red, 20]**

Out[6]= {■, ■}

If you successively apply a function that adds 1, you just get successive integers.

Nestedly add 1, getting successive numbers:

In[7]:= **NestList[♯+1 &, 1, 15]**

Out[7]= {1, 2, 3, 4, 5, 6, 7, 8, 9, 10, 11, 12, 13, 14, 15, 16}

Nestedly multiply by 2, getting powers of 2.

The result doubles each time, giving a list of powers of 2:

In[8]:= **NestList[2 ∗ ♯ &, 1, 15]**

Out[8]= {1, 2, 4, 8, 16, 32, 64, 128, 256, 512, 1024, 2048, 4096, 8192, 16 384, 32 768}

Nested squaring very soon leads to big numbers:

In[9]:= **NestList[♯^2 &, 2, 6]**

Out[9]= {2, 4, 16, 256, 65 536, 4 294 967 296, 18 446 744 073 709 551 616}

You can make nested square roots too.

Nestedly apply square root:

In[10]:= **NestList[Sqrt[1+♯] &, 1, 5]**

$$\text{Out[10]}= \left\{1, \sqrt{2}, \sqrt{1+\sqrt{2}}, \sqrt{1+\sqrt{1+\sqrt{2}}}, \right.$$

$$\left. \sqrt{1+\sqrt{1+\sqrt{1+\sqrt{2}}}}, \sqrt{1+\sqrt{1+\sqrt{1+\sqrt{1+\sqrt{2}}}}} \right\}$$

The decimal version of the result converges quickly (to the *golden ratio*):

In[11]:= **NestList[Sqrt[1+♯] &, 1, 10] // N**

Out[11]= {1., 1.41421, 1.55377, 1.59805, 1.61185, 1.61612, 1.61744, 1.61785, 1.61798, 1.61802, 1.61803}

RandomChoice randomly chooses from a list. You can use it to create a pure function that, say, randomly either adds $+1$ or -1.

Randomly add or subtract 1 at each step, starting from 0:

In[12]:= **NestList[# + RandomChoice[{+1, −1}] &, 0, 20]**

Out[12]= {0, 1, 0, −1, −2, −3, −4, −5, −6, −5, −6, −5, −4, −5, −4, −3, −4, −3, −2, −1, −2}

This generates 500 steps in a "random walk":

In[13]:= **ListLinePlot[NestList[# + RandomChoice[{+1, −1}] &, 0, 500]]**

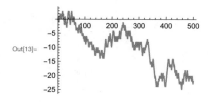

Out[13]=

So far, we've used NestList *iteratively*—effectively to perform a chain of applications of a particular function. But you can also use it for *recursion*, in which the very pattern of applications of the function is itself nested.

This does a chain of applications of the function f:

In[14]:= **NestList[f[#] &, x, 3]**

Out[14]= {x, f[x], f[f[x]], f[f[f[x]]]}

The pattern of applications of f is more complicated here:

In[15]:= **NestList[f[#, #] &, x, 3]**

Out[15]= {x, f[x, x], f[f[x, x], f[x, x]], f[f[f[x, x], f[x, x]], f[f[x, x], f[x, x]]]}

Adding frames makes it a little easier to see what's going on:

In[16]:= **NestList[Framed[f[#, #]] &, x, 3]**

Out[16]= {x, f[x, x] , f[f[x, x] , f[x, x]] , f[f[f[x, x] , f[x, x]] , f[f[x, x] , f[x, x]]] }

Putting everything in columns shows the nested pattern of function applications.

The nested boxes are recursively combined in twos at each level:

In[17]:= **NestList[Framed[Column[{#, #}]] &, x, 3]**

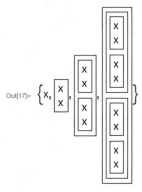

This gives a sequence of recursively nested grids:

In[18]:= **NestList[Framed[Grid[{{#, #}, {#, #}}]] &, x, 3]**

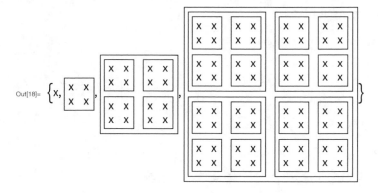

This forms the beginning of a fractal structure:

In[19]:= **NestList[Framed[Grid[{{0, #}, {#, #}}]] &, x, 3]**

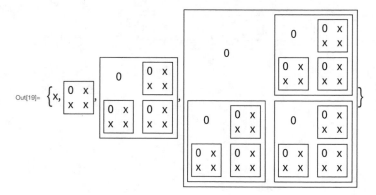

It's easy to get some pretty ornate recursive structures:

In[20]:= **NestList[Flatten[{⌗, Rotate[⌗, 90 °], Rotate[⌗, 270 °]}] &, "R", 4]**

Out[20]= {R, {R, ⊏, ⊐}, {R, ⊏, ⊐, ⅄, Ɽ}, {R, ⊏, ⊐, ⅄, Ɽ, ...

Not all results from recursion are so complicated. Here's an example that successively adds two shifted copies of a list together, as in {0, 1, 2, 1} + {1, 2, 1, 0}.

Prepend and append 0 to a list, then add together:

In[21]:= **NestList[Join[{0}, ⌗] + Join[⌗, {0}] &, {1}, 5]**

Out[21]= {{1}, {1, 1}, {1, 2, 1}, {1, 3, 3, 1}, {1, 4, 6, 4, 1}, {1, 5, 10, 10, 5, 1}}

If you put the result in a grid, it forms *Pascal's triangle* of *binomial coefficients*:

In[22]:= **NestList[Join[{0}, ⌗] + Join[⌗, {0}] &, {1}, 8] // Grid**

Out[22]=
```
1
1  1
1  2  1
1  3  3  1
1  4  6  4  1
1  5  10 10  5  1
1  6  15 20 15  6  1
1  7  21 35 35 21  7  1
1  8  28 56 70 56 28  8  1
```

Here's another example of recursion with NestList.

Form a recursive structure with two functions f and g:

In[23]:= **NestList[{f[#], g[#]} &, x, 3]**

Out[23]= {x, {f[x], g[x]}, {f[{f[x], g[x]}], g[{f[x], g[x]}]},
{f[{f[{f[x], g[x]}], g[{f[x], g[x]}]}], g[{f[{f[x], g[x]}], g[{f[x], g[x]}]}]}}

Even if things are arranged in columns, it's still quite difficult to understand the structure that's been created.

Arrange the recursive structure in columns:

In[24]:= **NestList[Column[{f[#], g[#]}] &, x, 3]**

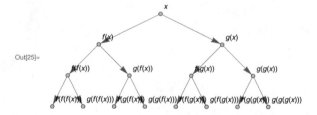

NestGraph is basically like NestList, except that it makes a graph rather than a list. It repeatedly applies a function to determine what nodes a particular node should connect to. In this case, it produces a tree of nodes, making it clearer what's going on.

Start from x, then repeatedly connect to the list of nodes obtained by applying the function:

In[25]:= **NestGraph[{f[#], g[#]} &, x, 3, VertexLabels → All]**

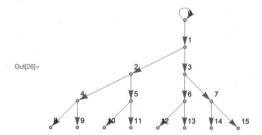

Repeatedly apply a numerical function to form another tree structure:

In[26]:= **NestGraph[{2 #, 2 # + 1} &, 0, 4, VertexLabels → All]**

Out[26]=

You can use **NestGraph** to effectively "crawl" outward creating a network. As an example, we can repeatedly apply a function that for any country gives a list of countries that border it. The result is a network that connects bordering countries, here starting with Switzerland.

"Crawl" outward 2 steps from Switzerland, connecting each country to all those that border it:

In[27]:= **NestGraph[⌗["BorderingCountries"] &, 🬭 switzerland , 2, VertexLabels → All]**

Out[27]=

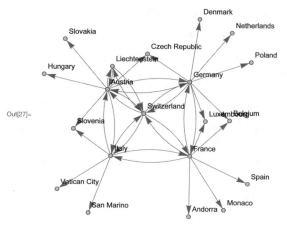

As another example, start from the word "hello" and successively connect every word to 3 words in the list of common words that **Nearest** considers nearest to it.

Create a network of nearby words with respect to 1-letter changes:

In[28]:= **NestGraph[Nearest[WordList[], ⌗, 3] &, "hello", 4, VertexLabels → All]**

Out[28]=

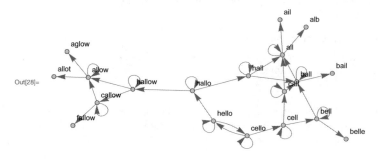

Vocabulary

NestList[f, x, n **]**	make a list of applying f to x up to n times
Nest[f, x, n **]**	give the result of applying f to x exactly n times
NestGraph[f, x, n **]**	make a graph by nestedly applying f starting with x

Exercises

27.1   Make a list of the results of nesting Blur up to 10 times, starting with a rasterized size-30 "X".

27.2   Start with x, then make a list by nestedly applying Framed up to 10 times, using a random background color each time.

27.3   Start with a size-50 "A", then make a list of nestedly applying a frame and a random rotation 5 times.

27.4   Make a line plot of 100 iterations of the *logistic map iteration* $4\,\#\,(1-\#)\,\&$, starting from 0.2.

27.5   Find the numerical value of the result from 30 iterations of $1+1/\#\,\&$ starting from 1.

27.6   Create a list of the first 10 powers of 3 (starting at 0) by nested multiplication.

27.7   Make a list of the result of nesting the (*Newton's method*) function $(\#+2/\#)/2\,\&$ up to 5 times starting from 1.0, and then subtract $\sqrt{2}$ from all the results.

27.8   Make graphics of a 1000-step 2D random walk which starts at $\{0, 0\}$, and in which at each step a pair of random numbers between −1 and +1 are added to the coordinates.

27.9   Make an array plot of 50 steps of Pascal's triangle modulo 2 by starting from $\{1\}$ and nestedly joining $\{0\}$ at the beginning and at the end, and adding these results together modulo 2.

27.10   Generate a graph by starting from 0, then nestedly 10 times connecting each node with value n to ones with values $n+1$ and $2\,n$.

27.11   Generate a graph obtained by nestedly finding bordering countries starting from the United States, and going 4 iterations.

Q&A

What's the difference between iteration and recursion?

If one does one thing repeatedly, it's iteration. When one takes the result of an operation and applies the same operation to it wherever it is, that's recursion. It's slightly confusing, because simple cases of recursion are just iteration. NestList always does recursion, but if only one slot appears in the function, the recursion can be "unrolled" into iteration.

What is the relation between nesting, recursion and fractals?

They are very closely related. The definitions aren't precise, but fractals are basically geometrical forms that exhibit some type of nested or recursive structure.

What is Pascal's triangle?

It's a very common structure discussed in elementary mathematics. Its definition is very close to the Wolfram Language code here: at each row each number is computed as the sum of the numbers directly above it and above it to its right. Each row gives the coefficients in the expansion of $(1+x)\,\hat{}\,n$.

Is NestGraph like a web crawler?

Conceptually yes. One can think of it as doing the analog of starting from a webpage and then visiting links from that page, and continuing recursively with that process. We'll see an example of this in Section 44.

Why do some but not all countries have arrows both ways in the bordering countries graph?

If NestGraph was run for enough steps, all countries would have arrows both ways, since if A borders B, then B borders A. But here we're stopping after just 2 steps, so many of the reverse connections haven't been reached.

Why use NestList for something like NestList[2 ∗ ♯ &, 1, 15]?

You don't need to. You can just use Power, as in Table[2 ^ n, {n, 0, 15}]. But it's nice to see the sequence Plus, Times, Power arise from successive nesting (e.g. NestList[2 + ♯ &, 0, 15] is Table[2 ∗ n, {n, 0, 15}]).

Is there a way to keep applying a function until nothing is changing?

Yes. Use FixedPoint or FixedPointList (see Section 41).

Tech Note

- The nearest words example can be made much more efficient by first computing a NearestFunction, then using this repeatedly, rather than computing Nearest from scratch for every word. This example is also closely related to NearestNeighborGraph, discussed in Section 22.

More to Explore

Guide to Functional Iteration in the Wolfram Language (wolfr.am/eiwl-27-more)

28 | Tests and Conditionals

Is $2+2$ equal to 4? Let's ask the Wolfram Language.

Test whether 2+2 is equal to 4:

In[1]:= **2 + 2 == 4**

Out[1]= True

Not surprisingly, testing whether $2+2$ is equal to 4 gives True.

We can also test whether 2×2 is greater than 5. We do that using $>$.

Test whether 2×2 is greater than 5:

In[2]:= **2 * 2 > 5**

Out[2]= False

The function If lets you choose to give one result if a test is True, and another if it's False.

Since the test gives True, the result of the If is x:

In[3]:= **If[2 + 2 == 4, x, y]**

Out[3]= x

By using a pure function with /@, we can apply an If to every element of a list.

If an element is less than 4, make it x, otherwise make it y:

In[4]:= **If[# < 4, x, y] & /@ {1, 2, 3, 4, 5, 6, 7}**

Out[4]= {x, x, x, y, y, y, y}

You can also test for less than or equal using $\leq$, which is typed as <=.

If an element is less than or equal to 4, make it x; otherwise, make it y:

In[5]:= **If[# ≤ 4, x, y] & /@ {1, 2, 3, 4, 5, 6, 7}**

Out[5]= {x, x, x, x, y, y, y}

This makes an element x only if it is equal to 4:

In[6]:= **If[# == 4, x, y] & /@ {1, 2, 3, 4, 5, 6, 7}**

Out[6]= {y, y, y, x, y, y, y}

You can test whether two things are not equal using ≠, which is typed as !=.

If an element is not equal to 4, make it x; otherwise, make it y:

In[7]:= **If[# ≠ 4, x, y] &/@ {1, 2, 3, 4, 5, 6, 7}**

Out[7]= {x, x, x, y, x, x, x}

It's often useful to select elements in a list that satisfy a test. You can do this by using Select, and giving your test as a pure function.

Select elements in the list that are greater than 3:

In[8]:= **Select[{1, 2, 3, 4, 5, 6, 7}, # > 3 &]**

Out[8]= {4, 5, 6, 7}

Select elements that are between 2 and 5:

In[9]:= **Select[{1, 2, 3, 4, 5, 6, 7}, 2 ≤ # ≤ 5 &]**

Out[9]= {2, 3, 4, 5}

Beyond size comparisons like <, > and ==, the Wolfram Language includes many other kinds of tests. Examples are EvenQ and OddQ, which test whether numbers are even or odd. (The "Q" indicates that the functions are asking a question.)

4 is an even number:

In[10]:= **EvenQ[4]**

Out[10]= True

Select even numbers from the list:

In[11]:= **Select[{1, 2, 3, 4, 5, 6, 7, 8, 9}, EvenQ[#] &]**

Out[11]= {2, 4, 6, 8}

In this case, we don't need the explicit pure function:

In[12]:= **Select[{1, 2, 3, 4, 5, 6, 7, 8, 9}, EvenQ]**

Out[12]= {2, 4, 6, 8}

IntegerQ tests whether something is an integer; PrimeQ tests whether a number is prime.

Select prime numbers:

In[13]:= **Select[{1, 2, 3, 4, 5, 6, 7, 8, 9, 10}, PrimeQ]**

Out[13]= {2, 3, 5, 7}

Sometimes we need to combine tests. && represents "and", || represents "or" and ! represents "not".

Select elements of the list that are both even and greater than 2:

In[14]:= **Select[{1, 2, 3, 4, 5, 6, 7}, EvenQ[#] && # > 2 &]**

Out[14]= {4, 6}

Select elements that are either even or greater than 4:

In[15]:= **Select[{1, 2, 3, 4, 5, 6, 7}, EvenQ[#] || # > 4 &]**

Out[15]= {2, 4, 5, 6, 7}

Select elements that are not either even or greater than 4:

In[16]:= **Select[{1, 2, 3, 4, 5, 6, 7}, ! (EvenQ[#] || # > 4) &]**

Out[16]= {1, 3}

There are many other "Q functions" that ask various kinds of questions. LetterQ tests whether a string consists of letters.

The space between letters isn't a letter; nor is "!":

In[17]:= **{LetterQ["a"], LetterQ["bc"], LetterQ["a b"], LetterQ["!"]}**

Out[17]= {True, True, False, False}

Turn a string into a list of characters, then test which are letters:

In[18]:= **LetterQ /@ Characters["30 is the best!"]**

Out[18]= {False, False, False, True, True, False, True, True, True, False, True, True, True, True, False}

Select the characters that are letters:

In[19]:= **Select[Characters["30 is the best!"], LetterQ]**

Out[19]= {i, s, t, h, e, b, e, s, t}

Select letters that appear after position 10 in the alphabet:

In[20]:= **Select[Characters["30 is the best!"], LetterQ[#] && LetterNumber[#] > 10 &]**

Out[20]= {s, t, s, t}

You can use Select to find words in English that are *palindromes*, meaning that they are the same if you reverse them.

In[21]:= **Select[WordList[ ], StringReverse[#] == # &]**

Out[21]= {a, aha, bib, bob, boob, civic, dad, deed, dud, ere, eve, ewe, eye, gag, gig, huh, kayak, kook, level, ma'am, madam, minim, mom, mum, nan, non, noon, nun, oho, pap, peep, pep, pip, poop, pop, pup, radar, refer, rotor, sis, tat, tenet, toot, tot, tut, wow}

MemberQ tests whether something appears as an element, or member, of a list.

5 appears in the list {1, 3, 5, 7}:

In[22]:= **MemberQ[{1, 3, 5, 7}, 5]**

Out[22]= True

Select numbers in the range 1 to 100 whose digit sequences contain 2:

In[23]:= **Select[Range[100], MemberQ[IntegerDigits[#], 2] &]**

Out[23]= {2, 12, 20, 21, 22, 23, 24, 25, 26, 27, 28, 29, 32, 42, 52, 62, 72, 82, 92}

ImageInstanceQ is a machine-learning-based function that tests whether an image is an instance of a particular kind of thing, like a cat.

Test if an image is of a cat:

In[24]:= **ImageInstanceQ[**  **]**

Out[24]= True

Select images of cats:

In[25]:= **Select[{**  **},**

ImageInstanceQ[#, ⊟ cat] &]

Out[25]= { }

Here's a geographic example of Select: find which cities in a list are less than 3000 miles from San Francisco.

Select cities whose distance from San Francisco is less than 3000 miles:

In[26]:= **Select[{** 🔲 london **,** 🔲 nyc **,** 🔲 tokyo **,** 🔲 chicago **},**
GeoDistance[#, 🔲 san francisco **] <** 🔲 3000 miles **&]**

Out[26]= **{** New York City **,** Chicago **}**

Vocabulary

$a == b$	test for equality
$a < b$	test whether less
$a > b$	test whether greater
$a \leq b$	test whether less or equal
$a \geq b$	test whether greater or equal
If[*test, u, v*]	give *u* if *test* is True and *v* if False
Select[*list, f*]	select elements that pass a test
EvenQ[*x*]	test whether even
OddQ[*x*]	test whether odd
IntegerQ[*x*]	test whether an integer
PrimeQ[*x*]	test whether a prime number
LetterQ[*string*]	test whether there are only letters
MemberQ[*list, x*]	test whether *x* is a member of *list*
ImageInstanceQ[*image, category*]	test whether *image* is an instance of *category*

Exercises

28.1 Test whether 123^321 is greater than 456^123.

28.2 Get a list of numbers up to 100 whose digits add up to less than 5.

28.3 Make a list of the first 20 integers, with prime numbers styled red.

28.4 Find words in WordList[] that both begin and end with the letter "p".

28.5 Make a list of the first 100 primes, keeping only ones whose last digit is less than 3.

28.6 Find Roman numerals up to 100 that do not contain "I".

28.7 Get a list of Roman numerals up to 1000 that are palindromes.

28.8 Find names of integers up to 100 that begin and end with the same letter.

28.9 Get a list of words longer than 15 characters from the Wikipedia article on words.

28.10 Starting from 1000, divide by 2 if the number is even, and compute 3 # + 1 & if the number is odd; do this repeatedly 200 times (*Collatz problem*).

28.11 Make a word cloud of 5-letter words in the Wikipedia article on computers.

28.12 Find words in WordList[ ] whose first 3 letters are the same as their last 3 read backward, but where the whole string is not a palindrome.

28.13 Find all 10-letter words in WordList[ ] for which the total of LetterNumber values is 100.

Q&A

Why does one test equality with == not =?

Because = means something else in the Wolfram Language. You'll get very strange results if you use = instead of == by mistake. (= is for assigning values of variables.) To avoid possible confusion, == is often read as "double equals".

Why is "and" written as &&, not &?

Because & means other things in the Wolfram Language. For example it's what ends a pure function.

How are ==, >, &&, etc. interpreted?

== is Equal, ≠ (!=) is Unequal, > is Greater, ≥ is GreaterEqual, < is Less, && is And, || is Or and ! is Not.

When do I need to use parentheses with &&, ||, etc.?

There's an order of operations that's a direct analog of arithmetic. && is like ×, || is like +, and ! is like −. So ! p && q means "(not p) and q"; ! (p && q) means "not (p and q)".

What's special about "Q" functions?

They ask a question that normally has an answer of True or False.

What are some other "Q" functions?

NumberQ, StringContainsQ, BusinessDayQ and ConnectedGraphQ are a few.

Is there a better way to find real-world entities with certain properties than using Select?

Yes. You can do things like Entity["Country", "Population" → GreaterThan[10^7 people]] to find "implicit entities", then use EntityList to get explicit lists of entities.

Tech Notes

- True and False are typically called *Booleans* in computer science, after George Boole from the mid-1800s. Expressions with &&, ||, etc. are often called *Boolean expressions*.

- In the Wolfram Language, True and False are *symbols*, and are not represented by 1 and 0 as in many other computer languages.

- If is often called a *conditional*. In If[*test, then, else*], the *then* and *else* aren't computed unless the *test* says their condition is met.

- PalindromeQ directly tests if a string is a palindrome.

- In the Wolfram Language, x is a *symbol* (see Section 33) that could represent anything, so x == 1 is just an *equation*, that isn't immediately True or False. x === 1 ("triple equals") tests whether x is *the same* as 1, and since it isn't, it gives False.

More to Explore

Guide to Functions That Apply Tests in the Wolfram Language (wolfr.am/eiwl-28-more)

Guide to Boolean Computation in the Wolfram Language (wolfr.am/eiwl-28-more2)

29 | More about Pure Functions

We've seen how to make lists and arrays with Table. There's also a way to do it using pure functions—with Array.

Generate a 10-element array with an abstract function f:

In[1]:= **Array[f, 10]**

Out[1]= {f[1], f[2], f[3], f[4], f[5], f[6], f[7], f[8], f[9], f[10]}

Use a pure function to generate a list of the first 10 squares:

In[2]:= **Array[# ^ 2 &, 10]**

Out[2]= {1, 4, 9, 16, 25, 36, 49, 64, 81, 100}

Table can give the same result, though you have to introduce the variable n:

In[3]:= **Table[n ^ 2, {n, 10}]**

Out[3]= {1, 4, 9, 16, 25, 36, 49, 64, 81, 100}

Array[f, 4] makes a single list of 4 elements. Array[f, {3, 4}] makes a 3×4 array.

Make a list of length 3, each of whose elements is a list of length 4:

In[4]:= **Array[f, {3, 4}]**

Out[4]= {{f[1, 1], f[1, 2], f[1, 3], f[1, 4]}, {f[2, 1], f[2, 2], f[2, 3], f[2, 4]}, {f[3, 1], f[3, 2], f[3, 3], f[3, 4]}}

Display it in a grid:

In[5]:= **Array[f, {3, 4}] // Grid**

Out[5]=
f[1, 1] f[1, 2] f[1, 3] f[1, 4]
f[2, 1] f[2, 2] f[2, 3] f[2, 4]
f[3, 1] f[3, 2] f[3, 3] f[3, 4]

If the function is Times, Array makes a multiplication table:

In[6]:= **Grid[Array[Times, {5, 5}]]**

Out[6]=
1   2   3   4   5
2   4   6   8   10
3   6   9   12 15
4   8   12 16 20
5   10 15 20 25

What if we want to use a pure function in place of Times? When we compute Times[3, 4], we say that Times is applied to two *arguments*. (In Times[3, 4, 5], Times is applied to three arguments, etc.) In a pure function, #1 represents the first argument, #2 the second argument and so on.

#1 represents the first argument, #2 the second argument:

In[7]:= **f[#1, #2] &[55, 66]**

Out[7]= f[55, 66]

#1 always picks out the first argument, and #2 the second argument:

In[8]:= **f[#2, #1, {#2, #2, #1}] &[55, 66]**

Out[8]= f[66, 55, {66, 66, 55}]

Now we can use #1 and #2 inside a function in Array.

Use a pure function to make a multiplication table:

In[9]:= **Array[#1 * #2 &, {5, 5}] // Grid**

1	2	3	4	5
2	4	6	8	10
3	6	9	12	15
4	8	12	16	20
5	10	15	20	25

Out[9]=

Use a different pure function that puts in x whenever the numbers are equal:

In[10]:= **Array[If[#1 == #2, x, #1 * #2] &, {5, 5}] // Grid**

x	2	3	4	5
2	x	6	8	10
3	6	x	12	15
4	8	12	x	20
5	10	15	20	x

Out[10]=

Here's the equivalent computation with Table:

In[11]:= **Table[If[i == j, x, i * j], {i, 5}, {j, 5}] // Grid**

x	2	3	4	5
2	x	6	8	10
3	6	x	12	15
4	8	12	x	20
5	10	15	20	x

Out[11]=

Now that we've discussed pure functions with more than one argument, we're in a position to talk about FoldList. You can think of FoldList as a 2-argument generalization of NestList.

NestList takes a single function, say f, and successively nests it:

In[12]:= **NestList[f, x, 5]**

Out[12]= {x, f[x], f[f[x]], f[f[f[x]]], f[f[f[f[x]]]], f[f[f[f[f[x]]]]]}

It's easier to understand when the function we use is Framed:

In[13]:= **NestList[Framed, x, 5]**

Out[13]= {x, x, x, x, x, x}

NestList just keeps on applying a function to whatever result it got before. FoldList does the same, except that it also "folds in" a new element each time.

Here's FoldList with an abstract function f:

In[14]:= **FoldList[f, x, {1, 2, 3, 4, 5}]**

Out[14]= {x, f[x, 1], f[f[x, 1], 2], f[f[f[x, 1], 2], 3], f[f[f[f[x, 1], 2], 3], 4], f[f[f[f[f[x, 1], 2], 3], 4], 5]}

Including Framed makes it a little easier to see what's going on:

In[15]:= **FoldList[Framed[f[#1, #2]] &, x, {1, 2, 3, 4, 5}]**

At first, this may look complicated and obscure, and it might seem hard to imagine how it could be useful. But actually, it's very useful, and surprisingly common in real programs.

FoldList is good for progressively accumulating things. Let's start with a simple case: progressively adding up numbers.

At each step FoldList folds in another element (#2), adding it to the result so far (#1):

In[16]:= **FoldList[#1 + #2 &, 0, {1, 1, 1, 2, 0, 0}]**

Out[16]= {0, 1, 2, 3, 5, 5, 5}

Here's the computation it's doing:

In[17]:= {0, 0 + 1, (0 + 1) + 1, ((0 + 1) + 1) + 1, (((0 + 1) + 1) + 1) + 2,
        ((((0 + 1) + 1) + 1) + 2) + 0, (((((0 + 1) + 1) + 1) + 2) + 0) + 0}

Out[17]= {0, 1, 2, 3, 5, 5, 5}

Or equivalently:

In[18]:= {0, 0 + 1, 0 + 1 + 1, 0 + 1 + 1 + 1, 0 + 1 + 1 + 1 + 2, 0 + 1 + 1 + 1 + 2 + 0, 0 + 1 + 1 + 1 + 2 + 0 + 0}

Out[18]= {0, 1, 2, 3, 5, 5, 5}

It may be easier to see what's going on with symbols:

In[19]:= **FoldList[#1 + #2 &, 0, {a, b, c, d, e}]**

Out[19]= {0, a, a + b, a + b + c, a + b + c + d, a + b + c + d + e}

Of course, this case is simple enough that you don't actually need a pure function:

In[20]:= **FoldList[Plus, 0, {a, b, c, d, e}]**

Out[20]= {0, a, a + b, a + b + c, a + b + c + d, a + b + c + d + e}

A classic use of FoldList is to successively "fold in" digits to reconstruct a number from its list of digits.

Successively construct a number from its digits, starting the folding process with its first digit:

In[21]:= **FoldList[10 #1 + #2 &, {8, 7, 6, 1, 2, 3, 9, 8, 7}]**

Out[21]= {8, 87, 876, 8761, 87 612, 876 123, 8 761 239, 87 612 398, 876 123 987}

Finally, let's use FoldList to "fold in" progressive images from a list, at each point adding them with ImageAdd to the image obtained so far.

Progressively "fold in" images from a list, combining them with ImageAdd:

In[22]:= **FoldList[ImageAdd,**

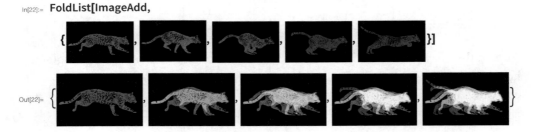

The concept of FoldList is not at first the easiest to understand. But when you've got it, you've learned an extremely powerful *functional programming* technique that's an example of the kind of elegant abstraction possible in the Wolfram Language.

Vocabulary

Array[f, n **]**	make an array by applying a function
Array[f, {m, n} **]**	make an array in 2D
FoldList[f, x, *list* **]**	successively apply a function, folding in elements of a list

Exercises

29.1 Use Prime and Array to generate a list of the first 100 primes.

29.2 Use Prime and Array to find successive differences between the first 100 primes.

29.3 Use Array and Grid to make a 10 by 10 addition table.

29.4 Use FoldList, Times and Range to successively multiply numbers up to 10 (making factorials).

29.5 Use FoldList and Array to compute the successive products of the first 10 primes.

29.6 Use FoldList to successively ImageAdd regular polygons with between 3 and 8 sides, and with opacity 0.2.

Q&A

What does # alone mean?

It's equivalent to #1—a slot to be filled from the first argument of a function.

How does one say #1?

Either "slot 1" (reflecting its role in a pure function), or "hash 1" (reflecting how it's written—the "#" is usually called "hash").

Can one name arguments to a pure function?

Yes. It's done with Function[{x, y}, x+y], etc. It's sometimes nice to do this for code readability, and it's sometimes necessary when pure functions are nested.

Can Array make more deeply nested structures?

Yes—as deep as you want. Lists of lists of lists... for any number of levels.

What is functional programming?

It's programming where everything is based on evaluating functions and combinations of functions. It's actually the only style of programming we've seen so far in this book. In Section 38 we'll see *procedural programming*, which is about going through a procedure and progressively changing values of variables.

Tech Notes

- Fold gives the last element of FoldList, just like Nest gives the last element of NestList.

- FromDigits reconstructs numbers from lists of digits, effectively doing what we used FoldList for above.

- Accumulate[*list*] is FoldList[Plus, *list*].

- Array and FoldList, like NestList, are examples of what are called *higher-order functions*, that take functions as input. (In mathematics, they're also known as *functionals* or *functors*.)

- You can set up pure functions that take any number of arguments at a time using ##, etc.

- You can animate lists of images using ListAnimate, and show the images stacked in 3D using Image3D.

More to Explore

Guide to Functional Programming in the Wolfram Language (wolfr.am/eiwl-29-more)

30 | Rearranging Lists

It's common for lists that come out of one computation to have to be rearranged before going into another computation. For example, one might have a list of pairs, and need to convert it into a pair of lists, or vice versa.

Transpose a list of pairs so it becomes a pair of lists:

In[1]:= **Transpose[{{1, 2}, {3, 4}, {5, 6}, {7, 8}, {9, 10}}]**

Out[1]= {{1, 3, 5, 7, 9}, {2, 4, 6, 8, 10}}

Transpose the pair of lists back to a list of pairs:

In[2]:= **Transpose[{{1, 3, 5, 7, 9}, {2, 4, 6, 8, 10}}]**

Out[2]= {{1, 2}, {3, 4}, {5, 6}, {7, 8}, {9, 10}}

Thread is a closely related operation, often useful for generating input to Graph.

"Thread" → across the elements of two lists:

In[3]:= **Thread[{1, 3, 5, 7, 9} → {2, 4, 6, 8, 10}]**

Out[3]= {1 → 2, 3 → 4, 5 → 6, 7 → 8, 9 → 10}

Partition takes a list, and partitions it into blocks of a specified size.

Partition a 12-element list into blocks of size 3:

In[4]:= **Partition[Range[12], 3]**

Out[4]= {{1, 2, 3}, {4, 5, 6}, {7, 8, 9}, {10, 11, 12}}

Partition a list of characters to display them in a grid:

In[5]:= **Grid[Partition[Characters["An array of text made in the Wolfram Language"], 9],**
Frame → All]

Out[5]=

If you don't tell it otherwise, Partition breaks a list up into non-overlapping blocks. But you can also tell it to break the list into blocks that have some specified offset.

Partition a list into blocks of size 3 with offset 1:

In[6]:= **Partition[Range[10], 3, 1]**

Out[6]= {{1, 2, 3}, {2, 3, 4}, {3, 4, 5}, {4, 5, 6}, {5, 6, 7}, {6, 7, 8}, {7, 8, 9}, {8, 9, 10}}

Partition a list of characters into blocks with an offset of 1:

In[7]:= **Grid[Partition[Characters["Wolfram Language"], 12, 1], Frame → All]**

W	o	l	f	r	a	m		L	a	n	g
o	l	f	r	a	m		L	a	n	g	u
l	f	r	a	m		L	a	n	g	u	a
f	r	a	m		L	a	n	g	u	a	g
r	a	m		L	a	n	g	u	a	g	e

Out[7]=

Use an offset of 2 instead:

In[8]:= **Grid[Partition[Characters["Wolfram Language"], 12, 2], Frame → All]**

W	o	l	f	r	a	m		L	a	n	g
l	f	r	a	m		L	a	n	g	u	a
r	a	m		L	a	n	g	u	a	g	e

Out[8]=

Partition takes a list and breaks it into sublists. Flatten "flattens out" sublists.

Make a list of lists from digits of successive integers:

In[9]:= **IntegerDigits /@ Range[20]**

Out[9]= {{1}, {2}, {3}, {4}, {5}, {6}, {7}, {8}, {9}, {1, 0}, {1, 1},
　　　{1, 2}, {1, 3}, {1, 4}, {1, 5}, {1, 6}, {1, 7}, {1, 8}, {1, 9}, {2, 0}}

Make a flattened version:

In[10]:= **Flatten[IntegerDigits /@ Range[20]]**

Out[10]= {1, 2, 3, 4, 5, 6, 7, 8, 9, 1, 0, 1, 1, 1, 2, 1, 3, 1, 4, 1, 5, 1, 6, 1, 7, 1, 8, 1, 9, 2, 0}

Make a plot from the sequence of digits:

In[11]:= **ListLinePlot[Flatten[IntegerDigits /@ Range[20]]]**

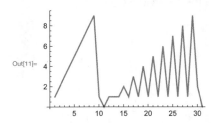

Out[11]=

Flatten will normally flatten out all levels of lists. But quite often you only want to flatten, say, one level of lists. This makes a 4×4 table in which each element is itself a list.

Make a list of lists of lists:

In[12]:= **Table[IntegerDigits[i ^ j], {i, 4}, {j, 4}]**

Out[12]= {{{1}, {1}, {1}, {1}}, {{2}, {4}, {8}, {1, 6}}, {{3}, {9}, {2, 7}, {8, 1}}, {{4}, {1, 6}, {6, 4}, {2, 5, 6}}}

Flatten everything out:

In[13]:= **Flatten[Table[IntegerDigits[i^j], {i, 4}, {j, 4}]]**

Out[13]= {1, 1, 1, 1, 2, 4, 8, 1, 6, 3, 9, 2, 7, 8, 1, 4, 1, 6, 6, 4, 2, 5, 6}

Flatten out only one level of list:

In[14]:= **Flatten[Table[IntegerDigits[i^j], {i, 4}, {j, 4}], 1]**

Out[14]= {{1}, {1}, {1}, {1}, {2}, {4}, {8}, {1, 6}, {3}, {9}, {2, 7}, {8, 1}, {4}, {1, 6}, {6, 4}, {2, 5, 6}}

ArrayFlatten is a generalization of Flatten, which takes arrays of arrays, and flattens them into individual arrays.

This generates a deeply nested structure that's hard to understand:

In[15]:= **NestList[{{#, 0}, {#, #}} &, {{1}}, 2]**

Out[15]= {{{1}}, {{{{1}}, 0}, {{{1}}, {{1}}}},
      {{{{{1}}}, 0}, {{{1}}, {{1}}}}, 0}, {{{{{1}}}, 0}, {{{1}}, {{1}}}}, {{{{1}}, 0}, {{{1}}, {{1}}}}}}}

ArrayFlatten makes a structure that's a little easier to understand:

In[16]:= **NestList[ArrayFlatten[{{#, 0}, {#, #}}] &, {{1}}, 2]**

Out[16]= {{{1}}, {{1, 0}, {1, 1}}, {{1, 0, 0, 0}, {1, 1, 0, 0}, {1, 0, 1, 0}, {1, 1, 1, 1}}}

With ArrayPlot, it's considerably easier to see what's going on:

In[17]:= **ArrayPlot/@NestList[ArrayFlatten[{{#, 0}, {#, #}}] &, {{1}}, 4]**

Out[17]=

Generate a *fractal Sierpinski pattern* with 8 levels of nesting:

In[18]:= **ArrayPlot[Nest[ArrayFlatten[{{#, 0}, {#, #}}] &, {{1}}, 8]]**

Out[18]=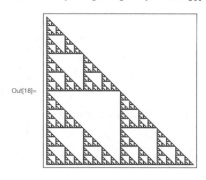

There are many other ways to rearrange lists. For example, Split splits a list into runs of identical elements.

Split a list into sequences of successive identical elements:

In[19]:= **Split[{1, 1, 1, 2, 2, 1, 1, 3, 1, 1, 1, 2}]**

Out[19]= {{1, 1, 1}, {2, 2}, {1, 1}, {3}, {1, 1, 1}, {2}}

Gather, on the other hand, gathers identical elements together, wherever they appear.

Gather identical elements together in lists:

In[20]:= **Gather[{1, 1, 1, 2, 2, 1, 1, 3, 1, 1, 1, 2}]**

Out[20]= {{1, 1, 1, 1, 1, 1, 1, 1}, {2, 2, 2}, {3}}

GatherBy gathers elements according to the result of applying a function to them. Here it's using LetterQ, so that it gathers separately letters and non-letters.

Gather characters according to whether they are letters or not:

In[21]:= **GatherBy[Characters["It's true that 2+2 is equal to 4!"], LetterQ]**

Out[21]= {{I, t, s, t, r, u, e, t, h, a, t, i, s, e, q, u, a, l, t, o}, {', , , , 2, +, 2, , , , , , 4, !}}

SortBy sorts according to the result of applying a function.

Sort normally sorts shorter lists before longer ones:

In[22]:= **Sort[Table[IntegerDigits[2 ^ n], {n, 10}]]**

Out[22]= {{2}, {4}, {8}, {1, 6}, {3, 2}, {6, 4}, {1, 2, 8}, {2, 5, 6}, {5, 1, 2}, {1, 0, 2, 4}}

Here SortBy is told to sort by the first element in each list:

In[23]:= **SortBy[Table[IntegerDigits[2 ^ n], {n, 10}], First]**

Out[23]= {{1, 6}, {1, 2, 8}, {1, 0, 2, 4}, {2}, {2, 5, 6}, {3, 2}, {4}, {5, 1, 2}, {6, 4}, {8}}

Sort sorts a list in order. Union also removes any repeated elements.

Find all the distinct elements that appear:

In[24]:= **Union[{1, 9, 5, 3, 1, 4, 3, 1, 3, 3, 5, 3, 9}]**

Out[24]= {1, 3, 4, 5, 9}

You can use Union to find the "union" of elements that appear in any of several lists.

Get a list of all elements that appear in any of the lists:

In[25]:= **Union[{2, 1, 3, 7, 9}, {4, 5, 1, 2, 3, 3}, {3, 1, 2, 8, 5}]**

Out[25]= {1, 2, 3, 4, 5, 7, 8, 9}

Find which elements are common to all the lists:

In[26]:= **Intersection[{2, 1, 3, 7, 9}, {4, 5, 1, 2, 3, 3}, {3, 1, 2, 8}]**

Out[26]= {1, 2, 3}

Find which elements are in the first list but not the second one:

In[27]:= **Complement[{4, 5, 1, 2, 3, 3}, {3, 1, 2, 8}]**

Out[27]= {4, 5}

Find letters that appear in any of English, Swedish and Turkish:

In[28]:= **Union[Alphabet["English"], Alphabet["Swedish"], Alphabet["Turkish"]]**

Out[28]= {ğ, ş, a, å, ä, b, c, ç, d, e, f, g, h, i, ı, j, k, l, m, n, o, ö, p, q, r, s, t, u, ü, v, w, x, y, z}

Letters that appear in Swedish but not English:

In[29]:= **Complement[Alphabet["Swedish"], Alphabet["English"]]**

Out[29]= {å, ä, ö}

Another of the many functions you can apply to lists is Riffle, which inserts things between successive elements of a list.

Riffle x in between the elements of a list:

In[30]:= **Riffle[{1, 2, 3, 4, 5}, x]**

Out[30]= {1, x, 2, x, 3, x, 4, x, 5}

Riffle −− into a list of characters:

In[31]:= **Riffle[Characters["WOLFRAM"], "−−"]**

Out[31]= {W, −−, O, −−, L, −−, F, −−, R, −−, A, −−, M}

Join everything together in a single string:

In[32]:= **StringJoin[Riffle[Characters["WOLFRAM"], "−−"]]**

Out[32]= W−−O−−L−−F−−R−−A−−M

Functions like Partition let you take a list and break it into sublists. Sometimes you'll instead just want to start from a collection of possible elements, and form lists from them.

Permutations gives all possible orderings, or *permutations*, of a list.

Generate a list of the 3!=3×2×1=6 possible orderings of 3 elements:

In[33]:= **Permutations[{Red, Green, Blue}]**

Out[33]= {{■, ■, ■}, {■, ■, ■}, {■, ■, ■}, {■, ■, ■}, {■, ■, ■}, {■, ■, ■}}

Generate all $2^3 = 8$ possible subsets of a list of 3 elements:

In[34]:= **Subsets[{Red, Green, Blue}]**

Out[34]= {{}, {■}, {■}, {■}, {■, ■}, {■, ■}, {■, ■}, {■, ■, ■}}

Tuples takes a list of elements, and generates all possible combinations of a given number of those elements.

Generate a list of all possible triples of red and green:

In[35]:= **Tuples[{Red, Green}, 3]**

Out[35]= {{■, ■, ■}, {■, ■, ■}, {■, ■, ■}, {■, ■, ■}, {■, ■, ■}, {■, ■, ■}, {■, ■, ■}, {■, ■, ■}}

RandomChoice lets you make a random choice from a list of elements.

Make a single random choice from a list:

In[36]:= **RandomChoice[{Red, Green, Blue}]**

Out[36]= ■

Make a list of 20 random choices:

In[37]:= **RandomChoice[{Red, Green, Blue}, 20]**

Out[37]= {■, ■, ■, ■, ■, ■, ■, ■, ■, ■, ■, ■, ■, ■, ■, ■, ■, ■, ■, ■}

Make 5 lists of 3 random choices:

In[38]:= **RandomChoice[{Red, Green, Blue}, {5, 3}]**

Out[38]= {{■, ■, ■}, {■, ■, ■}, {■, ■, ■}, {■, ■, ■}, {■, ■, ■}}

RandomSample picks a random sample of elements from a list, never picking any particular element more than once.

Pick 20 elements from the range 1 to 100, never picking any number more than once:

In[39]:= **RandomSample[Range[100], 20]**

Out[39]= {82, 3, 93, 92, 39, 45, 63, 32, 79, 75, 34, 1, 11, 59, 98, 67, 38, 44, 28, 76}

If you don't say how many elements to pick you get a random ordering of the whole list:

In[40]:= **RandomSample[Range[10]]**

Out[40]= {2, 5, 1, 7, 4, 6, 3, 8, 9, 10}

Vocabulary

Transpose[*list***]**	transpose inner and outer lists
Thread[*list$_1$* → *list$_2$***]**	thread across elements of lists
Partition[*list***, *n***]**	partition into blocks of size *n*
Flatten[*list***]**	flatten out all sublists
Flatten[*list***, *k***]**	flatten out *k* levels of sublists
ArrayFlatten[*list***]**	flatten arrays of arrays
Split[*list***]**	split into runs of identical elements
Gather[*list***]**	gather identical elements into lists
GatherBy[*list***, *f***]**	gather according to results of applying *f*
SortBy[*list***, *f***]**	sort according to results of applying *f*
Riffle[*list***, *x***]**	riffle *x* between elements of *list*
Union[*list***]**	distinct elements in *list*
Union[*list$_1$***, *list$_2$***, ...]**	elements that appear in any of the lists
Intersection[*list$_1$***, *list$_2$***, ...]**	elements that appear in all the lists
Complement[*list$_1$***, *list$_2$***]**	elements that appear in *list$_1$* but not *list$_2$*
Permutations[*list***]**	all possible permutations (orderings)
Subsets[*list***]**	all possible subsets
Tuples[*list***, *n***]**	all possible combinations of *n* elements
RandomChoice[*list***]**	random choice from *list*
RandomChoice[*list***, *n***]**	*n* random choices
RandomSample[*list***, *n***]**	*n* random non-repeating samples
RandomSample[*list***]**	random ordering of a list

Exercises

30.1   Use **Thread** to make a list of rules with each letter of the alphabet going to its position in the alphabet.

30.2   Make a 4×6 grid of the first 24 letters of the alphabet.

30.3   Make a grid of the digits in 2^1000, with 50 digits per row, and put frames around everything.

30.4   Make a grid of the first 400 characters in the Wikipedia article for "computers", with 20 characters per row, and frames around everything.

30.5   Make a line plot of the flattened list of the digits from the numbers from 0 to 200 (*Champernowne sequence*).

30.6   Make 4 steps in the *"Menger sponge"* analog of the fractal Sierpinski pattern from the text, but with a "kernel" of the form {{⊞, ⊞, ⊞}, {⊞, 0, ⊞}, {⊞, ⊞, ⊞}}.

30.7   Find *Pythagorean triples* involving only integers by selecting {x, y, Sqrt[x^2+y^2]} with x and y up to 20.

30.8   Find the lengths of the longest sequences of identical digits in 2^n for n up to 100.

30.9   Take the names of integers up to 100 and gather them into sublists according to their first letters.

30.10   Sort the first 50 words in **WordList[ ]** by their last letters.

30.11   Make a list of the first 20 squares, sorted by their first digits.

30.12   Sort integers up to 20 by the length of their names in English.

30.13   Get a random sample of 20 words from **WordList[ ]**, and gather them into sublists by length.

30.14   Find letters that appear in Ukrainian but not Russian.

30.15   Use **Intersection** to find numbers that appear both among the first 100 squares and cubes.

30.16   Find the list of countries that are in both NATO and the G8.

30.17   Make a grid in which all possible permutations of the numbers 1 through 4 appear as successive columns.

30.18   Make a list of all the different strings that can be obtained by permuting the characters in "hello".

30.19   Make an array plot of the sequence of possible 5-tuples of 0 and 1.

30.20   Generate a list of 10 random sequences of 5 letters.

30.21   Find a simpler form for **Flatten** [Table[{i, j, k}, {i, 2}, {j, 2}, {k, 2}], 2].

Q&A

What does Partition do if the blocks don't fit perfectly?

If it's not told otherwise, it'll only include complete blocks, so it'll just drop elements that appear only in incomplete blocks. However, if you say for example Partition [*list*, UpTo [4]], it'll make blocks *up to* length 4, with the last block being shorter if necessary.

Tech Note

- Transpose can be thought of as transposing rows and columns in a matrix.

- ArrayFlatten flattens an array of arrays into a single array, or alternatively, a matrix of matrices into a single matrix.

- DeleteDuplicates[*list*] does the same as Union [*list*], except it doesn't reorder elements.

More to Explore

Guide to Rearranging & Restructuring Lists in the Wolfram Language (wolfr.am/eiwl-30-more)

31 | Parts of Lists

Part lets you pick out an element of a list.

Pick out element 2 from a list:

In[1]:= **Part[{a, b, c, d, e, f, g}, 2]**

Out[1]= b

[[...]] is an alternative notation.

Use [[2]] to pick out element 2 from a list:

In[2]:= **{a, b, c, d, e, f, g}[[2]]**

Out[2]= b

Negative part numbers count from the end of a list:

In[3]:= **{a, b, c, d, e, f, g}[[-2]]**

Out[3]= f

You can ask for a list of parts by giving a list of part numbers.

Pick out parts 2, 4 and 5:

In[4]:= **{a, b, c, d, e, f, g}[[{2, 4, 5}]]**

Out[4]= {b, d, e}

;; lets you ask for a *span* or sequence of parts.

Pick out parts 2 through 5:

In[5]:= **{a, b, c, d, e, f, g}[[2 ;; 5]]**

Out[5]= {b, c, d, e}

Take the first 4 elements from a list:

In[6]:= **Take[{a, b, c, d, e, f, g}, 4]**

Out[6]= {a, b, c, d}

Take the last 2 elements from a list:

In[7]:= **Take[{a, b, c, d, e, f, g}, -2]**

Out[7]= {f, g}

Drop the last 2 elements from a list:

In[8]:= **Drop[{a, b, c, d, e, f, g}, -2]**

Out[8]= {a, b, c, d, e}

Let's now talk about lists of lists, or arrays. Each sublist acts as a *row* in the array.

In[9]:= **{{a, b, c}, {d, e, f}, {g, h, i}} // Grid**

Out[9]=
```
a b c
d e f
g h i
```

Pick out the second sublist, corresponding to the second row, in the array:

In[10]:= **{{a, b, c}, {d, e, f}, {g, h, i}}[[2]]**

Out[10]= {d, e, f}

This picks out element 1 on row 2:

In[11]:= **{{a, b, c}, {d, e, f}, {g, h, i}}[[2, 1]]**

Out[11]= d

It's also often useful to pick out *columns* in an array.

Pick out the first column, by getting element 1 on all rows:

In[12]:= **{{a, b, c}, {d, e, f}, {g, h, i}}[[All, 1]]**

Out[12]= {a, d, g}

The function Position finds the list of positions at which something appears.

Here there's only one d, and it appears at position 2, 1:

In[13]:= **Position[{{a, b, c}, {d, e, f}, {g, h, i}}, d]**

Out[13]= {{2, 1}}

This gives a list of all positions at which x appears:

In[14]:= **Position[{{x, y, x}, {y, y, x}, {x, y, y}, {x, x, y}}, x]**

Out[14]= {{1, 1}, {1, 3}, {2, 3}, {3, 1}, {4, 1}, {4, 2}}

The positions at which "a" occurs in a list of characters:

In[15]:= **Position[Characters["The Wolfram Language"], "a"]**

Out[15]= {{10}, {14}, {18}}

Find the positions at which 0 occurs in the digit sequence of 2^500:

In[16]:= **Flatten[Position[IntegerDigits[2 ^ 500], 0]]**

Out[16]= {7, 9, 19, 20, 44, 47, 50, 65, 75, 88, 89, 96, 103, 115, 116, 119, 120, 137}

The function ReplacePart lets you replace parts of a list:

Replace part 3 with x:

In[17]:= **ReplacePart[{a, b, c, d, e, f, g}, 3 → x]**

Out[17]= {a, b, x, d, e, f, g}

Replace two parts:

In[18]:= **ReplacePart[{a, b, c, d, e, f, g}, {3 → x, 5 → y}]**

Out[18]= {a, b, x, d, y, f, g}

Replace 5 randomly chosen parts with "−−":

In[19]:= **ReplacePart[Characters["The Wolfram Language"],**
   Table[RandomInteger[{1, 20}] → "−−", 5]]

Out[19]= {T, h, e, , W, −−, l, f, r, a, m, −−, −−, −−, n, g, u, a, g, −−}

Sometimes one wants particular parts of a list to just disappear. One can do this by replacing them with Nothing.

Nothing just disappears:

In[20]:= **{1, 2, Nothing, 4, 5, Nothing}**

Out[20]= {1, 2, 4, 5}

Replace parts 1 and 3 with Nothing:

In[21]:= **ReplacePart[{a, b, c, d, e, f, g}, {1 → Nothing, 3 → Nothing}]**

Out[21]= {b, d, e, f, g}

Take 50 random words, dropping ones longer than 5 characters, and reversing others:

In[22]:= **If[StringLength[⌗] > 5, Nothing, StringReverse[⌗]] &/@ RandomSample[WordList[], 50]**

Out[22]= {yllud, yciuj, poons, tsioh}

Take takes a specified number of elements in a list based on their position. TakeLargest and TakeSmallest take elements based on their size.

Take the 5 largest elements from a list:

In[23]:= **TakeLargest[Range[20], 5]**

Out[23]= {20, 19, 18, 17, 16}

TakeLargestBy and TakeSmallestBy take elements based on applying a function.

From the first 100 Roman numerals take the 5 that have the largest string length:

In[24]:= **TakeLargestBy[Array[RomanNumeral, 100], StringLength, 5]**

Out[24]= {LXXXVIII, LXXXIII, XXXVIII, LXXVIII, LXXXVII}

Vocabulary

Part[*list, n***]**	part *n* of a list
list[[*n*]]	short notation for part *n* of a list
list[[{*n*₁, *n*₂, ...}]]	list of parts $n_1, n_2, ...$
list[[*n*₁ ;; *n*₂]]	span (sequence) of parts n_1 through n_2
list[[*m, n*]]	element from row *m*, column *n* of an array
list[[All, *n*]]	all elements in column *n*
Take[*list, n***]**	take the first *n* elements of a list
TakeLargest[*list, n***]**	take the largest *n* elements of a list
TakeSmallest[*list, n***]**	take the smallest *n* elements of a list
TakeLargestBy[*list, f, n***]**	take elements largest by applying *f*
TakeSmallestBy[*list, f, n***]**	take elements smallest by applying *f*
Position[*list, x***]**	all positions of *x* in *list*
ReplacePart[*list, n → x***]**	replace part *n* of *list* with *x*
Nothing	a list element that is automatically removed

Exercises

31.1   Find the last 5 digits in 2^1000.

31.2   Pick out letters 10 through 20 in the alphabet.

31.3   Make a list of the letters at even-numbered positions in the alphabet.

31.4   Make a line plot of the second to last digit in the first 100 powers of 12.

31.5   Join lists of the first 20 squares and cubes, and get the 10 smallest elements of the combined list.

31.6   Find the positions of the word "software" in the Wikipedia entry for "computers".

31.7   Make a histogram of where the letter "e" occurs in the words in WordList[ ].

31.8   Make a list of the first 100 cubes, with every one whose position is a square replaced by Red.

31.9   Make a list of the first 100 primes, dropping ones whose first digit is less than 5.

31.10   Make a grid starting with Range[10], then at each of 9 steps randomly removing another element.

31.11   Find the longest 10 words in WordList[ ].

31.12   Find the 5 longest integer names for integers up to 100.

31.13   Find the 5 English names for integers up to 100 that have the largest number of "e"s in them.

Q&A

How does one read *list*[[*n*]] out loud?

Usually "*list* part *n*" or "*list* sub *n*". The second form (with "sub" short for "subscript") comes from thinking about math and extracting components of vectors.

What happens if one asks for a part of a list that doesn't exist?

One gets a message, and the original computation is returned undone.

Can I just get the first position at which something appears in a list?

Yes. Use FirstPosition.

Tech Notes

- First and Last are equivalent to [[1]] and [[-1]].

- In specifying parts, 1 ;; −1 is equivalent to All.

More to Explore

Guide to Parts of Lists in the Wolfram Language (wolfr.am/eiwl-31-more)

32 | Patterns

Patterns are a fundamental concept in the Wolfram Language. The pattern _ (read "blank") stands for anything.

MatchQ tests whether something matches a pattern.

{a, x, b} matches the pattern {_, x, _}:

In[1]:= **MatchQ[{a, x, b}, {_, x, _}]**

Out[1]= True

{a, b, c} doesn't match, because it has b in the middle, rather than x:

In[2]:= **MatchQ[{a, b, c}, {_, x, _}]**

Out[2]= False

Any list with two elements matches the pattern {_, _}:

In[3]:= **MatchQ[{a, a}, {_, _}]**

Out[3]= True

A list with three elements doesn't match the pattern {_, _}:

In[4]:= **MatchQ[{a, a, a}, {_, _}]**

Out[4]= False

MatchQ lets you test one thing at a time against a pattern. Cases lets you pick out all the elements ("cases") in a list that match a particular pattern.

Find all elements that match the pattern {_, _}:

In[5]:= **Cases[{{a, a}, {b, a}, {a, b, c}, {b, b}, {c, a}, {b, b, b}}, {_, _}]**

Out[5]= {{a, a}, {b, a}, {b, b}, {c, a}}

Find all elements that match {b, _} (i.e. cases of b followed by something):

In[6]:= **Cases[{{a, a}, {b, a}, {a, b, c}, {b, b}, {c, a}, {b, b, b}}, {b, _}]**

Out[6]= {{b, a}, {b, b}}

This is what you get if you test whether each element matches {b, _}:

In[7]:= **MatchQ[#, {b, _}] &/@{{a, a}, {b, a}, {a, b, c}, {b, b}, {c, a}, {b, b, b}}**

Out[7]= {False, True, False, True, False, False}

Using Select to select what matches gives the same result as Cases:

In[8]:= **Select[{{a, a}, {b, a}, {a, b, c}, {b, b}, {c, a}, {b, b, b}}, MatchQ[#, {b, _}] &]**

Out[8]= {{b, a}, {b, b}}

In a pattern, a | b indicates "either a or b".

Find all cases of either a or b, followed by something:

In[9]:= **Cases[{{a, a}, {b, a}, {a, b, c}, {b, b}, {c, a}, {b, b, b}}, {a | b, _}]**

Out[9]= {{a, a}, {b, a}, {b, b}}

Let's look at another example, based on creating a list, then picking out elements that match particular patterns.

Create a list by getting the digits of a range of numbers:

In[10]:= **IntegerDigits[Range[100, 500, 55]]**

Out[10]= {{1, 0, 0}, {1, 5, 5}, {2, 1, 0}, {2, 6, 5}, {3, 2, 0}, {3, 7, 5}, {4, 3, 0}, {4, 8, 5}}

Find cases that end in 5:

In[11]:= **Cases[IntegerDigits[Range[100, 500, 55]], {_, _, 5}]**

Out[11]= {{1, 5, 5}, {2, 6, 5}, {3, 7, 5}, {4, 8, 5}}

Find cases with 1 or 2 in the middle:

In[12]:= **Cases[IntegerDigits[Range[100, 500, 55]], {_, 1 | 2, _}]**

Out[12]= {{2, 1, 0}, {3, 2, 0}}

The notation __ ("double blank") in a pattern indicates any sequence of things.

Find cases consisting of any sequence, ending with b:

In[13]:= **Cases[{{a, a}, {b, a}, {a, b, c}, {b, b}, {c, a}, {b, b, b}}, {__, b}]**

Out[13]= {{b, b}, {b, b, b}}

Find sequences ending with a or b, or beginning with c:

In[14]:= **Cases[{{a, a}, {b, a}, {a, b, c}, {b, b}, {c, a}, {b, b, b}}, {__, a | b} | {c, __}]**

Out[14]= {{a, a}, {b, a}, {b, b}, {c, a}, {b, b, b}}

Patterns aren't just about lists; they can involve anything.

Pick out cases that match the pattern f[_]:

In[15]:= **Cases[{f[1], g[2, 3], {a, b, c}, f[x], f[x, x]}, f[_]]**

Out[15]= {f[1], f[x]}

One of the many uses of patterns is to define replacements. /. ("slash dot") performs a replacement.

Replace b with Red in a list:

In[16]:= **{a, b, a, a, b, b, a, b} /. b → Red**

Out[16]= {a, ■, a, a, ■, ■, a, ■}

Replace all occurrences of 2-element lists that begin with 1:

In[17]:= **{{1, a}, {1, b}, {1, a, b}, {2, b, c}, {2, b}} /. {1, _} → Red**

Out[17]= {■, ■, {1, a, b}, {2, b, c}, {2, b}}

You can give a list of replacements to use:

In[18]:= **{{1, a}, {1, b}, {1, a, b}, {2, b, c}, {2, b}} /. {{1, _} → Red, {_ _, b} → Yellow}**

Out[18]= {■, ■, □, {2, b, c}, □}

The "blank" pattern _ matches absolutely anything. This means, for example, that {_, _} matches any list of two elements. But what if you want to insist that the two elements be the same? You can do that using a pattern like {x_, x_}.

{_, _} matches any list of two elements, whether the elements are the same or not:

In[19]:= **Cases[{{a, a, a}, {a, a}, {a, b}, {a, c}, {b, a}, {b, b}, {c}, {a}, {b}}, {_, _}]**

Out[19]= {{a, a}, {a, b}, {a, c}, {b, a}, {b, b}}

{x_, x_} matches only lists of two identical elements:

In[20]:= **Cases[{{a, a, a}, {a, a}, {a, b}, {a, c}, {b, a}, {b, b}, {c}, {a}, {b}}, {x_, x_}]**

Out[20]= {{a, a}, {b, b}}

x_ is an example of a *named pattern*. Named patterns are especially important in replacements, because they give one way to make use of parts of what one's replacing.

Use the named pattern x_ in a replacement:

In[21]:= **{{1, ■}, {1, ■}, {1, ■, ■}, {2, ■, ■}, {2, ■}} /. {1, x_} → {x, x, Yellow, x, x}**

Out[21]= {{■, ■, □, ■, ■}, {■, ■, □, ■, ■}, {1, ■, ■}, {2, ■, ■}, {2, ■}}

The form *a→b* is usually called a *rule*. If x_ appears on the left-hand side of a rule, then whatever the x_ matches can be referred to on the right-hand side as x.

Use x in the right-hand side of the rule to refer to what x_ matches:

In[22]:= **{f[1], g[2], f[2], f[6], g[3]} /. f[x_] → x + 10**

Out[22]= {11, g[2], 12, 16, g[3]}

You can use rules inside Cases as well.

Pick out elements in the list that match f[x_], and give the result of replacing them by x + 10:

In[23]:= **Cases[{f[1], g[2], f[2], f[6], g[3]}, f[x_] → x + 10]**

Out[23]= {11, 12, 16}

Later on, we'll see how named patterns are crucial to defining your own functions in the Wolfram Language.

Vocabulary

_	pattern standing for anything ("blank")
__	pattern standing for any sequence ("double blank")
$x\_$	pattern named x
$a \mid b$	pattern matching a or b
MatchQ[$expr, pattern$**]**	test whether $expr$ matches a pattern
Cases[$list, pattern$**]**	find cases of a pattern in a list
$lhs \rightarrow rhs$	rule for transforming lhs into rhs
$expr$ /. $lhs \rightarrow rhs$	replace lhs by rhs in $expr$

Exercises

32.1   Find lists beginning with 1 and ending with 9 in IntegerDigits[Range[1000]].

32.2   Find lists of three identical elements in IntegerDigits[Range[1000]].

32.3   In the digit lists for the first 1000 squares, find those that begin with 9 and end with 0 or 1.

32.4   In IntegerDigits[Range[100]] replace all 0's by Gray and all 9's by Orange.

32.5   Make a list of the digits of 2^1000, replacing all zeros by Red.

32.6   Remove the vowels a, e, i, o and u from the list of characters in "The Wolfram Language".

32.7   Find a simpler form for Select[IntegerDigits[2 ^ 1000], ♯ == 0 || ♯ == 1 &].

32.8   Find a simpler form for Select[IntegerDigits[Range[100, 999]], First[♯] == Last[♯] &].

Q&A

Do the names of pattern variables (x_, etc.) matter?

No. They just have to be consistent inside a given pattern. Different patterns can reuse the same name for different purposes, and the name can also appear outside the pattern.

What else can be used to define patterns?

We'll discuss several more things in Section 41.

What's the difference between | and ||?

p | q is a pattern construct, that matches either p or q. p || q is a logic construct, that tests whether p or q is True.

How does one say a|b?

Either "a or b" or "a vertical bar b".

How is /. interpreted?

It's the function ReplaceAll. Replace tries to replace a whole expression. ReplaceList gives a list of results from all possible ways to match a particular pattern.

If /. has several replacements, which one will it use?

It uses the first one that applies. If replacements apply to multiple levels of an expression, /. will use it on the outermost level.

Tech Notes

- Patterns for strings are discussed in Section 42.

- Pattern matching in the Wolfram Language takes account of facts such as the equivalence of $x + y$ and $y + x$, or $x + (y + z)$ and $(x + y) + z$. See Section 41.

- In writing $lhs \rightarrow rhs$, the *lhs* stands for "left-hand side" and the *rhs* for "right-hand side".

- Patterns are *scoping constructs*, in the sense that they localize names like the x in x_ to just the scope of the pattern.

- In the rare case that /. is followed by a digit (like 0), you need to leave a space before the digit to avoid confusion with division.

More to Explore

Guide to Patterns in the Wolfram Language (wolfr.am/eiwl-32-more)

33 | Expressions and Their Structure

We've now seen all sorts of things that exist in the Wolfram Language: lists, graphics, pure functions and much more. And now we're ready to discuss a very fundamental fact about the Wolfram Language: that each of these things—and in fact everything the language deals with—is ultimately constructed in the same basic kind of way. Everything is what's called a *symbolic expression*.

Symbolic expressions are a very general way to represent structure, potentially with meaning associated with that structure. f[x, y] is a simple example of a symbolic expression. On its own, this symbolic expression doesn't have any particular meaning attached, and if you type it into the Wolfram Language, it'll just come back unchanged.

f[x, y] is a symbolic expression with no particular meaning attached:

In[1]:= **f[x, y]**

Out[1]= f[x, y]

{x, y, z} is another symbolic expression. Internally, it's List[x, y, z], but it's displayed as {x, y, z}.

The symbolic expression List[x, y, z] displays as {x, y, z}:

In[2]:= **List[x, y, z]**

Out[2]= {x, y, z}

Symbolic expressions are often nested:

In[3]:= **List[List[a, b], List[c, d]]**

Out[3]= {{a, b}, {c, d}}

FullForm shows you the internal form of any symbolic expression.

In[4]:= **FullForm[{{a, b}, {c, d}}]**

Out[4]//FullForm= List[List[a, b], List[c, d]]

Graphics[Circle[{0, 0}]] is another symbolic expression, that just happens to display as a picture of a circle. FullForm shows its internal structure.

This symbolic expression displays as a circle:

In[5]:= **Graphics[Circle[{0, 0}]]**

Out[5]=

FullForm shows its underlying symbolic expression structure:

In[6]:= **FullForm[** 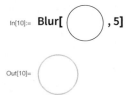 **]**

Out[6]//FullForm= Graphics[Circle[List[0, 0]]]

Symbolic expressions often don't just display in special ways, they actually *evaluate* to give results.

A symbolic expression that evaluates to give a result:

In[7]:= **Plus[2, 2]**

Out[7]= 4

The elements of the list evaluate, but the list itself stays symbolic:

In[8]:= **{Plus[3, 3], Times[3, 3], Power[3, 3]}**

Out[8]= {6, 9, 27}

Here's the symbolic expression structure of the list:

In[9]:= **{Plus[3, 3], Times[3, 3], Power[3, 3]} // FullForm**

Out[9]//FullForm= List[6, 9, 27]

This is just a symbolic expression that happens to evaluate:

In[10]:= **Blur[** ◯ **, 5]**

Out[10]= ◯

You could write it like this:

In[11]:= **Blur[Graphics[Circle[{0, 0}]], 5]**

Out[11]= ◯

What are the ultimate building blocks of symbolic expressions? They're called *atoms* (after the building blocks of physical materials). The main kinds of atoms are numbers, strings and *symbols*.

Things like x, y, f, Plus, Graphics and Table are all symbols. Every symbol has a unique name. Sometimes it'll also have a meaning attached. Sometimes it'll be associated with evaluation. Sometimes it'll just be part of defining a structure that other functions can use. But it doesn't have to have any of those things; it just has to have a name.

A crucial defining feature of the Wolfram Language is that it can handle symbols purely as symbols—"symbolically"—without them having to evaluate, say to numbers.

In the Wolfram Language, x can just be x, without having to evaluate to anything:

In[12]:= **X**

Out[12]= **X**

x does not evaluate, but the addition is still done, here according to the laws of algebra:

In[13]:= **x + x + x + 2 y + y + x**

Out[13]= **4 x + 3 y**

Given symbols like x, y and f, one can build up an infinite number of expressions from them. There's f[x], and f[y], and f[x, y]. Then there's f[f[x]] or f[x, f[x, y]], or, for that matter, x[x][y, f[x]] or whatever.

In general, each expression corresponds to a tree, whose ultimate "leaves" are atoms. You can display an expression as a tree using TreeForm.

An expression shown in tree form:

In[14]:= **TreeForm[{f[x, f[x, y]], {x, y, f[1]}}]**

Out[14]//TreeForm=

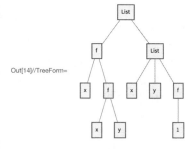

Here's a graphics expression shown in tree form:

In[15]:= **TreeForm[Graphics[{Circle[{0, 0}], Hue[0.5], Disk[{1, 1}]}]]**

Out[15]//TreeForm=

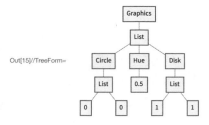

Because expressions ultimately have a very uniform structure, operations in the Wolfram Language operate in a very uniform way on them.

For example, any expression has parts, just like a list, and you can extract them using [[...]].

This is equivalent to {x, y, z}[[2]], which extracts the second element in a list:

In[16]:= **List[x, y, z][[2]]**

Out[16]= y

Extracting parts works exactly the same way for this expression:

In[17]:= **f[x, y, z][[2]]**

Out[17]= y

This extracts the circle from the graphics:

In[18]:= **Graphics[Circle[{0, 0}]][[1]]**

Out[18]= Circle[{0, 0}]

This goes on and extracts the coordinates of its center:

In[19]:= **Graphics[Circle[{0, 0}]][[1, 1]]**

Out[19]= {0, 0}

This works exactly the same:

In[20]:= **[[1, 1]]**

Out[20]= {0, 0}

In f[x, y], f is called the *head* of the expression. x and y are called *arguments*. The function Head extracts the head of an expression.

The head of a list is List:

In[21]:= **Head[{x, y, z}]**

Out[21]= List

Every part of an expression has a head, even its atoms.

The head of an integer is Integer:

In[22]:= **Head[1234]**

Out[22]= Integer

The head of an approximate real number is Real:

In[23]:= **Head[12.45]**

Out[23]= Real

The head of a string is String:

In[24]:= **Head["hello"]**

Out[24]= String

Even symbols have a head: Symbol.

In[25]:= **Head[x]**

Out[25]= Symbol

In patterns, you can ask to match expressions with particular heads. _ Integer represents any integer, _ String any string and so on.

_ Integer is a pattern that matches only objects with head Integer:

In[26]:= **Cases[{x, y, 3, 4, z, 6, 7}, _Integer]**

Out[26]= {3, 4, 6, 7}

Named patterns can have specified heads too:

In[27]:= **Cases[{99, x, y, z, 101, 102}, n_Integer → {n, n}]**

Out[27]= {{99, 99}, {101, 101}, {102, 102}}

In using the Wolfram Language, most of the heads you'll see are symbols. But there are important cases where there are more complicated heads. One such case is pure functions—where when you apply a pure function, the pure function appears as the head.

Here is the full form of a pure function (# is Slot[1]):

In[28]:= **FullForm[# ^ 2 &]**

Out[28]//FullForm= Function[Power[Slot[1], 2]]

When you apply the pure function, it appears as a head:

In[29]:= **Function[Power[Slot[1], 2]] [1000]**

Out[29]= 1 000 000

As you become more sophisticated in Wolfram Language programming, you'll encounter more and more examples of complicated heads. In fact, many functions that we've already discussed have *operator forms* where they appear as heads—and using them in this way leads to very powerful and elegant styles of programming.

Select appears as a head here:

In[30]:= **Select[# > 4 &][{1, 2.2, 3, 4.5, 5, 6, 7.5, 8}]**

Out[30]= {4.5, 5, 6, 7.5, 8}

Both Cases and Select appear as heads here:

In[31]:= **Cases[_Integer] @ Select[# > 4 &] @ {1, 2.2, 3, 4.5, 5, 6, 7.5, 8}**

Out[31]= {5, 6, 8}

All the basic structural operations that we have seen for lists work exactly the same for arbitrary expressions.

Length does not care what the head of an expression is; it just counts arguments:

In[32]:= **Length[f[x, y, z]]**

Out[32]= 3

/@ does not care about the head of an expression either; it just applies a function to the arguments:

In[33]:= **f /@ g[x, y, z]**

Out[33]= g[f[x], f[y], f[z]]

Since there are lots of functions that generate lists, it's often convenient to build up structures as lists even if eventually one needs to replace the lists with other functions.

@@ effectively replaces the head of the list with f:

In[34]:= **f @@ {x, y, z}**

Out[34]= f[x, y, z]

This yields Plus[1, 1, 1, 1], which then evaluates:

In[35]:= **Plus @@ {1, 1, 1, 1}**

Out[35]= 4

This turns a list into a rule:

In[36]:= **#1 → #2 & @@ {x, y}**

Out[36]= x → y

Here's a simpler alternative, without the explicit pure function:

In[37]:= **Rule @@ {x, y}**

Out[37]= x → y

A surprisingly common situation is to have a list of lists, and to want to replace the inner lists with some function. It's possible to do this with @@ and /@. But @@@ provides a convenient direct way to do it.

Replace the inner lists with f:

In[38]:= **f @@@ {{1, 2, 3}, {4, 5, 6}}**

Out[38]= {f[1, 2, 3], f[4, 5, 6]}

Turn the inner lists into rules:

In[39]:= **Rule @@@ {{1, 10}, {2, 20}, {3, 30}}**

Out[39]= $\{1 \to 10, 2 \to 20, 3 \to 30\}$

Here's an example of how **@@@** can help construct a graph from a list of pairs.

This generates a list of pairs of characters:

In[40]:= **Partition[Characters["antidisestablishmentarianism"], 2, 1]**

Out[40]= {{a, n}, {n, t}, {t, i}, {i, d}, {d, i}, {i, s}, {s, e}, {e, s}, {s, t}, {t, a}, {a, b}, {b, l}, {l, i}, {i, s}, {s, h}, {h, m}, {m, e}, {e, n}, {n, t}, {t, a}, {a, r}, {r, i}, {i, a}, {a, n}, {n, i}, {i, s}, {s, m}}

Turn this into a list of rules:

In[41]:= **Rule @@@ Partition[Characters["antidisestablishmentarianism"], 2, 1]**

Out[41]= $\{a \to n, n \to t, t \to i, i \to d, d \to i, i \to s, s \to e, e \to s, s \to t, t \to a, a \to b, b \to l, l \to i, i \to s,$
$s \to h, h \to m, m \to e, e \to n, n \to t, t \to a, a \to r, r \to i, i \to a, a \to n, n \to i, i \to s, s \to m\}$

Form a *transition graph* showing how letters follow each other:

In[42]:= **Graph[Rule @@@ Partition[Characters["antidisestablishmentarianism"], 2, 1],**
VertexLabels → All]

Out[42]=

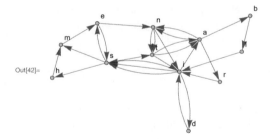

Vocabulary

FullForm[*expr***]**	show full internal form
TreeForm[*expr***]**	show tree structure
Head[*expr***]**	extract the head of an expression
_*head***	match any expression with a particular head
f **@@** *list*	replace the head of *list* with *f*
f **@@@** {*list₁*, *list₂*, ...}	replace heads of $list_1$, $list_2$, ... with *f*

Exercises

33.1 Find the head of the output from ListPlot.

33.2 Use @@ to compute the result of multiplying together integers up to 100.

33.3 Use @@@ and Tuples to generate {f[a, a], f[a, b], f[b, a], f[b, b]}.

33.4 Make a list of tree forms for the results of 4 successive applications of ♯^♯ & starting from x.

33.5 Find the unique cases where i^2/(j^2 + 1) is an integer, with i and j going up to 20.

33.6 Create a graph that connects successive pairs of numbers in Table[Mod[n^2+n, 100], {n, 100}].

33.7 Generate a graph showing which word can follow which in the first 200 words of the Wikipedia article on computers.

33.8 Find a simpler form for f@@@♯ &/@ {{1, 2}, {7, 2}, {5, 4}}.

Q&A

How are @@ and @@@ interpreted?

f @@ *expr* is Apply[*f*, *expr*]. *f* @@@ *expr* is Apply[*f*, *expr*, {1}]. They're usually just read as "double at" and "triple at".

Are all expressions in the Wolfram Language trees?

At a structural level, yes. When there are variables with values assigned (see Section 38), though, they can behave more like directed graphs. And of course one can use Graph to represent any graph as an expression in the Wolfram Language.

Tech Notes

- The basic concept of symbolic languages comes directly from work in mathematical logic stretching back to the 1930s and before, but other than in the Wolfram Language it's been very rare for it to be implemented in practice.

- Wolfram Language expressions are a bit like XML expressions (and can be converted to and from them). But unlike XML expressions, Wolfram Language expressions can evaluate so that they automatically change their structure.

- Things like Select[*f*] that are set up to be applied to expressions are called *operator forms*, by analogy with operators in mathematics. Using Select[*f*][*expr*] instead of Select[*expr*, *f*] is often called *currying*, after a logician named Haskell Curry.

- Symbols like x can be used to represent algebraic variables or "unknowns". This is central to doing many kinds of mathematics in the Wolfram Language.

- LeafCount gives the total number of atoms at the leaves of an expression tree. ByteCount gives the number of bytes needed to store the expression.

More to Explore

Guide to Expressions in the Wolfram Language (wolfr.am/eiwl-33-more)

34 | Associations

Associations are a kind of generalization of lists, in which every element has a key as well as a value. Counts is a typical function that produces an association.

Counts gives an association that reports how many times each different element occurs:

In[1]:= **Counts[{a, a, b, c, a, a, b, c, c, a, a}]**

Out[1]= **<| a → 6, b → 2, c → 3 |>**

You can get the value associated with a particular key using [...].

Find the value associated with c in the association:

In[2]:= **<| a → 6, b → 2, c → 3 |> [c]**

Out[2]= 3

Operations that work on lists typically also work on associations—but apply themselves only to the values, not the keys.

This adds 500 to each value in the association:

In[3]:= **<| a → 6, b → 2, c → 3 |> +500**

Out[3]= **<| a → 506, b → 502, c → 503 |>**

/@ applies a function to each value in the association:

In[4]:= **f /@ <| a → 6, b → 2, c → 3 |>**

Out[4]= **<| a → f[6], b → f[2], c → f[3] |>**

Total gives the total of the values:

In[5]:= **Total[<| a → 6, b → 2, c → 3 |>]**

Out[5]= 11

Sort operates on the values:

In[6]:= **Sort[<| a → 6, b → 2, c → 3 |>]**

Out[6]= **<| b → 2, c → 3, a → 6 |>**

KeySort operates on the keys:

In[7]:= **KeySort[<| c → 1, b → 2, a → 4 |>]**

Out[7]= **<| a → 4, b → 2, c → 1 |>**

The functions Keys and Values extract the keys and values of an association.

Get the list of keys in the association:

In[8]:= **Keys[<| a → 6, b → 2, c → 3 |>]**

Out[8]= {a, b, c}

Get the list of values in the association:

In[9]:= **Values[<| a → 6, b → 2, c → 3 |>]**

Out[9]= {6, 2, 3}

Normal turns an association into a normal list of rules. Association makes an association from a list of rules.

In[10]:= **Normal[<| a → 6, b → 2, c → 3 |>]**

Out[10]= {a → 6, b → 2, c → 3}

In[11]:= **Association[{a → 6, b → 2, c → 3}]**

Out[11]= <| a → 6, b → 2, c → 3 |>

LetterCounts counts how many times letters occur in a string.

Count how many times each letter occurs in the Wikipedia article on computers:

In[12]:= **LetterCounts[WikipediaData["computers"]]**

Out[12]= <| e → 4833, t → 3528, a → 3207, o → 3059, r → 2907, i → 2818, n → 2747, s → 2475, c → 1800,
l → 1673, m → 1494, h → 1473, u → 1357, d → 1329, p → 1153, g → 818, f → 766,
y → 594, b → 545, w → 456, v → 391, k → 174, T → 150, A → 110, I → 101, C → 84,
M → 82, x → 77, S → 68, P → 64, q → 58, U → 55, B → 45, H → 43, E → 42, R → 41,
L → 41, z → 38, O → 38, D → 37, W → 30, N → 29, F → 28, j → 25, G → 23, J → 17,
K → 14, V → 10, Z → 8, Q → 4, ū → 4, ī → 4, ö → 2, ā → 2, Y → 1, X → 1, é → 1, â → 1 |>

KeyTake picks out elements of an association that appear in a list of keys you specify. Here we're taking the elements whose keys are letters in the (lowercase) alphabet.

Take only those elements in the association whose keys appear as letters in the alphabet:

In[13]:= **KeyTake[LetterCounts[WikipediaData["computers"]], Alphabet[]]**

Out[13]= <| a → 3207, b → 545, c → 1800, d → 1329, e → 4833, f → 766, g → 818, h → 1473,
i → 2818, j → 25, k → 174, l → 1673, m → 1494, n → 2747, o → 3059, p → 1153, q → 58,
r → 2907, s → 2475, t → 3528, u → 1357, v → 391, w → 456, x → 77, y → 594, z → 38 |>

BarChart plots the values in an association. With the option ChartLabels → Automatic, it uses the keys as labels.

Make a bar chart of how many times each letter appears; "e" is the most common:

In[14]:= **BarChart[KeyTake[LetterCounts[WikipediaData["computers"]], Alphabet[]],
       ChartLabels → Automatic]**

Out[14]=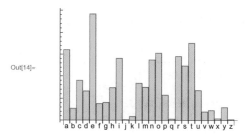

Here's a direct way to apply a pure function to an association:

Apply a pure function to an association:

In[15]:= **f[♯["apples"], ♯["oranges"]] &[<| "apples" → 10, "oranges" → 12, "pears" → 4 |>]**

Out[15]= **f[10, 12]**

It's very common to have keys that are strings, and the Wolfram Language has a special way to handle these when it comes to pure functions: you can just use ♯key to refer to an element whose key is "key".

Use the simpler notation for association elements whose keys are strings:

In[16]:= **f[♯apples, ♯oranges] &[<| "apples" → 10, "oranges" → 12, "pears" → 4 |>]**

Out[16]= **f[10, 12]**

As a more realistic example, apply a pure function that extracts the value for "e" from the letter counts, and divides by the total. The N gives the result as a decimal.

Compute the fraction of letters in the "computers" article that are "e":

In[17]:= **♯e / Total[♯] & @LetterCounts[WikipediaData["computers"]] // N**

Out[17]= **0.11795**

Vocabulary

$<\vert\ key_1 \to value_1, key_2 \to value_2, ...\ \vert>$	an association
Association[*rules***]**	turn a list of rules into an association
*assoc***[***key***]**	extract an element of an association
Keys[*assoc***]**	list of keys in an association
Values[*assoc***]**	list of values in an association
Normal[*assoc***]**	turn an association into a list of rules
KeySort[*assoc***]**	sort an association by its keys
KeyTake[*assoc***, *keys***]**	take elements with particular keys
#*key*	function slot for an element with key "*key*"
Counts[*list***]**	an association with counts of distinct elements
LetterCounts[*string***]**	an association with counts of distinct letters

Exercises

34.1 Make a list, in order, of the number of times each of the digits 0 through 9 occurs in 3^100.

34.2 Make a labeled bar chart of the number of times each of the digits 0 through 9 occurs in 2^1000.

34.3 Make a labeled bar chart of the number of times each possible first letter occurs in words from WordList[ ].

34.4 Make an association giving the 5 most common first letters of words in WordList[ ] and their counts.

34.5 Find the numerical ratio of the number of occurrences of "q" and "u" in the Wikipedia entry for computers.

34.6 Find the 10 most common words in ExampleData[{"Text", "AliceInWonderland"}].

Q&A

Why are associations called "associations"?

Because they *associate* values with keys. Other names used for the same concept are associative arrays, dictionaries, hashmaps, structs, key-value maps and symbolically indexed lists.

How does one type in an association?

Start with <| (< followed by |), then use -> for each →. Alternatively use Association[a -> 1, b -> 2].

Can an association have several elements with the same key?

No. Keys in an association are always unique.

What happens if I ask for a key that's not in an association?

Normally you get Missing[...]. But if you use Lookup to look up the key, you can specify what to return if the key is absent.

How can I do operations on the keys of an association?

Use KeyMap, or use functions like KeySelect and KeyDrop. AssociationMap creates an association by mapping a function over keys.

How can I combine several associations into one?

Use Merge. You have to give a function to say what to do if the same key occurs in multiple associations.

Can one use [[...]] to extract part of an association, like one extracts part of a list?

Yes, if you explicitly say *assoc*[[Key[*key*]]]. For example, *assoc*[[2]] will extract the second element of *assoc*, whatever key it has. *assoc*[[*key*]] is a special case that works the same as *assoc*[*key*].

What happens in pure functions if the keys in an association aren't strings?

You can't use #*key* anymore; you have to explicitly use #[*key*].

Tech Notes

- Most functions effectively operate on associations as if they were operating on lists of their values. Functions that thread themselves over lists typically do the same over associations.

- Associations are like tables in a relational database. JoinAcross does the analog of a database join.

More to Explore

Guide to Associations in the Wolfram Language (wolfr.am/eiwl-34-more)

35 | Natural Language Understanding

We saw earlier how to use ⌈ctrl =⌉ to enter natural language input. Now we're going to talk about how to set up functions that understand natural language.

Interpreter is the key to much of this. You tell Interpreter what type of thing you want to get, and it will take any string you provide, and try to interpret it that way.

Interpret the string "nyc" as a city:

In[1]:= **Interpreter["City"]["nyc"]**

Out[1]= ⎡ New York City ⎤

"The big apple" is a nickname for New York City:

In[2]:= **Interpreter["City"]["the big apple"]**

Out[2]= ⎡ New York City ⎤

Interpret the string "hot pink" as a color:

In[3]:= **Interpreter["Color"]["hot pink"]**

Out[3]= ▪

Interpreter converts natural language to Wolfram Language expressions that you can compute with. Here's an example involving currency amounts.

Interpret various currency amounts:

In[4]:= **Interpreter["CurrencyAmount"][**
     {"4.25 dollars", "34 russian rubles", "5 euros", "85 cents"}]

Out[4]= { $4.25 , py634 , €5 , 85¢ }

Compute the total, doing conversions at current exchange rates:

In[5]:= **Total[{ $4.25 , py634 , €5 , 85¢ }]**

Out[5]= $11.07

Here's another example, involving locations.

Interpreter gives the geo location of the White House:

In[6]:= **Interpreter["Location"]["White House"]**

Out[6]= GeoPosition[{38.8977, −77.0366}]

It can also work from a street address:

In[7]:= **Interpreter["Location"]["1600 Pennsylvania Avenue, Washington, DC"]**

Out[7]= GeoPosition[{38.8977, −77.0366}]

Interpreter handles many hundreds of different types of objects.

Interpret names of universities (which "U of I" is picked depends on geo location):

In[8]:= **Interpreter["University"][{"Harvard", "Stanford", "U of I"}]**

Out[8]= { Harvard University , Stanford University ,
University of Illinois at Urbana-Champaign }

Interpret names of chemicals:

In[9]:= **Interpreter["Chemical"][{"H2O", "aspirin", "CO2", "wolfram"}]**

Out[9]= { water , aspirin , carbon dioxide , tungsten }

Interpret names of animals, then get images of them:

In[10]:= **EntityValue[Interpreter["Animal"][{"cheetah", "tiger", "elephant"}], "Image"]**

Out[10]= {  ,  , }

Interpreter interprets whole strings. TextCases, on the other hand, tries to pick out instances of what you request from a string.

Pick out the nouns in a piece of text:

In[11]:= **TextCases["A sentence is a linguistic construct", "Noun"]**

Out[11]= {sentence, construct}

Pick out currency amounts:

In[12]:= **TextCases["Choose between $5, €5 and ¥5000", "CurrencyAmount"]**

Out[12]= {$5, €5, ¥5000}

You can use TextCases to pick out particular kinds of things from a piece of text. Here we pick out instances of country names in a Wikipedia article.

Generate a word cloud of country names from the Wikipedia article on the EU:

In[13]:= **WordCloud[TextCases[WikipediaData["EU"], "Country"]]**

Out[13]=

TextStructure shows you the whole structure of a piece of text.

Find how a sentence of English can be parsed into grammatical units:

In[14]:= **TextStructure["You can do so much with the Wolfram Language."]**

Out[14]=

You	can	do	so	much	with	the	Wolfram	Language	.
Pronoun	Verb	Verb	Adverb	Adverb	Preposition	Determiner	Proper Noun	Proper Noun	Punctuation

Noun Phrase · · Adverb Phrase · Noun Phrase · Prepositional Phrase · Verb Phrase · Verb Phrase · Sentence

An alternative representation, as a graph:

In[15]:= **TextStructure["You can do so much with the Wolfram Language.", "ConstituentGraphs"]**

Out[15]=

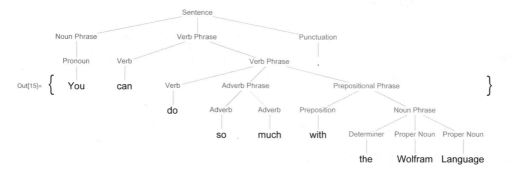

WordList[ ] gives a lists of common words. WordList["Noun"], etc. gives lists of words that can be used as particular parts of speech.

Give the first 20 in a list of common verbs in English:

In[16]:= **Take[WordList["Verb"], 20]**

Out[16]= {aah, abandon, abase, abash, abate, abbreviate, abdicate, abduct, abet, abhor, abide, abjure, ablate, abnegate, abolish, abominate, abort, abound, abrade, abridge}

It's easy to study properties of words. Here are histograms comparing the length distributions of nouns, verbs and adjectives in the list of common words.

Make histograms of the lengths of common nouns, verbs and adjectives:

In[17]:= **Histogram[StringLength[WordList[#]]] &/@{"Noun", "Verb", "Adjective"}**

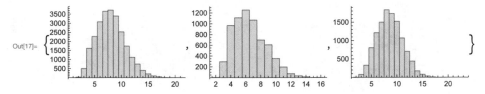

So far we've only talked about English. But the Wolfram Language also knows about other languages. For example, WordTranslation gives translations of words.

Translate "hello" into French:

In[18]:= **WordTranslation["hello", "French"]**

Out[18]= {bonjour, hello, holà, ohé}

Translate into Korean:

In[19]:= **WordTranslation["hello", "Korean"]**

Out[19]= {여보세요, 안녕하세요}

Translate into Korean, then transliterate to the English alphabet:

In[20]:= **Transliterate[WordTranslation["hello", "Korean"]]**

Out[20]= {yeoboseyo, annyeonghaseyo}

If you want to compare lots of different languages, give All as the language for WordTranslation. The result is an association which gives translations for different languages, with the languages listed roughly in order of decreasing worldwide usage.

Give translations of "hello" into the 5 most common languages in the world:

In[21]:= **Take[WordTranslation["hello", All], 5]**

Out[21]= ⟨| Mandarin → {表示問候的叫聲},

Hindi → {हलो, नमस्ते }, Spanish → {buenos días, hola},

Russian → {привет, приветствие, Здравствуйте}, Indonesian → {halo} |⟩

Let's take the top 100 languages, and look at the first character in the first translation for "hello" that appears. Here's a word cloud that shows that among these languages, "h" is the most common letter to start the word for "hello".

For the top 100 languages, make a word cloud of the first characters in the word for "hello":

In[22]:= `WordCloud[Values[StringTake[First[#], 1] &/@ Take[WordTranslation["hello", All], 100]]]`

Out[22]=

Vocabulary

Interpreter["*type*"]	specify a function to interpret natural language
TextCases["*text*", "*type*"]	find cases of a given type of object in *text*
TextStructure["*text*"]	find the grammatical structure of *text*
WordTranslation["*word*", "*language*"]	translate a word into another language

---

Exercises

35.1   Use **Interpreter** to find the location of the Eiffel Tower.

35.2   Use **Interpreter** to find a university referred to as "U of T".

35.3   Use **Interpreter** to find the chemicals referred to as C2H4, C2H6 and C3H8.

35.4   Use **Interpreter** to interpret the date "20140108".

35.5   Find universities that can be referred to as "U of X", where x is any letter of the alphabet.

35.6   Find which US state capital names can be interpreted as movie titles (use **CommonName** to get the string versions of entity names).

35.7   Find cities that can be referred to by permutations of the letters a, i, l and m.

35.8   Make a word cloud of country names in the Wikipedia article on "gunpowder".

35.9   Find all nouns in "She sells seashells by the sea shore."

35.10   Use **TextCases** to find the number of nouns, verbs and adjectives in the first 1000 characters of the Wikipedia article on computers.

35.11   Find the grammatical structure of the first sentence of the Wikipedia article about computers.

35.12   Find the 10 most common nouns in **ExampleData** [{"Text", "AliceInWonderland"}].

35.13   Make a community graph plot of the graph representation of the text structure of the first sentence of the Wikipedia article about language.

35.14   Make a list of numbers of nouns, verbs, adjectives and adverbs found by WordList in English.

35.15   Generate a list of the translations of numbers 2 through 10 into French.

Q&A

What possible types of interpreters are there?

It's a long list. Check out the documentation, or evaluate $InterpreterTypes to see the list.

Does Interpreter need a network connection?

In simple cases, such as dates or basic currency, no. But for full natural language input, yes.

When I say "4 dollars", how does it know if I want US dollars or something else?

It uses what it knows of your geo location to tell what kind of dollars you're likely to mean.

Can Interpreter deal with arbitrary natural language?

If something can be expressed in the Wolfram Language, then Interpreter should be able to interpret it. Interpreter["SemanticExpression"] takes any input, and tries to understand its meaning so as to get a Wolfram Language expression that captures it. What it's doing is essentially the first stage of what Wolfram|Alpha does.

Can I add my own interpreters?

Yes. GrammarRules lets you build up your own grammar, making use of whatever existing interpreters you want.

Can I find the meaning of a word?

WordDefinition gives dictionary definitions.

Can I find what part of speech a word is?

PartOfSpeech tells you *all* the parts of speech a word can correspond to. So for "fish" it gives noun and verb. Which of these is correct in a given case depends on how the word is used in a sentence—and that's what TextStructure figures out.

Can I translate whole sentences as well as words?

TextTranslation does this for some languages, usually by calling an external service.

What languages does WordTranslation handle?

It can translate lots of words for the few hundred most common languages. It can translate at least a few words for well over a thousand languages. LanguageData gives information on over 10,000 languages.

Tech Notes

- TextStructure requires complete grammatical text, but Interpreter uses many different techniques to also work with fragments of text.

- When you use ctrl = you can resolve ambiguous input interactively. With Interpreter you have to do it programmatically, using the option AmbiguityFunction.

More to Explore

Guide to Natural Language Interpreters in the Wolfram Language (wolfr.am/eiwl-35-more)

36 | Creating Websites and Apps

The Wolfram Language makes it easy to put anything you create onto the web.

Create some graphics:

In[1]:= **GeoGraphics[GeoRange → All, GeoProjection → "Albers"]**

Out[1]=

Deploy it to the cloud:

In[2]:= **CloudDeploy[GeoGraphics[GeoRange → All, GeoProjection → "Albers"]]**

Out[2]= CloudObject[https://www.wolframcloud.com/objects/9e1f3855–df3f–4d63–96f0–49c6bcd14138]

If you don't tell it otherwise, CloudDeploy will set up a new webpage, with a unique address. If you go to that webpage, you'll find your graphics there.

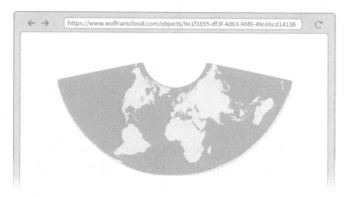

If you want the whole world to be able to see what you created, you can do that too (at least so long as you've got appropriate access to the Wolfram Cloud).

Deploy to the Wolfram Cloud, giving everyone permission to see what you've made:

In[3]:= **CloudDeploy[Graphics[{Red, Disk[]}], Permissions → "Public"]**

Out[3]= CloudObject[https://www.wolframcloud.com/objects/b76ab315–ee3a–4400–bed8–66c3c9b07c22]

Anyone who has the web address (URL) can now go there to see what you've made. URLShorten makes a short URL that's easier to tell to people.

Make a short URL for the webpage you've created:

In[4]:= **URLShorten[CloudDeploy[Graphics[{Red, Disk[ ]}], Permissions → "Public"]]**

Out[4]= https://wolfr.am/7vm~o2zC

You can deploy active content, like Manipulate, to the web too.

In[5]:= **CloudDeploy[Manipulate[**
    Graphics[Table[Circle[{0, 0}, r], {r, min, max}]], {min, 1, 30, 1}, {max, 1, 30, 1}]]

Out[5]= CloudObject[https://www.wolframcloud.com/objects/f113bc73–f933–4dc2–8359–7198c178a06b]

Now you'll get a webpage with active sliders and so on. You'll be able to use them in any standard web browser, though because they have to communicate over the internet, they'll run slower than if they were directly on your computer.

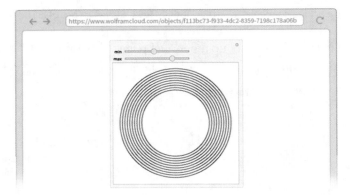

CloudDeploy normally works by first doing whatever computation it can, and then putting the result on the web. This means, for example, that CloudDeploy[Now] will make a webpage that always just shows the time when it was deployed. If instead you want to make a webpage that gives the current time every time the page is requested, you can do this with CloudDeploy[Delayed[Now]].

Use Delayed to make a clock that's regenerated every time the webpage is requested:

In[6]:= **CloudDeploy[Delayed[ClockGauge[Now]]]**

Out[6]= CloudObject[https://www.wolframcloud.com/objects/94aaf4ad–daea–4fe5–a50f–97b146a8b6ff]

Now every time you go to the webpage, it'll regenerate the clock in the Wolfram Cloud, and put a new version onto the webpage.

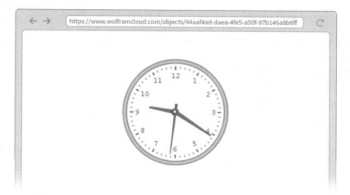

You can create a "real-time dashboard" by specifying an update interval.

Set up the webpage you create to automatically update itself every 2 seconds:

In[7]:= **CloudDeploy[Delayed[ClockGauge[Now], UpdateInterval → 2]]**

Out[7]= CloudObject[https://www.wolframcloud.com/objects/88e8fb8a–6d50–4474–b52a–6458a9aacca1]

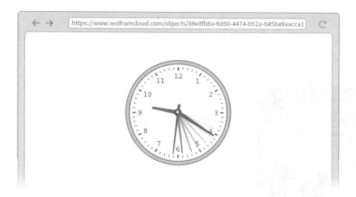

We've talked about things in terms of webpages. But actually, all of this works on mobile too, where you're for example viewing things through the Wolfram Cloud app.

But what about making your own apps on the web or on mobile? In the Wolfram Language it's for example easy to set up a form-based app.

The basic idea is to set up a FormFunction that defines both the structure of the form, and the action that's performed when the form is submitted.

Let's set up a form with one field labeled name that expects the name of an animal, then generates an image of that animal—and then deploys this to the cloud.

Set up a form-based app with a single input field for entering the name of an animal:

In[8]:= **CloudDeploy[FormFunction[{"name" → "Animal"}, ⌗name["Image"] &]]**

Out[8]= CloudObject[https://www.wolframcloud.com/objects/6925826b–776e–429a–bb0a–629be4594f35]

Now if you go to that web address, you'll see a form:

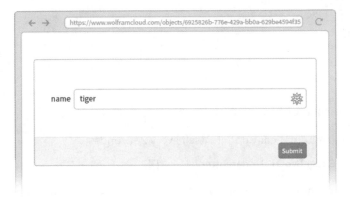

Submit the form and you'll get back a picture of a tiger:

You can have your form generate anything, including, for example, an active Manipulate.

Generate a Manipulate from a form:

In[9]:= **CloudDeploy[FormFunction[{"name" → "Animal"},**
     Manipulate[Rotate[#name["Image"], θ], {θ, 0, 360 °}] &]]

Out[9]= CloudObject[https://www.wolframcloud.com/objects/0870f086–37b1–4e3c–b078–510b9e95938b]

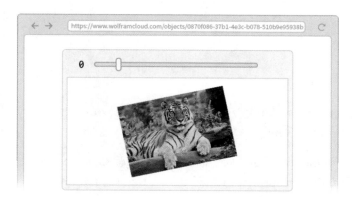

You can set up a form with any number of fields. For each field you say what type of input it should accept using the same specifications as Interpreter.

Deploy a form that accepts two numbers:

In[10]:= **CloudDeploy[FormFunction[{"x" → "Number", "y" → "Number"}, #x + #y &]]**

Out[10]= CloudObject[https://www.wolframcloud.com/objects/464eeeff–c7a0–4f93–b132–6721302a6048]

If you try to give this form an input that isn't a number, you'll get an error:

You can have fields that expect strings ("String") or integers ("Integer") or dates ("Date") or hundreds of other kinds of things.

When you ask for "real-world" types of input, like "Animal" or "City", CloudDeploy automatically sets up *smart fields* in your form, indicated by ❋, that use natural language understanding to interpret what's entered in them. But for more-abstract types of input, like numbers, you can for example choose between "Number", "SemanticNumber" and "ComputedNumber".

"Number" only allows explicit numbers, like 71. "SemanticNumber" also allows numbers in natural language, like "seventy-one". "ComputedNumber" also allows numbers that have to be computed, like "20th prime number".

Allow numbers specified by natural language:

In[11]:= **CloudDeploy[**
     FormFunction[{"x" → "SemanticNumber", "y" → "SemanticNumber"}, ♯x + ♯y &]]

Out[11]= CloudObject[https://www.wolframcloud.com/objects/662dc9bd–89ff–4c58–85c9–43ae1276082b]

"Seventy-one" works as a semantic number; to find the prime requires a computed number:

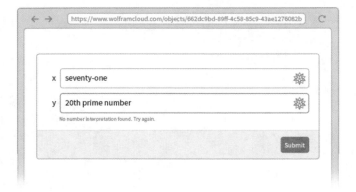

If you specify a type of input like "Image", you'll get special controls for acquiring the image—like direct access to the camera or photo gallery on a mobile device.

Deploy an edge-detection app for images:

In[12]:= **CloudDeploy[FormFunction[{"photo" → "Image"}, EdgeDetect[⌗photo] &]]**

Out[12]= CloudObject[https://www.wolframcloud.com/objects/727c12b9–6e42–496f–aa1d–0c5630c0fc5c]

On a mobile device, you can get the image from the camera:

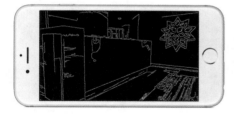

FormFunction lets you set up "one-shot" forms. You fill in a form, press Submit, then get a result. If you want to get another result, you have to go back to the form, and then submit it again. FormPage lets you set up pages that always include the form along with the result—like, for example, Wolfram | Alpha or a search engine would.

Create a form page that shows a map of a city:

In[13]:= **CloudDeploy[FormPage[{"city" → "City"}, GeoGraphics[⌗city] &]]**

Out[13]= CloudObject[https://www.wolframcloud.com/objects/0330658f–294c–43be–9d1f–3b7c1c455624]

You can change the field and submit again to get a new result:

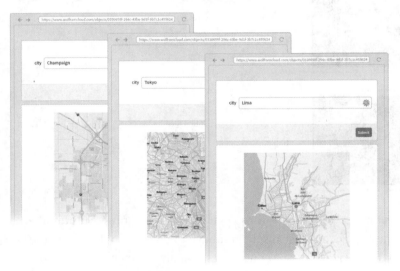

Vocabulary

CloudDeploy[*expr***]**	deploy to the cloud
Delayed[*expr***]**	computation delayed until it is requested
FormFunction[*form, function***]**	representation of a deployable form
FormPage[*form, function***]**	representation of a deployable form+result page
URLShorten[*url***]**	make a short version of a web URL

Exercises

36.1   Deploy a map of your current location to the web.

36.2   Deploy to the web a map that shows the current inferred location of the user.

36.3   Create a website that displays a new random number up to 1000 at size 100 every time it is visited.

36.4   Deploy a form on the web that takes a number x and returns $x \wedge x$.

36.5   Deploy a form on the web that takes numbers x and y and computes $x \wedge y$.

36.6   Deploy a form on the web that takes the topic of a Wikipedia page and gives a word cloud for the page.

36.7   Deploy a form page on the web that takes a string and repeatedly gives a reversed version at size 50.

36.8   Deploy a form page on the web that takes an integer n and repeatedly generates a picture of a polygon with random color and n sides.

36.9   Deploy a form page that takes a location and a number n and repeatedly gives a map of the n nearest volcanoes to the location.

Q&A

Why are the web addresses so long?

They're UUIDs (*universally unique identifiers*) that are long enough that with overwhelming probability no two identical ones will ever be created in the history of the universe.

How do I deploy to the cloud in a particular format?

Just ask for the format using ExportForm (or by giving the format inside FormFunction). Popular formats include "GIF", "PNG", "JPEG", "SVG", "PDF" and "HTMLFragment". (Note that "form" in ExportForm refers to a "form or type of output", not a "form to fill in".)

How can I embed a webpage generated by CloudDeploy?

Use EmbedCode to generate the necessary HTML.

How do I specify a label for a field in a form?

Just say e.g. {"s", "Enter a string here"} → "String". By default, the label shown for a field is just the name you use for the variable corresponding to the field. You can use any label you want for a field, including graphics, etc.

How do I specify initial or default values for a field in a form?

Say e.g. "n" → "Integer" → 100.

How do I restrict the values that can be entered in a particular field of a form?

Use Restricted. For example, Restricted["Number", {0, 10}] specifies a number between 0 and 10. Restricted["Location", ⊟ italy] specifies a location in Italy.

How do I specify the look of a form?

To start with, use options like FormTheme. For more control, you can put a FormObject inside a FormFunction, and give very detailed instructions. You can include any headers or text or styling that can appear in a notebook.

Can forms have checkboxes, sliders, etc.?

Yes. They can use the same controls as Manipulate, including checkboxes, radio buttons, popup menus, sliders, color pickers, etc.

Can I make extensible and multipage forms?

Yes. Field specifications can include constructs like RepeatingElement and CompoundElement. And forms can consist of lists of pages, including ones that are generated on the fly. (If the logic gets sufficiently complicated, you'll probably want to use AskFunction instead of FormFunction.)

When I deploy to the cloud, where are the computations actually done?

In the cloud ☺. Or in practice: on computers at centralized locations around the world.

How can I create a mobile app?

When you deploy to the cloud, you immediately have a mobile app that you can access from within the Wolfram Cloud app. You can specify a custom icon for your app using IconRules.

What about APIs?

APIFunction works very much like FormFunction, except it creates a web API that you can call by giving parameters in a URL query. EmbedCode lets you take an APIFunction, and generate code to call the API from many external programming languages and environments.

Tech Notes

- Hyperlink["*url*"] or Hyperlink[*label*, "*url*"] represents a hyperlink to deploy on the web. The label can be anything, including an image. GalleryView lets you make an array of hyperlinks.

- 3D graphics are by default deployed to be rotatable and zoomable.

- AutoRefreshed makes a webpage be automatically refreshed on a schedule, so it's ready if you ask for it.

- You can give detailed permissions for who can access something you deploy to the cloud, and what they can do with it. Setting $Permissions specifies a default choice of permissions.

More to Explore

Guide to Creating Web Sites and Apps in the Wolfram Language (wolfr.am/eiwl-36-more)

37 | Layout and Display

Earlier we saw how to use Framed to add a frame when one displays something.

Generate a number and put a frame around it:

In[1]:= **Framed[2 ^ 100]**

Out[1]= | 1 267 650 600 228 229 401 496 703 205 376 |

You can give options to Framed.

Specify a background color and a frame style:

In[2]:= **Framed[2 ^ 100, Background → LightYellow, FrameStyle → LightGray]**

Out[2]= | 1 267 650 600 228 229 401 496 703 205 376 |

Labeled lets you make things be labeled.

Add a label to the framed number:

In[3]:= **Labeled[Framed[2 ^ 100], "a big number"]**

Out[3]= | 1 267 650 600 228 229 401 496 703 205 376 |

a big number

This adds a label to a number styled with a yellow background:

In[4]:= **Labeled[Style[2 ^ 100, Background → Yellow], "a big number"]**

Out[4]= 1 267 650 600 228 229 401 496 703 205 376

a big number

This adds styling to the label:

In[5]:= **Labeled[Style[2 ^ 100, Background → Yellow], Style["a big number", Italic, Orange]]**

Out[5]= 1 267 650 600 228 229 401 496 703 205 376

a big number

You can use Labeled in graphics as well.

Make a pie chart in which some wedges are labeled:

In[6]:= **PieChart[**
         {Labeled[1, "one"], Labeled[2, "two"], Labeled[3, Red], Labeled[4, Orange], 2, 2}]

Out[6]=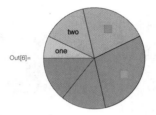

Plot labeled points:

In[7]:= **ListPlot[**
         {Labeled[1, "one"], Labeled[2, "two"], Labeled[3, Pink], Labeled[4, Yellow], 5, 6, 7}]

Out[7]=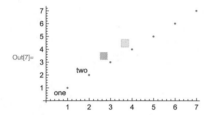

Plot the first few primes labeled with their values:

In[8]:= **ListPlot[Table[Labeled[Prime[n], Prime[n]], {n, 15}]]**

Out[8]=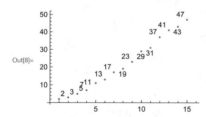

Labeled indicates something by putting a label right next to it. It's often nice instead to use "callouts", that have little lines pointing to whatever they're referring to. You can do this by using Callout rather than Labeled.

Callout creates "callouts" with little lines:

In[9]:= **ListPlot[Table[Callout[Prime[n], Prime[n]], {n, 15}]]**

Out[9]=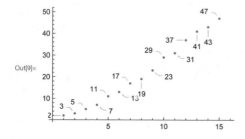

There are all sorts of ways to annotate graphics. Style directly inserts styling. Tooltip generates interactive tooltips that show themselves when the mouse hovers over them. Legended puts labels into a legend on the side.

Specify styles for the first three pie wedges:

In[10]:= **PieChart[{Style[3, Red], Style[2, Green], Style[1, Yellow], 1, 2}]**

Out[10]=
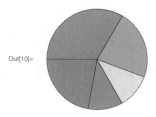

Set up words and colors as legends for pie wedges:

In[11]:= **PieChart[{Legended[1, "one"], Legended[2, "two"],
          Legended[3, Pink], Legended[4, Yellow], 2, 2}]**

Out[11]=
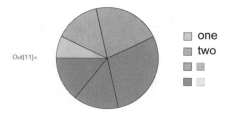

The default plot theme for the web is more brightly colored:

In[12]:= **PieChart[{1, 2, 3, 4, 2, 2}, PlotTheme → "Web"]**

Out[12]=
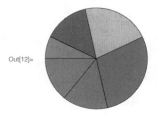

If you want the Wolfram Language to just automatically pick how to annotate things, then simply give the annotations with rules (→).

In ListPlot, annotations specified by rules are implemented with callouts:

In[13]:= **ListPlot[{1 → "one", 2 → "two", 3 → Pink, 4 → Yellow, 5, 6, 7}]**

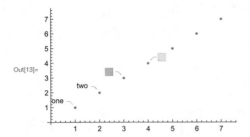

Out[13]=

In PieChart, strings are assumed to be labels, and colors to be styles:

In[14]:= **PieChart[{1 → "one", 2 → "two", 3 → Blue, 4 → Red}]**

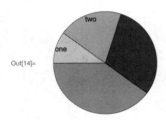

Out[14]=

It's common to want to combine different objects for presentation. Row, Column and Grid are convenient ways to do this.

Display a list of objects in a row:

In[15]:= **Row[{Yellow, Pink, Cyan}]**

Out[15]= ▨ ■ ▨

Display objects in a column:

In[16]:= **Column[{Yellow, Pink, Cyan}]**

Out[16]= ▨
▨
▨

Use GraphicsRow, GraphicsColumn and GraphicsGrid to arrange objects to fit in a certain overall size.

Generate an array of random pie charts, sized to fit:

In[17]:= **GraphicsGrid[Table[PieChart[RandomReal[10, 5]], 3, 6]]**

Out[17]=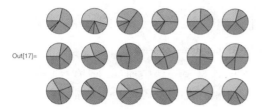

Do it with a frame around everything:

In[18]:= **GraphicsGrid[Table[PieChart[RandomReal[10, 5]], 3, 6], Frame → All]**

Out[18]=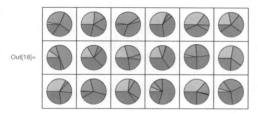

Vocabulary

Framed[*expr***]**	add a frame
Labeled[*expr, lab***]**	add a label
Callout[*expr, lab***]**	add a callout
Tooltip[*expr, lab***]**	add an interactive tooltip
Legended[*expr, lab***]**	add a legend
Row[{*expr₁, expr₂, ...***}]**	arrange in a row
Column[{*expr₁, expr₂, ...***}]**	arrange in a column
GraphicsRow[{*expr₁, expr₂, ...***}]**	arrange in a resizable row
GraphicsColumn[{*expr₁, expr₂, ...***}]**	arrange in a resizable column
GraphicsGrid[*array***]**	arrange in a resizable grid

Exercises

37.1 Make a list of numbers up to 100, with even numbers on yellow and odd numbers on light gray.

37.2 Make a list of numbers up to 100, with primes framed.

37.3 Make a list of numbers up to 100, with primes framed and labeled in light gray with their values modulo 4.

37.4 Create a 3×6 GraphicsGrid of randomly colored disks.

37.5 Make a pie chart of the GDPs of the countries in the G5, labeling each wedge.

37.6 Make a pie chart of the populations of the countries in the G5, giving a legend for each wedge.

37.7 Make a 5×5 GraphicsGrid of pie charts that give the relative frequencies of digits in $2 \wedge n$ with n starting at 1.

37.8 Make a graphics row of word clouds for Wikipedia articles on the G5 countries.

Q&A

Can I get rounded corners with Framed?

Yes. Use an option like RoundingRadius → 0.2.

What kinds of things can be in a label?

Anything you want. A label can be text or a graphic or, for that matter, a whole notebook.

Can I use Labeled to put labels in places other than at the bottom?

Yes. Use e.g. Labeled[*expr*, *label*, Left] or Labeled[*expr*, *label*, Right].

How do I determine where a legend goes?

Use Placed.

Can visualization be animated or dynamic?

Yes. ListAnimate creates an animation. Constructs from Tooltip to Manipulate can be used to set up dynamic visualizations.

Tech Notes

- The Wolfram Language tries to place labels where they won't interfere with the data that's being plotted.

- You can resize any graphic using Show[*graphic*, ImageSize → *width*] or Show[*graphic*, ImageSize → {*width*, *height*}]. ImageSize → Tiny, etc. also work.

- PlotTheme → "BlackBackground" may be useful for people with low vision. PlotTheme → "Monochrome" avoids using color.

- ListPlot, PieChart, etc. automatically work with associations (<| ... |>), taking keys to be coordinates when appropriate, but otherwise treating them as annotations.

- There are lots of different kinds of legends: LineLegend, BarLegend, etc.

More to Explore

Guide to Labeling & Annotation in the Wolfram Language (wolfr.am/eiwl-37-more)

38 | Assigning Names to Things

Particularly when you're doing quick experiments in the Wolfram Language, it's often convenient to use % to refer to the result of your most recent computation.

Do a simple computation:

In[1]:= **Range[10]**

Out[1]= {1, 2, 3, 4, 5, 6, 7, 8, 9, 10}

% gives the result of the previous computation:

In[2]:= **%**

Out[2]= {1, 2, 3, 4, 5, 6, 7, 8, 9, 10}

This squares the most recent result:

In[3]:= **% ^ 2**

Out[3]= {1, 4, 9, 16, 25, 36, 49, 64, 81, 100}

If you expect to refer to a result later, you can assign it a name. For example, you can say thing = Range[10] to assign thing as a name for the result of Range[10].

Assign thing to be the result of Range[10]:

In[4]:= **thing = Range[10]**

Out[4]= {1, 2, 3, 4, 5, 6, 7, 8, 9, 10}

Whenever thing appears, it'll be replaced by the result of Range[10]:

In[5]:= **thing**

Out[5]= {1, 2, 3, 4, 5, 6, 7, 8, 9, 10}

Square the value of thing:

In[6]:= **thing ^ 2**

Out[6]= {1, 4, 9, 16, 25, 36, 49, 64, 81, 100}

You can assign a name to the result of a computation even if you never display the result. End your input with ; (semicolon) to avoid seeing the result.

Assign a name to a list of a million elements, but don't display the list:

In[7]:= **millionlist = Range[1 000 000];**

Find the total of all the elements in the list:

In[8]:= **Total[millionlist]**

Out[8]= 500 000 500 000

When you assign a name to something, the name will stay until you explicitly clear it.

Assign x the value 42:

In[9]:= **x = 42**

Out[9]= 42

You might have thought this would be {x, y, z}—but x has value 42:

In[10]:= **{x, y, z}**

Out[10]= {42, y, z}

If you want to clear assignments, use Clear.

Clear any assignment for x:

In[11]:= **Clear[x]**

Now x, like y and z, isn't replaced:

In[12]:= **{x, y, z}**

Out[12]= {x, y, z}

Assigning a *global value* for x, like x = 42, is potentially a big deal, because it can affect everything you do in your session (at least until you clear x). Something that's much safer—and extremely useful—is just to assign a temporary, local value to x, inside a *module*.

This locally sets the value of x to be Range[10] inside the Module:

In[13]:= **Module[{x = Range[10]}, x^2]**

Out[13]= {1, 4, 9, 16, 25, 36, 49, 64, 81, 100}

Outside the module, x still has no value assigned:

In[14]:= **x**

Out[14]= x

You can have as many *local variables* inside a module as you want.

Define local variables x and n, then compute x ^ n using the values you've assigned:

In[15]:= **Module[{x = Range[10], n = 2}, x ^ n]**

Out[15]= {1, 4, 9, 16, 25, 36, 49, 64, 81, 100}

In the *functional* style of programming that we've used in most of this book, you carry out sequences of operations by applying sequences of functions. This is a very powerful and direct style of programming that's uniquely suited to the Wolfram Language.

But once one's defining variables, one can use a different style, in which one doesn't feed results directly from one function to another, but instead assigns them as values of variables to be used later. This kind of *procedural programming* is what's been used in lower-level languages since the very earliest days of computing.

It's still useful in the Wolfram Language, though in many ways it's eclipsed by functional programming, as well as by the *pattern-based* style of programming that we'll discuss later.

To specify sequences of actions in the Wolfram Language one just separates them by semicolons (;). (Putting a semicolon at the end is like specifying an empty final action, which is why this has the effect of not displaying a result.)

Do a sequence of operations; the result is what the last operation produces:

In[16]:= **x = Range[10]; y = x ^ 2; y = y + 10 000**

Out[16]= {10 001, 10 004, 10 009, 10 016, 10 025, 10 036, 10 049, 10 064, 10 081, 10 100}

This defined global values for x and y; don't forget to clear them:

In[17]:= **Clear[x, y]**

You can use semicolons to do sequences of operations inside Module.

This does a sequence of operations, with x and y maintained as local variables:

In[18]:= **Module[{x, y}, x = Range[10]; y = x ^ 2; y = y + 10 000]**

Out[18]= {10 001, 10 004, 10 009, 10 016, 10 025, 10 036, 10 049, 10 064, 10 081, 10 100}

You can mix local variables that do and don't have initial values:

In[19]:= **Module[{x, y, n = 2}, x = Range[10]; y = x ^ n; y = y + 10 000]**

Out[19]= {10 001, 10 004, 10 009, 10 016, 10 025, 10 036, 10 049, 10 064, 10 081, 10 100}

You can nest modules—which is useful if you're building large programs where you want to isolate different parts of your code.

Vocabulary

%	the most recent computation result
$x = value$	assign a value
Clear[x**]**	clear a value
Module[{$x = value$**}, ...]**	set up a temporary variable
$expr$;	do a computation, but don't display its result
$expr_1$; $expr_2$; ...	do a sequence of computations

Exercises

38.1 Use Module to compute x^2 + x where x is Range[10].

38.2 Use Module to generate a list of 10 random integers up to 100, then make a column giving the original list, and the results of applying Sort, Max and Total to it.

38.3 Use Module to generate an image collage from a picture of a giraffe, and the results of applying Blur, EdgeDetect and ColorNegate to it.

38.4 Inside a Module, let r = Range[10], then make a line plot of r joined with the reverse of r joined with r joined with the reverse of r.

38.5 Find a simpler form for {Range[10] + 1, Range[10] - 1, Reverse[Range[10]]}.

38.6 Find a simpler form for Module[{u = 10}, Join[{u}, Table[u = Mod[17 u + 2, 11], 20]]].

38.7 Generate 10 random strings made of 5 letters, in which consonants (non-vowels) alternate with vowels (aeiou).

Q&A

How come we're at Section 38, and only now introducing variable assignments?

Because, as we've seen, in the Wolfram Language one can go a very long way without introducing them. And it tends to be a lot cleaner to program without them.

Can I assign a name to anything?

Yes. Graphics, arrays, images, pure functions, whatever.

How does one read x = 4 out loud?

"x equals 4", or, more rarely, "assign x to 4", or "give x the value 4".

What are good principles for global names?

Use names that are specific and explicit. Don't worry if they're long; they'll get autocompleted when you type. For "informal" names, start with lowercase letters. For more carefully thought out names, consider using capitalization like built-in functions do.

% gives the previous result. What about the result before that, etc.?

%% gives the next to last, %%% gives the next-to-next-to-last, etc. % n gives the result on line n (i.e. the result labeled Out[n]).

Can I assign to several variables at once?

Yes. x = y = 6 assigns both x and y to 6. {x, y} = {3, 4} assigns x to 3 and y to 4. {x, y} = {y, x} swaps the values of x and y.

What happens if a variable escapes from a Module without having been assigned a value?

Try it! You'll find you'll get a new variable that's been given a unique name.

What about other procedural programming constructs, like Do and For?

The Wolfram Language has those. Do is sometimes worth using, particularly when your objective is side effects, like assigning variables or exporting data. For is almost always a bad idea, and can almost always be replaced by much cleaner code using constructs such as Table.

Tech Notes

- The result of x = 2 + 2 is just 4, but as a *side effect* an assignment is made for x.

- In pure functional programming, the only effect of any computation is to give the result. As soon as you're assigning values, there's effectively a hidden state that's set up by those assignments.

- x =. is an alternative to Clear[x].

- Module does *lexical scoping*, which means it effectively localizes the names of variables. Block does *dynamic scoping*, which means it localizes the values, but not the names, of variables. Both are useful in different circumstances. Table effectively uses Block.

- x ++ is equivalent to x = x + 1. x += n is equivalent to x = x + n. AppendTo[x, n] is equivalent to x = Append[x, n] or x = Join[x, {n}].

39 | Immediate and Delayed Values

There are two ways to assign a value to something in the Wolfram Language: *immediate assignment* (=), and *delayed assignment* (:=).

In immediate assignment, the value is computed immediately when the assignment is done, and is never recomputed. In delayed assignment, the computation of the value is delayed, and is done every time the value is requested.

As a simple example, consider the difference between value = RandomColor[] and value := RandomColor[].

In immediate assignment (=), a random color is immediately generated:

In[1]:= **value = RandomColor[ ]**

Out[1]= ■

Every time you ask for value, you get the same random color:

In[2]:= **value**

Out[2]= ■

In delayed assignment (:=), no random color is immediately generated:

In[3]:= **value := RandomColor[ ]**

Each time you ask for value, RandomColor[] is computed, and a new color is generated:

In[4]:= **value**

Out[4]= ▢

The color will typically be different every time:

In[5]:= **value**

Out[5]= ■

It's very common to use := if something isn't ready yet when you're defining a value.

You can make a delayed assignment for circles even though n doesn't yet have a value:

In[6]:= **circles := Graphics[Table[Circle[{x, 0}, x/2], {x, n}]]**

Give n a value:

In[7]:= **n = 6**

Out[7]= 6

Now you can ask for circles and the value you've given for n will be used:

In[8]:= **circles**

Out[8]=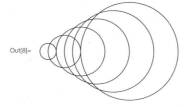

The idea of delayed assignment is directly analogous to the Delayed construct we discussed for deploying webpages. In delayed assignment we don't compute a value until we need it. Similarly, when we use CloudDeploy with Delayed we don't compute the content of a webpage until someone asks for it.

There's a notion of delayed rules too. $x \to rhs$ computes *rhs* immediately. But in a delayed rule $x :\to rhs$ (typed :>), *rhs* is instead recomputed every time it's requested.

This is an immediate rule, where a specific value for RandomReal[ ] is immediately computed:

In[9]:= **x → RandomReal[ ]**

Out[9]= x → 0.522293

You can replace four x's, but they'll all be the same:

In[10]:= **{x, x, x, x} /. x → RandomReal[ ]**

Out[10]= {0.821639, 0.821639, 0.821639, 0.821639}

This is a delayed rule, where the computation of RandomReal[ ] is delayed:

In[11]:= **x :→ RandomReal[ ]**

Out[11]= x :→ RandomReal[ ]

RandomReal[ ] is computed separately when each x is replaced, giving four different values:

In[12]:= **{x, x, x, x} /. x :→ RandomReal[ ]**

Out[12]= {0.536115, 0.84214, 0.242933, 0.514131}

Vocabulary

$x := value$	delayed assignment, evaluated every time x is requested
$x :\to value$	delayed rule, evaluated every time x is encountered (typed :>)

Exercises

39.1   Replace x in {x, x + 1, x + 2, x ^ 2} by the same random integer up to 100.

39.2   Replace each x in {x, x + 1, x + 2, x ^ 2} by a separately chosen random integer up to 100.

Q&A

Why not always use := ?

Because you don't want to have to recompute things unless it's necessary. It's more efficient to just compute something once, then use the result over and over again.

How does one read := and :> out loud?

:= is usually just "colon equals", though sometimes "delayed assignment". :> is usually "colon greater", though sometimes "delayed rule".

What happens if I do x = x + 1, with x not having a value?

You'll start an infinite loop that'll eventually get cut off by the system. x = {x} is the same story.

What's the significance of inputs being labeled In [n] := , and outputs Out[n] = ?

It indicates that inputs are assigned to In[n] and outputs to Out[n]. The := for input means the assignment is delayed, so that if you ask for In[n] the result will be recomputed.

Tech Notes

- In the Wolfram Language, the process of computing results is often called *evaluation*, because it involves finding values of things.

- The Wolfram Language has many ways of controlling evaluation. An example is the function **Hold**, which maintains an expression in "held" form until it is "released".

- The internal form of x = y is Set [x, y]. x := y is SetDelayed [x, y]. x :→ y is RuleDelayed [x, y].

40 | Defining Your Own Functions

As we've seen in this book, there's a huge amount that can be done with functions that are already built into the Wolfram Language. But you can go even further if you define your own functions too. And the Wolfram Language has a very flexible way of letting you do this.

Let's start with a typical, simple example of a function definition.

This defines a function pinks that takes any argument:

In[1]:= **pinks[n_] := Table[Pink, n]**

This uses the function definition:

In[2]:= **pinks[5]**

Out[2]= {■, ■, ■, ■, ■}

In[3]:= **pinks[10]**

Out[3]= {■, ■, ■, ■, ■, ■, ■, ■, ■, ■}

How does this function definition work? The idea is that the := defines a value for the pattern pinks[$n\_$]. When you ask for pinks[5], this matches the pinks[$n\_$] pattern, and the value you've defined for this is used.

But this is just the beginning of the story of function definition in the Wolfram Language. Because in the Wolfram Language, you can give a definition for anything.

Here's a list of expressions:

In[4]:= **{f[Red], f[Yellow], f[Green], f[Orange], f[Magenta]}**

Out[4]= {f[■], f[□], f[■], f[■], f[■]}

Define values for f[Red] and f[Green]:

In[5]:= **f[Red] = 1000; f[Green] = 2000;**

Now f[Red] and f[Green] are replaced by the values defined; the other cases are left unchanged:

In[6]:= **{f[Red], f[Yellow], f[Green], f[Orange], f[Blue]}**

Out[6]= {1000, f[□], 2000, f[■], f[■]}

Now let's add a definition for the pattern f[$x\_$]. The Wolfram Language will use this whenever the special definitions for f[Red] and f[Green] don't apply.

Define a value for f with any argument:

In[7]:= **f[x_] := Framed[Column[{x, ColorNegate[x]}]]**

If the special cases don't apply, the general definition is used:

In[8]:= **{f[Red], f[Yellow], f[Green], f[Orange], f[Blue]}**

Out[8]= $\left\{ 1000, \blacksquare, 2000, \blacksquare, \blacksquare \right\}$

Clear definitions for f to make sure nothing gets confused later:

In[9]:= **Clear[f]**

As another example, let's do the classic computer science exercise of defining the factorial function. Start by saying that factorial[1] = 1. Then define how to compute factorial[$n\_$] recursively in terms of another instance of factorial.

Give a recursive definition of factorial:

In[10]:= **factorial[1] = 1; factorial[n_Integer] := n * factorial[n − 1]**

Ask for factorial[50]:

In[11]:= **factorial[50]**

Out[11]= 30 414 093 201 713 378 043 612 608 166 064 768 844 377 641 568 960 512 000 000 000 000

There's also a built-in factorial function, which gives the same result:

In[12]:= **50 !**

Out[12]= 30 414 093 201 713 378 043 612 608 166 064 768 844 377 641 568 960 512 000 000 000 000

Instead of having definitions for factorial[1] and factorial[$n\_$] we could have had a single definition and used If. But having separate definitions for each case tends to make things much easier to read and understand.

An alternative definition using If:

In[13]:= **factorial[n_Integer] := If[n == 1, 1, n * factorial[n − 1]]**

It's nice to be able to break out special cases, but the real power of being able to make definitions for anything comes when one goes beyond simple *function*[*arguments*] cases.

As a simple example, consider making a definition for plusminus[{$x\_$, $y\_$}].

Define a value for a pattern:

In[14]:= **plusminus[{x_ , y_}] := {x + y, x − y}**

Use the definition:

In[15]:= **plusminus[{4, 1}]**

Out[15]= {5, 3}

A much less elegant form based on a traditional *function[argument]* definition:

In[16]:= **plusminus[v_] := {v[[1]] + v[[2]], v[[1]] − v[[2]]}**

It's very common to want to define a function that applies only to objects with a certain structure. This is easy to do with patterns. Here's an example.

A list with some Framed objects:

In[17]:= **{a, Framed[b], c, Framed[{d, e}], 100}**

Out[17]= $\left\{a, \boxed{b}, c, \boxed{\{d, e\}}, 100\right\}$

Define a function that applies only to framed objects:

In[18]:= **highlight[Framed[x_]] := Style[Labeled[x, "+"], 20, Background → LightYellow]**

Apply highlight to each element of a list; it knows what to do when it's given something framed:

In[19]:= **highlight /@ {a, Framed[b], c, Framed[{10, 20}], 100}**

Out[19]= $\left\{\text{highlight[a]}, \underset{+}{\text{b}}, \text{highlight[c]}, \underset{+}{\{10, 20\}}, \text{highlight[100]}\right\}$

This definition applies to anything with head List:

In[20]:= **highlight[list_List] := highlight /@ list**

Now you no longer have to use /@ :

In[21]:= **highlight[{a, Framed[b], c, Framed[{10, 20}], 100}]**

Out[21]= $\left\{\text{highlight[a]}, \underset{+}{\text{b}}, \text{highlight[c]}, \underset{+}{\{10, 20\}}, \text{highlight[100]}\right\}$

Give a general case, to use if none of the special cases apply:

In[22]:= **highlight[x_] := Style[Rotate[x, −30 Degree], 20, Orange]**

This uses the special cases when it can, then the general case when nothing else applies:

In[23]:= **highlight[{a, Framed[b], c, Framed[{10, 20}], 100}]**

Out[23]= $\left\{a, \underset{+}{\text{b}}, c, \{10, 20\}, \underset{+}{100}\right\}$

Exercises

Note: These exercises involve defining functions. Remember to use Clear to get rid of definitions once you're finished with each exercise.

40.1   Define a function f that computes the square of its argument.

40.2   Define a function poly that takes an integer, and makes a picture of an orange regular polygon with that number of sides.

40.3   Define a function f that takes a list of two elements and puts them in reverse order.

40.4   Create a function f that takes two arguments and gives the result of multiplying them and dividing by their sum.

40.5   Define a function f that takes a list of two elements and returns a list of their sum, difference and ratio.

40.6   Define a function evenodd that gives Black if its argument is even and White otherwise, but gives Red if its argument is 0.

40.7   Define a function f of three arguments where the second two arguments are added if the first argument is 1, multiplied if it's 2 and raised to a power if it's 3.

40.8   Define a Fibonacci function f with f[0] and f[1] both being 1, and f[n] for integer n being the sum of f[n-1] and f[n-2].

40.9   Create a function animal that takes a string, and gives a picture of an animal with that name.

40.10 Define a function nearwords that takes a string and an integer n, and gives the n words in WordList[ ] that are nearest to a given string.

Q&A

What kind of a pattern can be used in a function definition?

Absolutely any pattern you want. Even one where the head is itself a pattern.

How can I see the definitions made for a particular function?

Use ? f to see the definitions for f.

How do I overwrite an existing function definition?

Just make a new definition for the same pattern. Use Clear to remove all definitions.

How are different definitions for a particular function sorted?

Typically from most specific to least specific. If there are definitions that can't be ordered by specificity, definitions made later are put later. When definitions are used, the earlier ones are tried first. ? f shows the ordering of definitions for f.

Can I redefine built-in functions like Max or Plus?

Usually yes. First, though, you often have to say e.g. Unprotect[Max]. Then definitions you add will be used in preference to built-in ones. Some functions, like Plus, are so fundamental that the system locks them in a protected state. Even in this case, though, you can make "upvalue" definitions that are associated with particular structures of arguments.

Can I do object-oriented programming in the Wolfram Language?

A symbolic generalization of object-oriented programming, yes. Given an object "type" t, one wants to make definitions e.g. for f[t[...]] and g[t[...]]. One can associate such definitions with t by saying t /: f[t[...]] = ... In the Wolfram Language, this is called *defining an upvalue for t*.

Can I use = instead of := for function definitions?

Sometimes. f[n_] = n^2 will work fine, because the right-hand side doesn't evaluate when you make the assignment. f[n_] = Now and f[n_] := Now will give different results. And in many cases the right-hand side can't be meaningfully evaluated until specific arguments are given.

How can I share function definitions with other people?

Just send the code! A convenient way to do this through the cloud is to use CloudSave and CloudGet, as discussed in Section 43.

Tech Notes

- Many low-level languages require functions to have particular *static types* of arguments (e.g. integers, reals, strings). Some languages allow *dynamic typing*, with arguments allowed to have any of a certain set of types. The Wolfram Language generalizes this by allowing arguments to be defined by arbitrary symbolic structures.

- Having a pattern like {x_, y_} in a function definition allows immediate and convenient *destructuring* of the function argument.

- Definitions can be associated with the head of a function ("downvalues"), with the heads of its arguments ("upvalues"), or with the head of the head, etc. ("subvalues"). Upvalues are effectively a generalization of *methods* in object-oriented languages.

- f = (♯^2 &) and f[n_] := n^2 are two ways of defining a function, that for example give the same results for f[10]. Pure function definitions tend to be easier to combine with each other, but much coarser in their handling of argument structures.

More to Explore

Guide to Defining Functions in the Wolfram Language (wolfr.am/eiwl-40-more)

41 | More about Patterns

Within the Wolfram Language, there's a whole sublanguage of patterns. We've already seen some of its important elements.

_ ("blank") stands for anything. *x_* ("*x* blank") stands for anything, but calls it *x*. _*h* stands for anything with head *h*. And *x_h* stands for anything with head *h*, and calls it *x*.

Define a function whose argument is an integer named n:

In[1]:= **digitback[n_Integer] := Framed[Reverse[IntegerDigits[n]]]**

The function evaluates whenever the argument is an integer:

In[2]:= **{digitback[1234], digitback[6712], digitback[x], digitback[{4, 3, 2}], digitback[2 ^ 32]}**

Out[2]= { $\boxed{\{4, 3, 2, 1\}}$, $\boxed{\{2, 1, 7, 6\}}$, digitback[x], digitback[{4, 3, 2}], $\boxed{\{6, 9, 2, 7, 6, 9, 4, 9, 2, 4\}}$ }

Sometimes you may want to put a condition on a pattern. You can do this with /; ("slash semi"). n_Integer /; n > 0 means any integer that is greater than 0.

Give a definition which only applies when n > 0:

In[3]:= **pdigitback[n_Integer /; n > 0] := Framed[Reverse[IntegerDigits[n]]]**

The definition doesn't apply to negative numbers:

In[4]:= **{pdigitback[1234], pdigitback[−1234], pdigitback[x], pdigitback[2 ^ 40]}**

Out[4]= { $\boxed{\{4, 3, 2, 1\}}$, pdigitback[−1234], pdigitback[x], $\boxed{\{6, 7, 7, 7, 2, 6, 1, 1, 5, 9, 9, 0, 1\}}$ }

The /; can go anywhere—even at the end of the whole definition.

Define different cases of the check function:

In[5]:= **check[x_, y_] := Red /; x > y**

In[6]:= **check[x_, y_] := Green /; x ≤ y**

Some examples of the check function:

In[7]:= **{check[1, 2], check[2, 1], check[3, 4], check[50, 60], check[60, 50]}**

Out[7]= {■, ■, ■, ■, ■}

__ ("double blank") stands for any sequence of one or more arguments.
___ ("triple blank") stands for zero or more.

Define a function that looks for black and white (in that order) in a list.

The pattern matches black followed by white, with any elements before, between and after them:

In[8]:= **blackwhite[{ ___ , Black, m___ , White, ___}] := {1, m, 2, m, 3, m, 4}**

Pick out the (smallest) sequence between a black and a white:

In[9]:= **blackwhite[{▨, ■, ▨, ▨, ▨, □, ■, □}]**

Out[9]= {1, ■, ▨, ▨, ▨, 2, ■, ▨, ▨, 3, ■, ▨, ▨, 4}

By default, __ and ___ pick the shortest matches that work. You can use Longest to make them pick the longest instead.

Specify that the sequence between black and white should be as long as possible:

In[10]:= **blackwhitex[{ ___, Black, Longest[m___], White, ___}] := {1, m, 2, m, 3, m, 4}**

Now m grabs elements all the way to the last white:

In[11]:= **blackwhitex[{▨, ■, ▨, ▨, ▨, □, ■, □}]**

Out[11]= {1, ■, ▨, ▨, ▨, □, ■, 2, ■, ▨, ▨, ▨, □, ■, 3, ■, ▨, ▨, ▨, □, ■, 4}

x | y | z matches x, y or z. x .. matches any number of repetitions of x.

bwcut effectively cuts out the longest run containing only black and white:

In[12]:= **bwcut[{a___, Longest[(Black | White)..], b___}] := {{a}, Red, {b}}**

In[13]:= **bwcut[{▨, ▨, ■, □, □, ■, ■, □}]**

Out[13]= {{▨, ▨}, ■, {□}}

The pattern x_ is actually short for x : _, which means "match anything (i.e. _) and name the result x". You can use notations like x : for more complicated patterns too.

Set up a pattern named m that matches a list of two pairs:

In[14]:= **grid22[m : {{ _ , _ }, { _ , _ }}] := Grid[m, Frame → All]**

In[15]:= **{grid22[{{a, b}, {c, d}}], grid22[{{12, 34}, {56, 78}}],**
grid22[{123, 456}], grid22[{{1, 2, 3}, {4, 5, 6}}]}

Out[15]= $\left\{ \begin{array}{|c|c|} a & b \\ c & d \end{array}, \begin{array}{|c|c|} 12 & 34 \\ 56 & 78 \end{array}, \text{grid22}[\{123, 456\}], \text{grid22}[\{\{1, 2, 3\}, \{4, 5, 6\}\}] \right\}$

Name the sequence of black and white, so it can be used in the result:

In[16]:= **bwcut[{a___, r : Longest[(Black | White)..], b___}] := {{a}, Framed[Length[{r}]], {b}}**

In[17]:= **bwcut[{▨, ▨, ■, □, □, ■, ■, □}]**

Out[17]= $\left\{ \{▨, ▨\}, \boxed{5}, \{□\} \right\}$

As a final example, let's use patterns to implement the classic computer science algorithm of sorting a list by repeatedly swapping pairs of successive elements that are found to be out of order. It's easy to write each step in the algorithm as a replacement for a pattern.

Replace the first elements one finds out of order by ones that are in order:

In[18]:= **{5, 4, 1, 3, 2} /. {x___, b_, a_, y___} /; b > a → {x, a, b, y}**

Out[18]= {4, 5, 1, 3, 2}

Do the same operation 10 times, eventually sorting the list completely:

In[19]:= **NestList[(# /. {x___, b_, a_, y___} /; b > a → {x, a, b, y}) &, {4, 5, 1, 3, 2}, 10]**

Out[19]= {{4, 5, 1, 3, 2}, {4, 1, 5, 3, 2}, {1, 4, 5, 3, 2}, {1, 4, 3, 5, 2}, {1, 3, 4, 5, 2}, {1, 3, 4, 2, 5}, {1, 3, 2, 4, 5}, {1, 2, 3, 4, 5}, {1, 2, 3, 4, 5}, {1, 2, 3, 4, 5}, {1, 2, 3, 4, 5}}

At the beginning, we won't know how long it'll take to finish sorting a particular list. So the best thing is to use FixedPointList, which is like NestList, except that you don't have to tell it a specific number of steps, and instead it just goes on until the result reaches a *fixed point*, where nothing more is changing.

Do the operation until a fixed point is reached:

In[20]:= **FixedPointList[(# /. {x___, b_, a_, y___} /; b > a → {x, a, b, y}) &, {4, 5, 1, 3, 2}]**

Out[20]= {{4, 5, 1, 3, 2}, {4, 1, 5, 3, 2}, {1, 4, 5, 3, 2}, {1, 4, 3, 5, 2}, {1, 3, 4, 5, 2}, {1, 3, 4, 2, 5}, {1, 3, 2, 4, 5}, {1, 2, 3, 4, 5}, {1, 2, 3, 4, 5}}

Transpose to find the list of elements appearing first, second, etc. at successive steps:

In[21]:= **Transpose[%]**

Out[21]= {{4, 4, 1, 1, 1, 1, 1, 1, 1}, {5, 1, 4, 4, 3, 3, 3, 2, 2}, {1, 5, 5, 3, 4, 4, 2, 3, 3}, {3, 3, 3, 5, 5, 2, 4, 4, 4}, {2, 2, 2, 2, 2, 5, 5, 5, 5}}

ListLinePlot plots each list in a different color, showing how the sorting process proceeds:

In[22]:= **ListLinePlot[%]**

Out[22]=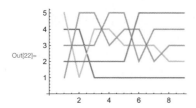

Here's the result for sorting a random length-20 list:

In[23]:= **ListLinePlot[Transpose[FixedPointList[**
**   (# /. {x___, b_, a_, y___} /; b > a → {x, a, b, y}) &, RandomSample[Range[20]]]]]**

Out[23]=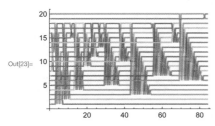

Vocabulary

patt /; *cond*	a pattern that matches if a condition is met
___	a pattern for any sequence of zero or more elements ("triple blank")
patt ..	a pattern for one or more repeats of *patt*
Longest[*patt* **]**	a pattern that picks out the longest sequence that matches
FixedPointList[f, x **]**	keep nesting f until the result no longer changes

---

Exercises

41.1   Find the list of digits for squares of numbers less than 100 that contain successive repeated digits.

41.2   In the first 100 Roman numerals, find those containing L, I and X in that order.

41.3   Define a function f that tests whether a list of integers is the same as its reverse.

41.4   Get a list of pairs of successive words in the Wikipedia article on alliteration that have identical first letters.

41.5   Use **Grid** to show the sorting process in this section for {4, 5, 1, 3, 2}, with successive steps going down the page.

41.6   Use **ArrayPlot** to show the sorting process in this section for a list of length 50, with successive steps going across the page.

41.7   Start with 1.0, then repeatedly apply the "*Newton's method*" function (#+2/#)/2 & until the result no longer changes.

41.8   Implement *Euclid's algorithm* for GCD in which {a, b} is repeatedly replaced by {b, Mod[a, b]} until b is 0, and apply the algorithm to 12 345, 54 321.

41.9   Define *combinators* using the rules s[x_][y_][z_] → x[z][y[z]], k[x_][y_] → x, then generate a list by starting with s[s][k][s[s[s]][s]][s] and applying these rules until nothing changes.

41.10   Remove all trailing 0's from the digit list for 100 !.

41.11   Start from {1, 0} then for 200 steps repeatedly remove the first 2 elements, and append {0, 1} if the first element is 1 and {1, 0, 0} if it is 0, and get a list of the lengths of the sequences produced (*tag system*).

41.12   Start from {0, 0} then for 200 steps repeatedly remove the first 2 elements, and append {2, 1} if the first element is 0, {0} if the first element is 1, and {0, 2, 1, 2} if it is 2, and make a line plot of the lengths of the sequences produced (*tag system*).

Q&A

What are other pattern constructs in the Wolfram Language?

Except[*patt*] matches anything except *patt*. PatternSequence[*patt*] matches a sequence of arguments in a function. OrderlessPatternSequence[*patt*] matches them in any order. f[x_: v] defines v as a default value, so f[ ] is matched, with x being v.

How can one see all the ways a pattern could match a particular expression?

Use ReplaceList. Replace gives the first match; ReplaceList gives a list of all of them.

What does FixedPointList do if there's no fixed point?

It'll eventually stop. There's an option that tells it how far to go. FixedPointList[f, x, n] stops after at most n steps.

Tech Notes

- In a repeating pattern *patt* .., don't forget to leave a space in e.g. 0 .. to avoid confusion with decimal numbers.

- Functions can have attributes that affect how pattern matching works. For example, Plus has attributes Flat and Orderless. Flat means that b + c can be pulled out of a + b + c + d. Orderless means that elements can be reordered, so a + c can be pulled out. (Flat is like the mathematical property of *associativity*; Orderless like *commutativity*.)

- The algorithm for sorting shown is usually called *bubble sort*. For a list of length n, it'll typically take about $n \wedge 2$ steps. The built-in Wolfram Language function Sort is much faster, and takes only a little over n steps.

More to Explore

Guide to Patterns in the Wolfram Language (wolfr.am/eiwl-41-more)

42 | String Patterns and Templates

String patterns work very much like other patterns in the Wolfram Language, except that they operate on sequences of characters in strings rather than parts of expressions. In a string pattern, you can combine pattern constructs like _ with strings like "abc" using ~~.

This picks out all instances of + followed by a single character:

In[1]:= **StringCases["+string +patterns are +quite +easy", "+" ~~ _]**

Out[1]= {+s, +p, +q, +e}

This picks out three characters after each +:

In[2]:= **StringCases["+string +patterns are +quite +easy", "+" ~~ _ ~~ _ ~~ _]**

Out[2]= {+str, +pat, +qui, +eas}

Use the name x for the character after each +, and return that character framed:

In[3]:= **StringCases["+string +patterns are +quite +easy", "+" ~~ x_ → Framed[x]]**

Out[3]= {| s |, | p |, | q |, | e |}

In a string pattern, _ stands for any single character. __ ("double blank") stands for any sequence of one or more characters, and ___ ("triple blank") stands for any sequence of zero or more characters. __ and ___ will normally grab as much of the string as they can.

Pick out the sequence of characters between [and]:

In[4]:= **StringCases["the [important] word", "[" ~~ x__ ~~ "]" → Framed[x]]**

Out[4]= {| important |}

__ normally matches as long a sequence of characters as it can:

In[5]:= **StringCases["now [several] important [words]", "[" ~~ x__ ~~ "]" → Framed[x]]**

Out[5]= {| several] important [words |}

Shortest forces the shortest match:

In[6]:= **StringCases["now [several] important [words]",**
         "[" ~~ Shortest[x__] ~~ "]" → Framed[x]]

Out[6]= {| several |, | words |}

StringCases picks out cases of a particular pattern in a string. StringReplace makes replacements.

Make replacements for characters in the string:

In[7]:= **StringReplace["now [several] important [words]", {"[" → "<<", "]" → ">>"}]**

Out[7]= now <<several>> important <<words>>

Make replacements for patterns, using :→ to compute ToUpperCase in each case:

In[8]:= **StringReplace["now [several] important [words]",**
"[" ~~ Shortest[x__] ~~ "]" :→ ToUpperCase[x]]

Out[8]= now SEVERAL important WORDS

Use NestList to apply a string replacement repeatedly:

In[9]:= **NestList[StringReplace[#, {"A" → "AB", "B" → "BA"}] &, "A", 5]**

Out[9]= {A, AB, ABBA, ABBABAAB, ABBABAABBAABABBA, ABBABAABBAABABBABAABABBAABBABAAB}

StringMatchQ tests whether a string matches a pattern.

Select common words that match the pattern of beginning with a and ending with b:

In[10]:= **Select[WordList[ ], StringMatchQ[#, "a" ~~ ___ ~~ "b"] &]**

Out[10]= {absorb, adsorb, adverb, alb, aplomb}

You can use | and .. in string patterns just like in ordinary patterns.

Pick out any sequence of A or B repeated:

In[11]:= **StringCases["the AAA and the BBB and the ABABBBABABABA", ("A" | "B")..]**

Out[11]= {AAA, BBB, ABABBBABABABA}

In a string pattern, LetterCharacter stands for any letter character, DigitCharacter for any digit character and Whitespace for any sequence of "white" characters such as spaces.

Pick out sequences of digit characters:

In[12]:= **StringCases["12 and 123 and 4567 and 0x456", DigitCharacter..]**

Out[12]= {12, 123, 4567, 0, 456}

Pick out sequences of digit characters "flanked" by whitespace:

In[13]:= **StringCases["12 and 123 and 4567 and 0x456",**
Whitespace ~~ DigitCharacter.. ~~ Whitespace]

Out[13]= { 123 , 4567 }

It's common in practice to want to go back and forth between strings and lists. You can split a string into a list of pieces using StringSplit.

Split a string into a list of pieces, by default breaking at spaces:

In[14]:= **StringSplit["a string to split"]**

Out[14]= {a, string, to, split}

This uses a string pattern to decide where to split:

In[15]:= **StringSplit["you+can+split−−at+any−−delimiter", "+" | "−−"]**

Out[15]= {you, can, split, at, any, delimiter}

Within strings, there's a special newline character which indicates where the string should break onto a new line. The newline character is represented within strings as \n.

Split at newlines:

In[16]:= **StringSplit["first line**
second line
third line", "\n"]

Out[16]= {first line, second line, third line}

StringJoin joins any list of strings together. In practice, though, one often wants to insert something between the strings before joining them. StringRiffle does this.

Join strings, riffling the string "−−−" in between them:

In[17]:= **StringRiffle[{"a", "list", "of", "strings"}, "−−−"]**

Out[17]= a−−−list−−−of−−−strings

In assembling strings, one often wants to turn arbitrary Wolfram Language expressions into strings. One can do this using TextString.

TextString turns numbers and other Wolfram Language expressions into strings:

In[18]:= **StringJoin["two to the ", TextString[50], " is ", TextString[2^50]]**

Out[18]= two to the 50 is 1125899906842624

A more convenient way to create strings from expressions is to use *string templates*. String templates work like pure functions in that they have slots into which arguments can be inserted.

In a string template each `` ` ` `` is a slot for a successive argument:

In[19]:= **StringTemplate["first `` ` ` `` then `` ` ` ``"][100, 200]**

Out[19]= first 100 then 200

Named slots pick elements from an association:

In[20]:= **StringTemplate["first: `a`; second `b`; first again `a`"][**
<| "a" → "AAAA", "b" → "BB BBB" |>]

Out[20]= first: AAAA; second BB BBB; first again AAAA

You can insert any expression within a string template by enclosing it with <*...*>. The value of the expression is computed when the template is applied.

Evaluate the <*...*> when the template is applied; no arguments are needed:

In[21]:= **StringTemplate["2 to the 50 is <* 2^50 *>"][]**

Out[21]= 2 to the 50 is 1125899906842624

Use slots in the template (` ` is the backquote character):

In[22]:= **StringTemplate["` 1 ` to the ` 2 ` is <* #1^#2 *>"][2, 50]**

Out[22]= 2 to the 50 is 1125899906842624

The expression in the template is evaluated when the template is applied:

In[23]:= **StringTemplate["the time now is <* Now *>"][ ]**

Out[23]= the time now is Wed 16 Sep 2015 16:50:43

Vocabulary

$patt_1$ ~~ $patt_2$	sequence of string patterns
Shortest[$patt$ **]**	shortest sequence that matches
StringCases[$string, patt$ **]**	cases within a string matching a pattern
StringReplace[$string, patt \to val$ **]**	replace a pattern within a string
StringMatchQ[$string, patt$ **]**	test whether a string matches a pattern
LetterCharacter	pattern construct matching a letter
DigitCharacter	pattern construct matching a digit
Whitespace	pattern construct matching spaces, etc.
\n	newline character
StringSplit[$string$ **]**	split a string into a list of pieces
StringJoin[{ $string_1, string_2, ...$ **}]**	join strings together
StringRiffle [{ $string_1, string_2, ...$ **}, m]**	join strings, inserting m between them
TextString[$expr$ **]**	make a text string out of anything
StringTemplate[$string$ **]**	create a string template to apply
` ` ` `	slot in a string template
<*...*>	expression to evaluate in a string template

Exercises

42.1 Replace each space in "1 2 3 4" with "−−−".

42.2 Get a sorted list of all sequences of 4 digits (representing possible dates) in the Wikipedia article on computers.

42.3 Extract "headings" in the Wikipedia article about computers, as indicated by strings starting and ending with "===".

42.4 Use a string template to make a grid of results of the form i + j = … for i and j up to 9.

42.5 Find names of integers below 50 that have an "i" somewhere before an "e".

42.6 Make any 2-letter word uppercase in the first sentence from the Wikipedia article on computers.

42.7 Make a labeled bar chart of the number of countries whose TextString names start with each possible letter.

42.8 Find simpler code for
Grid[Table[StringJoin[TextString[i], "^", TextString[j], "=", TextString[i^j]], {i, 5}, {j, 5}]].

Q&A

How should one read ~~ out loud?

It's usually read "tilde tilde". The underlying function is StringExpression.

How does one type `` to make a slot in a string template?

It's a pair of what are usually called backquote or backtick characters. On many keyboards, they're at the top left, along with ~ (tilde).

Can I write rules for understanding natural language?

Yes, but we didn't cover that here. The key function is GrammarRules.

What does TextString do when things don't have an obvious textual form?

It does its best to make something human readable, but if all else fails, it'll fall back on InputForm.

Tech Notes

- There's a correspondence between patterns for strings, and patterns for sequences in lists. SequenceCases is the analog for lists of StringCases for strings.

- The option Overlaps specifies whether or not to allow overlaps in string matching. Different functions have different defaults.

- String patterns by default match longest sequences, so you need to specify Shortest if you want it. Expression patterns by default match shortest sequences.

- Among string pattern constructs are Whitespace, NumberString, WordBoundary, StartOfLine, EndOfLine, StartOfString and EndOfString.

- Anywhere in a Wolfram Language symbolic string pattern, you can use RegularExpression to include regular expression syntaxes like $x*$ and $[abc][def]$.

- TextString tries to make a simple human-readable textual version of anything, dropping things like the details of graphics. ToString[InputForm[$expr$]] gives a complete version, suitable for subsequent input.

- You can compare strings using operations like SequenceAlignment. This is particularly useful in bioinformatics.

- FileTemplate, XMLTemplate and NotebookTemplate let you do the analog of StringTemplate for files, XML (and HTML) documents and notebooks.

- The Wolfram Language includes the function TextSearch, for searching text in large collections of files.

More to Explore

Guide to String Patterns in the Wolfram Language (wolfr.am/eiwl-42-more)

43 | Storing Things

The Wolfram Language makes it easy to store things either in the Wolfram Cloud, or locally on your computer system. Let's talk about the Wolfram Cloud first.

In the Wolfram Cloud everything is a *cloud object,* specified by a UUID (universally unique identifier).

Cloud objects are immediately assigned a UUID:

In[1]:= **CloudObject[]**

Out[1]= CloudObject[https://www.wolframcloud.com/objects/388b0fd0–7769–42e4–a992–7d1b9985fe55]

As soon as you create a cloud object, it's assigned a long randomly generated UUID. The great thing about UUIDs is that one can assume that there'll never be two of the same generated. (There are 300 trillion trillion trillion possible Wolfram UUIDs.)

Put a Wolfram Language expression into the cloud:

In[2]:= **CloudPut[{**  **}]**

Out[2]= CloudObject[https://www.wolframcloud.com/objects/715b04e7–e589–4ebb–8b88–dde32fe0718b]

Get the expression back from the cloud:

In[3]:= **CloudGet[%]**

Out[3]= {  }

If you've made definitions using = and :=, you can save these using CloudSave. (If your definitions depend on other definitions, these will get saved too.) You can load your definitions into a new session using CloudGet.

Make a definition:

In[4]:= **colorlist[n_Integer] := RandomColor[n]**

Save it in the cloud to be retrieved later using CloudGet:

In[5]:= **CloudSave[colorlist]**

Out[5]= CloudObject[https://www.wolframcloud.com/objects/b274c11e–88c2–44d9–b805–599dbf7f898e]

CloudPut lets you store single Wolfram Language expressions. But what if you want to progressively accumulate expressions—coming either from within the Wolfram Language, or, say, from an outside device or sensor?

The Wolfram Data Drop lets you do exactly this. You start by creating a databin. You can do this in the Wolfram Language using CreateDatabin.

Create a databin:

In[6]:= **bin = CreateDatabin[]**

Out[6]= Databin

You can add data to this databin from all sorts of outside devices and services—as well as using the DatabinAdd function in the Wolfram Language.

Add an entry to a databin:

In[7]:= **DatabinAdd[bin, {1, 2, 3, 4}]**

Out[7]= Databin

Add another entry to the same databin:

In[8]:= **DatabinAdd[bin, {a, b, c}]**

Out[8]= Databin

Get the values stored in the databin:

In[9]:= **Values[bin]**

Out[9]= {{1, 2, 3, 4}, {a, b, c}}

Here's a databin that's accumulated data from a little sensor on my desk. DateListPlot plots the time series of data.

Use a short ID to reference a databin connected to sensors on my desk:

In[10]:= **Databin["7m3ujLVf"]**

Out[10]= Databin

Plot time series from the databin:

In[11]:= **DateListPlot[Databin["7m3ujLVf"]]**

Out[11]=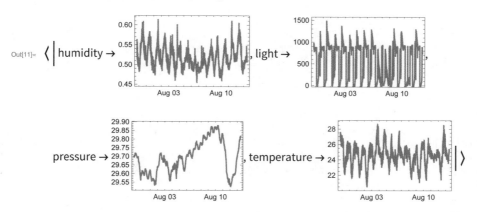

Wolfram Data Drop, like CloudPut and CloudSave, saves data into the cloud. But particularly if you're not connected to the cloud, you may instead want to store things on a local computer. If you figure out where in your filesystem you want the files to go, you can use Put, Save and Get to store and retrieve them.

It's also possible to get the Wolfram Language to automatically figure out an "anonymous" local location. You can do this with LocalObject.

Generate an "anonymous" location for Put, Save, etc.:

In[12]:= **LocalObject[ ]**

Out[12]= LocalObject[file:///Users/sw/Library/Wolfram/Objects/365e034d–9830–4842–8681–75d3714b3d19]

Put an image to the location:

In[13]:= **Put[** 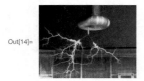 **, %]**

Out[13]= LocalObject[file:///Users/sw/Library/Wolfram/Objects/365e034d–9830–4842–8681–75d3714b3d19]

Get the image back:

In[14]:= **Get[%]**

Out[14]=

Vocabulary

CloudObject[ ]	create a cloud object
CloudPut[*expr*]	put into the cloud
CloudGet[*obj*]	get from the cloud
CloudSave[*s*]	save definitions to the cloud
Databin["*id*"]	a databin with accumulated data
CreateDatabin[ ]	create a new databin
DatabinAdd[*obj*, *value*]	add something to a databin
DateListPlot[*data*]	make a date list plot
LocalObject[ ]	create a local object
Put[*expr*, *obj*]	put into a local object
Get[*obj*]	get from a local object

Q&A

What do the letters and numbers in UUIDs mean?

They're digits in hexadecimal (base 16); the letters "a" through "f" are the hex digits 10 through 15. Each UUID has 32 hex digits, corresponding to $16 \wedge 32 \approx 3 \times 10^{38}$ possibilities.

How does the number of possible UUIDs compare to other things?

It's about the number of atoms in a cubic kilometer of water, or 100 trillion times the number of stars in the universe. If every one of 50 billion computers on Earth generated a UUID at 10 GHz, it'd take the age of the universe to run out of UUIDs.

How do UUIDs relate to short IDs?

All short IDs as generated by URLShorten are explicitly registered, and guaranteed to be unique, a bit like domain names on the internet. UUIDs are long enough that they can be assumed to be unique, even without any kind of central registration.

Can I specify a file name in CloudObject, CloudPut, etc.?

Yes. And the file name will be taken to be relative to your home directory in the cloud. The file will also get a URL, that includes the base of the cloud you're using, and your user ID.

Can other people access what I store in a cloud object?

Not usually. But if you set the option Permissions → "Public" then everyone can access it, just like we discussed for web apps in Section 36. You can also define exactly who you want to allow to do what with it.

Can I work with databins without using the Wolfram Language?

Yes. You can use the web and many other systems to create and add to databins.

Is there a way to manipulate an expression in the cloud, without getting the whole expression?

Yes. Make it a cloud expression (using CreateCloudExpression). Then all the usual ways of getting and setting parts of the expression will work, but the expression will be persistently stored in the cloud.

Tech Notes

- When you work in the cloud, Wolfram Notebook documents are automatically stored after every change you make—unless you say not to do this.

- You can save large objects more efficiently with **DumpSave** than **Save**, but then the file you create is binary, not text.

- **LocalCache[CloudObject[...]]** is a way to refer to a cloud object, but to use a local cache of its contents if that's available (and create it if it's not).

- Databins can have *data signatures*, that specify how data in them should be interpreted, for example in terms of units, date formats, etc.

- An assignment like x = 3 lasts only for the duration of a Wolfram Language session. But you can use things like **PersistentValue["x"]** = 3 to store values with different degrees of persistence (on a single computer; whenever you log in; for a certain time; etc.)

More to Explore

Guide to Files in the Wolfram Language (wolfr.am/eiwl-43-more)

Wolfram Data Drop (wolfr.am/eiwl-43-more2)

44 | Importing and Exporting

Everything we've done so far in this book has been done entirely within the Wolfram Language and the Wolfram Knowledgebase. But sometimes you need to get things from the outside. Needless to say, they often won't be as clean and organized as what we're used to inside the Wolfram Language—and they may change without warning.

As a first example, let's import the text from the front page of the United Nations website. We can do this using the function Import.

Import a text version of the front page of the UN website (it might be different now):

In[1]:= **Import["http://un.org"]**

Out[1]= عالمك إنها — المتحدة الأمم
联合国，您的世界！
United Nations — It's your world!
Nations Unies — C'est votre monde!
Организация Объединенных Наций — это ваш мир!
Las Naciones Unidas son su mundo

The result is a string, possibly with some blank lines. Let's start by splitting the string at newlines.

Split at newlines to get a list of strings:

In[2]:= **StringSplit[Import["http://un.org"], "\n"]**

Out[2]= {عالمك إنها — المتحدة الأمم , 联合国，您的世界！ ,
United Nations — It's your world!, Nations Unies — C'est votre monde!,
Организация Объединенных Наций — это ваш мир!,
Las Naciones Unidas son su mundo}

Identify the language for each string (blank lines are considered English):

In[3]:= **LanguageIdentify[StringSplit[Import["http://un.org"], "\n"]]**

Out[3]= { Arabic , Chinese , English , French , Russian , Spanish }

Import lets you import a wide variety of different elements. "Hyperlinks" gets hyperlinks that appear on a webpage; "Images" gets images.

Get a list of the hyperlinks on the front of the UN website:

In[4]:= **Import["http://un.org", "Hyperlinks"]**

Out[4]= {//www.un.org/ar/index.html, //www.un.org/zh/index.html, //www.un.org/en/index.html,
//www.un.org/fr/index.html, //www.un.org/ru/index.html, //www.un.org/es/index.html}

Get the images on the front page of Wikipedia:

In[5]:= **Import["http://wikipedia.org", "Images"]**

Out[5]= {  }

As a more sophisticated example, here's a graph of the hyperlinks in part of my website. To keep it manageable, I've taken just the first 5 hyperlinks at each level, and gone only 3 levels.

Compute part of the hyperlink graph for my website:

In[6]:= **NestGraph[Take[Import[♯, "Hyperlinks"], 5] &, "http://stephenwolfram.com", 3]**

Out[6]=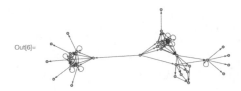

The Wolfram Language can import hundreds of formats—including spreadsheets, images, sounds, geometry, databases, log files and more. Import will automatically look at the file extension (.png, .xls, etc.) to determine what to do.

Import a picture from my website:

In[7]:= **Import[**
"http://www.stephenwolfram.com/img/homepage/stephen–wolfram–portrait.png"]

Out[7]=

The Wolfram Language recognizes me!

In[8]:= **Classify["NotablePerson", %]**

Out[8]= Stephen Wolfram

As well as importing from the web, Import can also import from your own files, stored in your computer system or in the Wolfram Cloud.

The Wolfram Language lets you not only deal with webpages and files, but also with *services* or *APIs*. For example, SocialMediaData lets you get data from social media services—at least once you've authorized them to send the data.

Find the network of my Facebook friends who give access to their connection data:

In[9]:= **SocialMediaData["Facebook", "FriendNetwork"]**

Out[9]=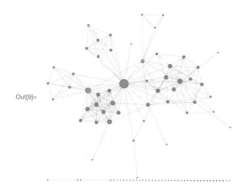

Another external service the Wolfram Language can access is web search.

Search for images on the web using the keywords "colorful birds":

In[10]:= **WebImageSearch["colorful birds"]**

Out[10]=

Thumbnail	PageTitle	PageHyperlink
	Colorful Birds Wallpapers 1024x768	http://free1024wallpapers.
	Life is Better with a Cute Outfit: Colorful Birds Wallpapers	http://lifeisbetterwithacute
	Colorful Birds Wallpapers 1024x768	http://free1024wallpapers.
	... colorful birds beautiful colorful birds beautiful colorful birds	http://lifeiz4fun.blogspot.c
	these colorful birds were great posers for photography. And they are ...	http://trans-pond.blogspot
	GALLERY FUNNY GAME: Beautiful Colorful Birds gallery	http://galleryfunnygame.bl
	AJORBAHMAN'S COLLECTION: COLORFUL BIRDS	http://ajorbahman.blogsp
	The Pate Potpourri: Colorful Birds Make Ava Happy Too!	http://thepatepotpourri.bl
	Colorful Birds Wallpapers 1024x768	http://free1024wallpapers.
	Cool Daily Pics: Beautiful Colorful Birds	http://cooldailypics.blogsp

Request image thumbnails:

In[11]:= **WebImageSearch["colorful birds", "Thumbnails"]**

Out[11]=

They're recognized as different kinds of birds:

In[12]:= **ImageIdentify/@%**

Out[12]=

An important source of external data for the Wolfram Language is the Wolfram Data Repository. The data in this repository comes from many places—but it's all been set up to be easy to work with in the Wolfram Language.

You can find out what's available by browsing the Wolfram Data Repository.

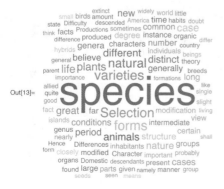

Once you've found something you want, just use ResourceData["*name*"] to get it into the Wolfram Language.

Get the full text of Darwin's *On the Origin of Species*, then make a word cloud of it:

In[13]:= **WordCloud[ResourceData["On the Origin of Species"]]**

Out[13]=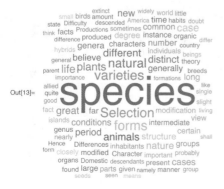

In addition to getting things into the Wolfram Language, you can also send things out. For example, SendMail sends email from the Wolfram Language.

Send oneself a message by email (for me it's sending to me):

In[14]:= **SendMail["Hello from the Wolfram Language!"]**

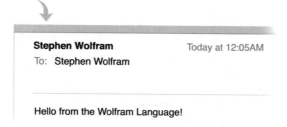

If you want to interact with external programs and services, you'll often have to *export* things from the Wolfram Language.

Send email to a test account with subject "Wolf" and a picture of a wolf attached:

In[15]:= **SendMail["test@wolfram.com", {"Wolf", "Here's a wolf...",** **}]**

If you want to interact with external programs and services, you'll often have to *export* things from the Wolfram Language.

Export a graphic of a circle to the cloud in PDF format:

In[16]:= **CloudExport[Graphics[Circle[]], "PDF"]**

Out[16]= CloudObject[https://www.wolframcloud.com/objects/6d93f2de–6597–4d9f–9edb–7cdc342571b8]

You can also export to local files using Export.

Export a table of primes and their powers to a local spreadsheet file:

In[17]:= **Export["primepowers.xls", Table[Prime[m]^n, {m, 10}, {n, 4}]]**

Out[17]= primepowers.xls

Here's part of the resulting file:

	A	B	C	D	E	F
1	2	4	8	16		
2	3	9	27	81		
3	5	25	125	625		
4	7	49	343	2401		
5	11	121	1331	14641		
6	13	169	2197	28561		
7	17	289	4913	83521		
8	19	361	6859	130321		
9	23	529	12167	279841		
10	29	841	24389	707281		
11						
12						

Import the contents of the file back into the Wolfram Language:

In[18]:= **Import["primepowers.xls"]**

Out[18]= {{{2., 4., 8., 16.}, {3., 9., 27., 81.}, {5., 25., 125., 625.}, {7., 49., 343., 2401.},
{11., 121., 1331., 14641.}, {13., 169., 2197., 28561.}, {17., 289., 4913., 83521.},
{19., 361., 6859., 130321.}, {23., 529., 12167., 279841.}, {29., 841., 24389., 707281.}}}

The Wolfram Language can import and export hundreds of formats, of many different kinds.

Export 3D geometry in a format suitable for 3D printing:

In[19]:= **Export["spikey.stl", ▤ rhombic hexecontahedron ["Image"]]**

Out[19]= spikey.stl

Here's the result of 3D printing from the spikey.stl file:

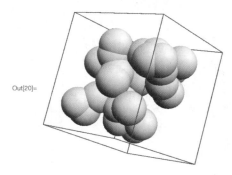

Creating 3D geometry in a form suitable for printing can be quite complicated. The function Printout3D does all the steps automatically—and it can also send the final geometry to a 3D printing service (or to your own 3D printer, if you have one).

Make a random clump of spheres:

In[20]:= **Graphics3D[Sphere[RandomReal[5, {30, 3}]]]**

Out[20]=

Send this for 3D printing to the Sculpteo service:

In[21]:= **Printout3D[%, "Sculpteo"]**

Out[21]=

Status	Successful
Service	sculpteo
Image	
Size	2.1 in × 2.0 in × 2.1 in
Material	Metal (Laser melting)
URL	http://www.sculpteo.com/gallery/design/ext/423MbGJ...
Report	...

Vocabulary

Import[*loc***]**	import from an external location
SocialMediaData[...]	get data from social media networks
WebImageSearch[*"keyword"***]**	do an image search on the web
ResourceData[*"name"***]**	get data from the Wolfram Data Repository
SendMail[*expr***]**	send email
CloudExport[*expr, format***]**	export in a certain format to the cloud
Export[*file, expr***]**	export to a file
Printout3D[*source, "service"***]**	send *source* to a 3D printer service

Exercises

44.1 Import the images from http://google.com.

44.2 Make an image collage of disks with the dominant colors from images on http://google.com.

44.3 Make a word cloud of the text on http://bbc.co.uk.

44.4 Make an image collage of the images on http://nps.gov.

44.5 Use ImageInstanceQ to find pictures on https://en.wikipedia.org/wiki/Ostrich that are of birds.

44.6 Use TextCases with "Country" to find instances of country names on http://nato.int, and make a word cloud of them.

44.7 Find the number of links on https://en.wikipedia.org.

44.8 Send yourself mail with a map of your current location.

44.9 Send yourself mail with an icon of the current phase of the moon.

Q&A

Why do I get different results when I run the website examples?

Because the websites have changed! You'll get whatever they have on them now.

Why doesn't Import retrieve elements that I see when I visit a webpage in a browser?

Probably because they're not directly present in the HTML source of the webpage, which is what Import looks at. They're probably being dynamically added using JavaScript.

Can I import a local file from my computer if I'm using the cloud?

Yes. Use the upload ⬆ button in the cloud system to upload the file into your cloud file system, then use Import.

What formats can Import handle?

See the list at wolfr.am/ref-importexport or evaluate $ImportFormats.

How do Import and Export figure out what format to use?

You can explicitly tell them. Or they can determine it from file extensions, like .gif or .mbox.

Where does Export put the files it creates?

If you don't give a directory in the file name you specify, it'll go in your current directory. You can open it as your operating system would using SystemOpen, and you can delete it with DeleteFile.

What is an API?

An application program interface. It's an interface that a program exposes to other programs, rather than to humans. The Wolfram Language has several APIs, and lets you create your own using APIFunction.

How do I authorize a connection to an external account of mine?

When you use SocialMediaData or ServiceConnect, you'll typically be prompted to authorize the Wolfram Connection app for that particular service.

Tech Notes

- **ImportString** lets you "import" from a string rather than from an external file or URL. **ExportString** "exports" to a string.

- **SendMail** uses either mail server preferences you set up, or a proxy in the Wolfram Cloud.

- The Wolfram Language supports many external services. Typically it uses mechanisms like OAuth to authenticate them.

- Another way to get (and send) data is through direct connection from your computer to a sensor, Arduino, etc. The Wolfram Language has a whole framework for dealing with such things, including functions such as **DeviceReadTimeSeries**.

- If you're running everything locally on your computer, you can have the Wolfram Language start external programs, and exchange data with them, for example using **RunProcess**. In simple cases, you'll often be able to just *pipe* data straight in from a program, say with **Import**["!program", …].

- The Wolfram Language supports asynchronous reading and writing of data. A simple case is **URLSubmit**, but **ChannelListen**, etc. allow you to set up a complete brokered *publish-subscribe* system.

More to Explore

Guide to Importing and Exporting in the Wolfram Language (wolfr.am/eiwl-44-more)

45 | Datasets

Especially in larger organizations, computing often centers around dealing with large amounts of structured data. The Wolfram Language has a very powerful way to deal with structured data, using what it calls *datasets*.

A simple example of a dataset is formed from an association of associations.

Create a simple dataset that can be viewed as having 2 rows and 3 columns:

In[1]:= **data = Dataset[**
⟨| "a" → ⟨| "x" → 1, "y" → 2, "z" → 3 |⟩, "b" → ⟨| "x" → 5, "y" → 10, "z" → 7 |⟩ |⟩]

Out[1]=
	x	y	z
a	1	2	3
b	5	10	7

The Wolfram Language displays most datasets in tabular form. You can extract parts from datasets just like you would from associations.

Get the element from "row b" and "column z":

In[2]:= **data["b", "z"]**

Out[2]= 7

You can first extract the whole "b row", then get the "z" element of the result:

In[3]:= **data["b"]["z"]**

Out[3]= 7

You can also just get the whole "b row" of the dataset. The result is a new dataset, which for ease of reading happens to be displayed in this case as a column.

Generate a new dataset from the "b row" of the original dataset:

In[4]:= **data["b"]**

Out[4]=
x	5
y	10
z	7

Here is the dataset that corresponds to the "z column" for all "rows".

Generate a dataset consisting of the "z column" for all rows:

In[5]:= **data[All, "z"]**

Out[5]=
a	3
b	7

Extracting parts of datasets is just the beginning. Anywhere you can ask for a part you can also give a function that will be applied to all parts at that level.

Get totals for each row by applying Total to all columns for all the rows:

In[6]:= **data[All, Total]**

Out[6]=

a	6
b	22

If we use f instead of Total, we can see what's going on: the function is being applied to each of the "row" associations.

Apply the function f to each row:

In[7]:= **data[All, f]**

Out[7]=

a	f [⟨| "x" → 1, "y" → 2, "z" → 3 |⟩]
b	f [⟨| "x" → 5, "y" → 10, "z" → 7 |⟩]

Apply a function that adds the x and z elements of each association:

In[8]:= **data[All, #x + #z &]**

Out[8]=

a	4
b	12

You can use any function; here's PieChart:

In[9]:= **data[All, PieChart]**

Out[9]=

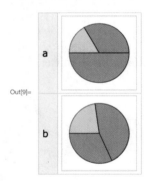

You can give a function to apply to all rows too.

This extracts the value of each "z column", then applies f to the association of results:

In[10]:= **data[f, "z"]**

Out[10]= f[⟨\| a → 3, b → 7 \|⟩]

Apply f to the totals of all columns:

In[11]:= **data[f, Total]**

Out[11]= f[⟨\| a → 6, b → 22 \|⟩]

Find the maximum of these totals:

In[12]:= **data[Max, Total]**

Out[12]= 22

You can always "chain" queries, for example first finding the totals for all rows, then picking out the result for the "b row".

Find totals for all rows, then pick out the total for the "b row":

In[13]:= **data[All, Total]["b"]**

Out[13]= 22

It's equivalent to this:

In[14]:= **data["b", Total]**

Out[14]= 22

Particularly when one's dealing with large datasets, it's common to want to select parts based on a criterion. The *operator form* of Select provides a very convenient way to do this.

Select numbers greater than 5 from a list:

In[15]:= **Select[{1, 3, 6, 8, 2, 5, 9, 7}, ⌗ > 5 &]**

Out[15]= {6, 8, 9, 7}

Another way to get the same answer, using the operator form of Select:

In[16]:= **Select[⌗ > 5 &][{1, 3, 6, 8, 2, 5, 9, 7}]**

Out[16]= {6, 8, 9, 7}

The operator form of Select is a function which can be applied to actually perform the Select operation.

Make a dataset by selecting only rows whose "z column" is greater than 5:

In[17]:= **data[Select[⌗z > 5 &]]**

Out[17]=

	x	y	z
b	5	10	7

For each row, select columns whose values are greater than 5, leaving a ragged structure:

In[18]:= **data[All, Select[⌗ > 5 &]]**

Out[18]=

Normal turns the dataset into an ordinary association of associations:

In[19]:= **Normal[%]**

Out[19]= ⟨| a → ⟨| |⟩ , b → ⟨| y → 10, z → 7 |⟩ |⟩

Many Wolfram Language functions have operator forms.

Sort according to the values of a function applied to each element:

In[20]:= **SortBy[{1, 3, 6, 8, 2, 5, 9, 7}, If[EvenQ[#], #, 10+#] &]**

Out[20]= {2, 6, 8, 1, 3, 5, 7, 9}

SortBy has an operator form:

In[21]:= **SortBy[If[EvenQ[#], #, 10+#] &][{1, 3, 6, 8, 2, 5, 9, 7}]**

Out[21]= {2, 6, 8, 1, 3, 5, 7, 9}

Sort rows according to the value of the difference of the x and y columns:

In[22]:= **data[SortBy[#x − #y &]]**

Out[22]=

	x	y	z
b	5	10	7
a	1	2	3

Sort the rows, and find the total of all columns:

In[23]:= **data[SortBy[#x − #y &], Total]**

Out[23]=

b	22
a	6

Sometimes you want to apply a function to each element in the dataset.

Apply f to each element in the dataset:

In[24]:= **data[All, All, f]**

Out[24]=

	x	y	z
a	f[1]	f[2]	f[3]
b	f[5]	f[10]	f[7]

Sort the rows before totaling the squares of their elements:

In[25]:= **data[SortBy[#x − #y &], Total, #^2 &]**

Out[25]=

b	174
a	14

Datasets can contain arbitrary mixtures of lists and associations. Here's a dataset that can be thought of as a *list of records* with named *fields*.

A dataset formed from a list of associations:

In[26]:= **Dataset[{ <| "x" → 2, "y" → 4, "z" → 6 |> , <| "x" → 11, "y" → 7, "z" → 1 |> }]**

Out[26]=

x	y	z
2	4	6
11	7	1

It's OK for entries to be missing:

In[27]:= **Dataset[{ <| "x" → 2, "y" → 4, "z" → 6 |> , <| "x" → 11, "y" → 7 |> }]**

Out[27]=

x	2
y	4
3 total >	
x	11
y	7

Now that we've seen some simple examples, it's time to look at something slightly more realistic. Let's import a dataset giving properties of planets and moons. The dataset has a hierarchical structure, with each planet having a mass and radius of its own, and then also having a collection of moons, each of which have their own properties. This general structure is extremely common in practice (think students and grades, customers and orders, etc.).

Get a hierarchical dataset of planets and moons from the cloud:

In[28]:= **planets = CloudGet["http://wolfr.am/7FxLgPm5"]**

Out[28]=

	Mass	Radius	Moons		
				Mass	Radius
Mercury	3.30104×10^{23} kg	2439.7 km			
Venus	4.86732×10^{24} kg	6051.9 km			
Earth	5.9721986×10^{24} kg	6371.0088 km	Moon	7.3459×10^{22} kg	1737.5 km
Mars	6.41693×10^{23} kg	3386. km	Deimos	1.5×10^{15} kg	6.2 km
			Phobos	1.072×10^{16} kg	11.1 km
Jupiter	1.89813×10^{27} kg	69911 km	Adrastea	$7. \times 10^{15}$ kg	8.2 km
			Aitne	$4. \times 10^{13}$ kg	1.5 km
			67 total >		
Saturn	5.68319×10^{26} kg	57316. km	Aegaeon	—	0.25 km
			Aegir	—	3.0 km
			62 total >		
Uranus	8.68103×10^{25} kg	25266. km	Ariel	1.35×10^{21} kg	578.9 km
			Belinda	3.57×10^{17} kg	40.3 km
			27 total >		
Neptune	1.02410×10^{26} kg	24553. km	Despina	2.1×10^{18} kg	75. km
			Galatea	3.7×10^{18} kg	88. km
			14 total >		

Find the radii of all the planets:

In[29]:= **planets[All, "Radius"]**

Out[29]=

Mercury	2439.7 km
Venus	6051.9 km
Earth	6371.0088 km
Mars	3386. km
Jupiter	69 911 km
Saturn	57 316. km
Uranus	25 266. km
Neptune	24 553. km

Make a bar chart of planet radii:

In[30]:= **BarChart[planets[All, "Radius"], ChartLabels → Automatic]**

Out[30]=

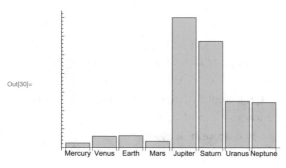

If we ask about the moons of Mars, we get a dataset, which we can then query further.

Get a dataset about the moons of Mars:

In[31]:= **planets["Mars", "Moons"]**

Out[31]=

	Mass	Radius
Deimos	1.5×10^{15} kg	6.2 km
Phobos	1.072×10^{16} kg	11.1 km

"Drill down" to make a table of radii of all the moons of Mars:

In[32]:= **planets["Mars", "Moons", All, "Radius"]**

Out[32]=

Deimos	6.2 km
Phobos	11.1 km

We can do computations about the moons of all planets. First, let's just find out how many moons are listed for each planet.

Make a dataset of the number of moons listed for each planet:

In[33]:= **planets[All, "Moons", Length]**

Out[33]=

Mercury	0
Venus	0
Earth	1
Mars	2
Jupiter	67
Saturn	62
Uranus	27
Neptune	14

Find the total mass of all moons for each planet:

In[34]:= **planets[All, "Moons", Total, "Mass"]**

Out[34]=

Mercury	0
Venus	0
Earth	7.3459×10^{22} kg
Mars	1.22×10^{16} kg
Jupiter	3.9301×10^{23} kg
Saturn	1.4051×10^{23} kg
Uranus	9.14×10^{21} kg
Neptune	2.1487×10^{22} kg

Get the same result, but only for planets with more than 10 moons:

In[35]:= **planets[Select[Length[#Moons] > 10 &], "Moons", Total, "Mass"]**

Out[35]=

Jupiter	3.9301×10^{23} kg
Saturn	1.4051×10^{23} kg
Uranus	9.14×10^{21} kg
Neptune	2.1487×10^{22} kg

Make a pie chart of the result:

In[36]:= **PieChart[%, ChartLegends → Automatic]**

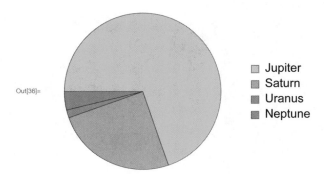

Out[36]=

Get a dataset with moons that are more than 1% of the mass of the Earth.

For all moons, select ones whose mass is greater than 0.01 times the mass of the Earth:

In[37]:= **planets[All, "Moons", Select[#Mass > ▤ .01 earth masses &]]**

Out[37]=

		Mass	Radius
Mercury			
Venus			
Earth	Moon	7.3459×10^{22} kg	1737.5 km
Mars			
Jupiter	Callisto	1.0757×10^{23} kg	2410.3 km
		3 total ›	
Saturn	Titan	1.3452×10^{23} kg	2575.5 km
Uranus			
Neptune			

Get the list of keys (i.e. moon names) in the resulting association for each planet:

In[38]:= **planets[All, "Moons", Select[#Mass > ▤ .01 earth masses &]][All, Keys]**

Out[38]=

Mercury	{}
Venus	{}
Earth	{Moon}
Mars	{}
Jupiter	{Callisto, Ganymede, Io}
Saturn	{Titan}
Uranus	{}
Neptune	{}

Get the underlying association:

In[39]:= **Normal[%]**

Out[39]= <| Mercury → {}, Venus → {}, Earth → {Moon}, Mars → {},
Jupiter → {Callisto, Ganymede, Io}, Saturn → {Titan}, Uranus → {}, Neptune → {} |>

Join together, or "catenate", the lists for all keys:

In[40]:= **Catenate[%]**

Out[40]= {Moon, Callisto, Ganymede, Io, Titan}

Here's the whole computation in one line:

In[41]:= **planets[All, "Moons", Select[♯Mass > ▤ .01 earth masses &]][Catenate, Keys] // Normal**

Out[41]= {Moon, Callisto, Ganymede, Io, Titan}

Here's one more example, where we find the logarithm of the mass of each moon, then make a number line plot of these values for each planet.

Make number line plots of the logarithms of masses for moons of each planet:

In[42]:= **planets[All, "Moons", NumberLinePlot[Values[♯]] &, Log[♯Mass/ ▤ 1 earth mass] &]**

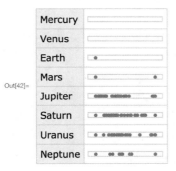

As a final example, let's make a word cloud of names of moons, sized according to the masses of the moons. To do this, we need a single association that associates the name of each moon with its mass.

When given an association, WordCloud determines sizes from values in the association:

In[43]:= **WordCloud[<| "A" → 5, "B" → 4, "C" → 3, "D" → 2, "E" → 1 |>]**

The function Association combines associations:

In[44]:= **Association[<| "a" → 1, "b" → 2 |>, <| "c" → 3 |>]**

Out[44]= <| a → 1, b → 2, c → 3 |>

Generate the word cloud of moon masses:

In[45]:= **planets[WordCloud[Association[Values[#]]] &, "Moons", All, "Mass"]**

Out[45]=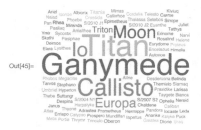

For what it does, the code here is surprisingly simple. But we can make it slightly more streamlined by using @* or /*.

We've seen before that we can write something like f[g[x]] as f @ g @ x or x // g // f. We can also write it f[g[#]] &[x]. But what about f[g[#]] &? Is there a short way to write this? The answer is that there is, in terms of the *function composition operators* @* and /*.

f @* g @* h represents a composition of functions to be applied right-to-left:

In[46]:= **(f @* g @* h)[x]**

Out[46]= f[g[h[x]]]

h /* g /* f represents a composition of functions to be applied left-to-right:

In[47]:= **(h /* g /* f)[x]**

Out[47]= f[g[h[x]]]

Here's the previous code rewritten using composition @*:

In[48]:= **planets[WordCloud @* Association @* Values, "Moons", All, "Mass"]**

Out[48]=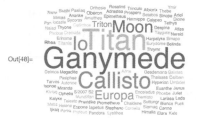

And using right composition /*:

In[49]:= **planets[Values /* Association /* WordCloud, "Moons", All, "Mass"]**

Out[49]=

As a final example, let's look at another dataset—this time coming straight from the Wolfram Data Repository. Here's a webpage (about big meteors) from the repository:

To get the main dataset that's mentioned here, just use ResourceData.

Get the dataset just by giving its name to ResourceData:

In[50]:= **fireballs = ResourceData["Fireballs and Bolides"]**

Out[50]=

PeakBrightness	Coordinates	NearestCity	Altitude	Velocity	VelocityXC
Thu 8 Oct 2009 02:57:00	4.2°S 120.6°E	Bone	19.1 km	19.2 km/s	14 km/s
Sat 21 Nov 2009 20:53:00	22.°S 29.2°E	Kobojango	38 km	32.1 km/s	3 km/s
Sat 25 Dec 2010 23:24:00	38.°N 158.°E	Kurilsk	26 km	18.1 km/s	18 km/s
Sat 21 Apr 2012 16:08:23	15.8°S 174.8°W	Hihifo	—	—	—
Mon 23 Apr 2012 22:01:10	36.2°N 107.4°E	Pingliang	25.2 km	—	—
Fri 4 May 2012 21:54:49	76.7°N 10.6°W	Illoqqortoormiut	—	—	—
Tue 15 May 2012 11:04:17	61.8°S 135.5°W	Owenga	33.3 km	—	−0.8 km/s
Fri 25 May 2012 11:31:24	41.8°S 36.2°W	Grytviken	—	—	—

K <   showing 1–8 of **92**   > >|

Extract the coordinates entry from each row, and plot the results:

In[51]:= **GeoListPlot[fireballs[All, "Coordinates"]]**

Out[51]=

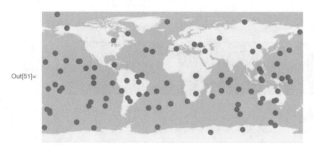

Make a histogram of the altitudes:

In[52]:= **Histogram[fireballs[All, "Altitude"]]**

Out[52]=

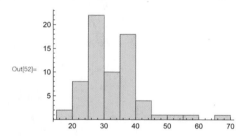

Vocabulary

Dataset[*data***]**	a dataset
Normal[*dataset***]**	convert a dataset to normal lists and associations
Catenate[{*assoc*$_1$**, ...}]**	catenate associations, combining their elements
f **@*** *g*	composition of functions (*f*[*g*[*x*]] when applied to *x*)
f **/*** *g*	right composition (*g*[*f*[x]] when applied to *x*)

Exercises

Note: These exercises use the dataset planets = CloudGet["http://wolfr.am/7FxLgPm5"].

45.1 Make a word cloud of the planets, with weights determined by their number of moons.

45.2 Make a bar chart of the number of moons for each planet.

45.3 Make a dataset of the masses of the planets, sorted by their number of moons.

45.4 Make a dataset of planets and the mass of each one's most massive moon.

45.5 Make a dataset of masses of planets, where the planets are sorted by the largest mass of their moons.

45.6 Make a dataset of the median mass of all moons for each planet.

45.7 For each planet, make a list of moons larger in mass than 0.0001 Earth masses.

45.8   Make a word cloud of countries in Central America, with the names of countries proportional to the lengths of the Wikipedia article about them.

45.9   Find the maximum observed altitude in the Fireballs & Bolides dataset.

45.10   Find a dataset of the 5 largest observed altitudes in the Fireballs & Bolides dataset.

45.11   Make a histogram of the differences in successive peak brightness times in the Fireballs & Bolides dataset.

45.12   Plot the nearest cities for the first 10 entries in the Fireballs & Bolides dataset, labeling each city.

45.13   Plot the nearest cities for the 10 entries with largest altitudes in the Fireballs & Bolides dataset, labeling each city.

Q&A

What kinds of data can datasets contain?

Any kinds. Not just numbers and text but also images, graphs and lots more. There's no need for all elements of a particular row or column to be the same type.

Can I turn spreadsheets into datasets?

Yes. SemanticImport is often a good way to do it.

What are databases and how do they relate to Dataset?

Databases are a traditional way to store structured data in a computer system. Databases are often set up to allow both reading and writing of data. Dataset is a way to represent data that might be stored in a database so that it's easy to manipulate with the Wolfram Language.

How does data in Dataset compare to data in an SQL (relational) database?

SQL databases are strictly based on tables of data arranged in rows and columns of particular types, with additional data linked in through "foreign keys". Dataset can have any mixture of types of data, with any number of levels of nesting, and any hierarchical structure, somewhat more analogous to a NoSQL database, but with additional operations made possible by the symbolic nature of the language.

Can I use datasets to set up entities and values for them?

Yes. If you've got a dataset that's an association of associations, with the outer keys being entities and the inner ones being properties, then you just have to put this inside EntityStore, and you'll pretty much have everything set up.

Tech Notes

- Dataset supports a new kind of *symbolic database structure* which generalizes both *relational* and *hierarchical databases*.

- Dataset has many additional mechanisms and capabilities that we haven't discussed.

- Everything that can be done with queries on datasets can also be done by using functions like **Map** and **Apply** on underlying lists and association—but it's typically much simpler with dataset queries.

- You can connect the Wolfram Language directly to SQL databases—and do queries with SQL syntax—using **DatabaseLink**.

More to Explore

Guide to Computation with Structured Datasets in the Wolfram Language (wolfr.am/eiwl-45-more)

46 | Writing Good Code

Writing good code is in many ways like writing good prose: you need to have your thoughts clear, and express them well. When you first start writing code, you'll most likely think about what your code does in English or whatever natural language you use. But as you become fluent in the Wolfram Language you'll start thinking directly in code, and it'll be faster for you to type a program than to describe what it does.

My goal as a language designer has been to make it as easy as possible to express things in the Wolfram Language. The functions in the Wolfram Language are much like the words in a natural language, and I've worked hard to choose them well.

Functions like Table or NestList or FoldList exist in the Wolfram Language because they express common things one wants to do. As in natural language, there are always many ways one can in principle express something. But good code involves finding the most direct and simple way.

To create a table of the first 10 squares in the Wolfram Language, there's an obvious good piece of code that just uses the function Table.

Simple and good Wolfram Language code for making a table of the first 10 squares:

In[1]:= **Table[n^2, {n, 10}]**

Out[1]= {1, 4, 9, 16, 25, 36, 49, 64, 81, 100}

Why would anyone write anything else? A common issue is not thinking about the "whole table", but instead thinking about the steps in building it. In the early days of computing, computers needed all the help they could get, and there was no choice but to give code that described every step to take.

A much worse piece of code that builds up the table step by step:

In[2]:= **Module[{list, i}, list = {}; For[i = 1, i ≤ 10, i++, list = Append[list, i^2]]; list]**

Out[2]= {1, 4, 9, 16, 25, 36, 49, 64, 81, 100}

But the point of the Wolfram Language is to let one express things at a higher level—and to create code that as directly as possible captures the concept of what one wants to do. Once one knows the language, it's vastly more efficient to operate at this level. And it leads to code that's easier for both computers and humans to understand.

In writing good code, it's important to ask frequently, "What's the big picture of what this code is trying to do?" Often you'll start off understanding only some part, and writing code just for that. But then you'll end up extending it, and adding more and more pieces to your code. But if you think about the big picture you may suddenly realize that there's some more powerful function—like a Fold—that you can use to make your code nice and simple again.

Make code to convert {*hundreds*, *tens*, *ones*} digits to a single integer:

In[3]:= **fromdigits[{h_ , t_ , o_ }] := 100 h + 10 t + o**

Run the code:

In[4]:= **fromdigits[{5, 6, 1}]**

Out[4]= 561

Write a generalization to a list of any length, using Table:

In[5]:= **fromdigits[list_List] := Total[Table[10 ^ (Length[list] − i) * list[[i]], {i, Length[list]}]]**

The new code works:

In[6]:= **fromdigits[{5, 6, 1, 7, 8}]**

Out[6]= 56 178

Simplify the code by multiplying the whole list of powers of 10 at the same time:

In[7]:= **fromdigits[list_List] := Total[10 ^ Reverse[Range[Length[list]] − 1] * list]**

Try a different, recursive, approach, after first clearing the earlier definitions:

In[8]:= **Clear[fromdigits]**

In[9]:= **fromdigits[{k_ }] := k**

In[10]:= **fromdigits[{digits_ _ _ , k_ }] := 10 * fromdigits[{digits}] + k**

The new approach works too:

In[11]:= **fromdigits[{5, 6, 1, 7, 8}]**

Out[11]= 56 178

But then you realize: it's actually all just a Fold!

In[12]:= **Clear[fromdigits]**

In[13]:= **fromdigits[list_] := Fold[10 * #1 + #2 &, list]**

In[14]:= **fromdigits[{5, 6, 1, 7, 8}]**

Out[14]= 56 178

Of course, there's a built-in function that does it too:

In[15]:= **FromDigits[{5, 6, 1, 7, 8}]**

Out[15]= 56 178

Why is it good for code to be simple? First, because it's more likely to be correct. It's much easier for a mistake to hide in a complicated piece of code than a simple one. Code that's simple is also usually more general, so it'll tend to cover even cases you didn't think of, and avoid you having to write more code. And finally, simple code tends to be much easier to read and understand. (Simpler isn't always the same as shorter, and in fact short "code poetry" can get hard to understand.)

An overly short version of fromdigits, that's starting to be difficult to understand:

In[16]:= **fromdigits = Fold[{10, 1}.{♯ ♯♯} &, ♯♯] & ;**

It still works though:

In[17]:= **fromdigits[{5, 6, 1, 7, 8}]**

Out[17]= 56 178

If what you're trying to do is complicated, then your code may inevitably need to be complicated. Good code, though, is broken up into functions and definitions that are each as simple and self-contained as possible. Even in very large Wolfram Language programs, there may be no individual definitions longer than a handful of lines.

Here's a single definition that combines several cases:

In[18]:= **fib[n_] := If[! IntegerQ[n] || n < 1, "Error", If[n == 1 || n == 2, 1, fib[n − 1] + fib[n − 2]]]**

It's much better to break it up into several simpler definitions:

In[19]:= **fib[1] = fib[2] = 1;**

In[20]:= **fib[n_Integer] := fib[n − 1] + fib[n − 2]**

A very important aspect of writing good code is choosing good names for your functions. For the built-in functions of the Wolfram Language, I've made a tremendous effort over the course of decades to pick names well—and to capture in their short names the essence of what the functions do, and how to think about them.

When you're writing code, it's common to first define a new function because you need it in some very specific context. But it's almost always worth trying to give it a name that you'll understand even outside that context. And if you can't find a good name, it's often a sign that it's not quite the right function to define in the first place.

A sign of a good function name is that when you read it in a piece of code, you immediately know what the code does. And indeed, it's an important feature of the Wolfram Language that it's typically easier to read and understand well-written code directly than from any kind of textual description of it.

How would one describe this in plain English?

In[21]:= **Graphics[**
         {White, Riffle[NestList[Scale[Rotate[♯, 0.1], 0.9] &, Rectangle[], 40], {Pink, Yellow}]}]

Out[21]=

When you write Wolfram Language code, you'll sometimes have to choose between using a single rare built-in function that happens to do exactly what you want—and building up the same functionality from several more common functions. In this book, I've sometimes chosen to avoid rare functions so as to minimize vocabulary. But the best code tends to use single functions whenever it can—because the name of the function explains the intent of the code in a way that individual pieces cannot.

Use a small piece of code to reverse the digits in an integer:

In[22]:= **FromDigits[Reverse[IntegerDigits[123 456]]]**

Out[22]= 654 321

Using a single built-in function explains the intent more clearly:

In[23]:= **IntegerReverse[123 456]**

Out[23]= 654 321

Good code needs to be correct and easy to understand. But it also needs to run efficiently. And in the Wolfram Language, simpler code is typically better here too— because by explaining your intent more clearly, it makes it easier for the Wolfram Language to optimize how the computations you need are done internally.

With every new version, the Wolfram Language does better at automatically figuring out how to make your code run fast. But you can always help by structuring your algorithms well.

Timing gives the timing of a computation (in seconds), together with its result:

In[24]:= **Timing[fib[20]]**

Out[24]= {0.021843, 6765}

Plot the time to compute fib[n] according to the definitions above.

With the definitions of fib above, the time grows very rapidly:

In[25]:= **ListLinePlot[Table[First[Timing[fib[n]]], {n, 20}]]**

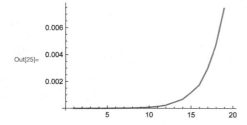

The algorithm we used happens to do an exponential amount of unnecessary work recomputing what it's already computed before. We can avoid this by making the definition for fib[n_] always do an assignment for fib[n], so it stores the result of each intermediate computation.

Redefine the fib function to remember every value it computes:

In[26]:= **fib[1] = fib[2] = 1;**

In[27]:= **fib[n_Integer] := fib[n] = fib[n − 1] + fib[n − 2]**

Now even up to 1000 each new value takes only microseconds to compute:

In[28]:= **ListLinePlot[Table[First[Timing[fib[n]]], {n, 1000}]]**

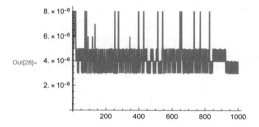

Out[28]=

Vocabulary

FromDigits[*list***]**	assemble an integer from its digits
IntegerReverse[*n***]**	reverse the digits in an integer
Timing[*expr***]**	do a computation, timing how long it takes

---

Exercises

46.1   Find a simpler form for Module[{a, i}, a = 0; For[i = 1, i ≤ 1000, i ++, a = i ∗ (i + 1) + a]; a].

46.2   Find a simpler form for Module[{a, i}, a = x; For[i = 1, i ≤ 10, i ++, a = 1 / (1 + a)]; a].

46.3   Find a simpler form for
Module[{i, j, a}, a = {}; For[i = 1, i ≤ 10, i ++, For[j = 1, j ≤ 10, j ++, a = Join[a, {i, j}]]]; a].

46.4   Make a line plot of the timing for computing n ^ n for n up to 10000.

46.5   Make a line plot of the timing for Sort to sort Range[n] from a random order, for n up to 200.

What does i ++ mean?

It's a short notation for i = i + 1. It's the same notation that C and many other low-level computer languages use for this increment operation.

What does the For function do?

It's a direct analog of the for (...) statement in C. For[*start*, *test*, *step*, *body*] first executes *start*, then checks *test*, then executes *step*, then *body*. It does this repeatedly until *test* no longer gives True.

Why can shortened pieces of code be hard to understand?

The most common issue is that variables and sometimes even functions have been factored out, so there are fewer names to read that might give clues about what the code is supposed to do.

What's the best IDE for authoring Wolfram Language code?

For everyday programming, Wolfram Notebooks are best. Make sure to add sections, text and examples right alongside your code. For large multi-developer software projects, Wolfram Workbench provides an Eclipse-based IDE.

What does Timing actually measure?

It measures the CPU time spent in the Wolfram Language actually computing your result. It doesn't include time to display the result. Nor does it include time spent on external operations, like fetching data from the cloud. If you want the absolute "wall clock" time, use AbsoluteTiming.

How can I get more accurate timings for code that runs fast?

Use RepeatedTiming, which runs code many times and averages the timings it gets. (This won't work if the code is modifying itself, like in the last definition of fib above.)

What are some tricks for speeding up code?

Beyond keeping the code simple, one thing is not to recompute anything you don't have to. Also, if you're dealing with lots of numbers, it may make sense to use N to force the numbers to be approximate. For some internal algorithms you can pick your PerformanceGoal, typically trading off speed and accuracy. There are also functions like Compile that force more of the work associated with optimization to be done up front, rather than during a computation.

- Complicated behavior can arise even from extremely simple code: that's what my 1280-page book *A New Kind of Science* is about. A good example is CellularAutomaton[30, {{1}, 0}].

- The fib function is computing Fibonacci [*n*]. The original definition always recurses down a whole tree of $O(\phi^n)$ values, where $\phi \approx 1.618$ is the golden ratio (GoldenRatio).

- Remembering values that a function has computed before is sometimes called memoization, sometimes dynamic programming and sometimes just caching.

- The function IntegerReverse was new in Version 10.3.

- For large programs, the Wolfram Language has a framework for isolating functions into *contexts* and *packages*.

- If[# 1 > 2, 2 # 0[# 1 – # 0[# 1 – 2]], 1] & /@ Range [50] is an example of short code that's seriously challenging to understand...

47 | Debugging Your Code

Even the most experienced programmers have to spend time debugging their code. It's an inevitable part of programming. But in the Wolfram Language it's particularly easy, especially if you follow a few principles.

The first and most important principle is to try out any piece of code you write. Because the Wolfram Language is interactive—and symbolic—you can always instantly do this. So even if you just make a tiny change, run your code again, and see if your test examples still work. If they don't, fix the code before you go on.

The Wolfram Language can sometimes tell as soon as you type something in that it's likely to be wrong—and then it'll color it red.

A piece of code with various problems, indicated with red:

```
WordCloud[Nest[Join[♯, Length[ ]+Reverse[♯, 1, 2]] &, {0}, m], Spacings → 0]
```

Once you run a piece of code, the Wolfram Language can also often tell if things have gone obviously wrong—in which case it'll display a message. The code here ends up, for example, asking for the first element of a length-0 list.

Something is obviously wrong when First is applied to the {} that's produced by Cases:

In[1]:= **First[Cases[{1, 2, 3, 4}, 777]]**

··· First: {} has zero length and no first element.

Out[1]= **First[{}]**

Sometimes the Wolfram Language may not know what to do with something, but it may not be sure there's a problem. In such cases, it'll just leave the input unchanged and return it in a symbolic form that can later get a definite value.

Without values for a, b and c, the Wolfram Language just returns this unchanged:

In[2]:= **Graph[{a, b, c}]**

Out[2]= Graph[{a, b, c}]

If you generate graphics with symbolic pieces that can't be rendered, you'll get a pink box:

In[3]:= **Graphics[{Circle[{0, 0}], Disk[{a, b}]}]**

Out[3]=

As you build up functions, it's quite common to have fragments of code that you want to test without finishing the function. You can do this by setting values of variables using With—which works like Module, except it doesn't allow values to be reset.

Use With to temporarily set m = 4 to test a fragment of code:

In[4]:= **With[{m = 4}, Nest[Join[#, Length[#] + Reverse[#]] &, {0}, m]]**

Out[4]= {0, 1, 3, 2, 6, 7, 5, 4, 12, 13, 15, 14, 10, 11, 9, 8}

When debugging takes a long time it's usually because one's made the wrong assumption about what one's code is doing. And in my experience, the best way to overcome this is just to systematically analyze how the code behaves, making tables of results, generating visualizations, testing out assertions and so on.

Make plots to see what the code is doing:

In[5]:= **ListLinePlot /@ Table[Nest[Join[#, Length[#] + Reverse[#]] &, {0}, m], {m, 6}]**

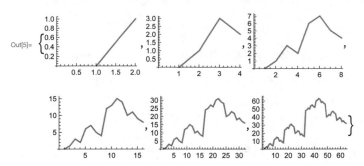

If this code is working correctly, the result should contain every number from 0 to 2^m − 1:

In[6]:= **Sort[With[{m = 4}, Nest[Join[#, Length[#] + Reverse[#]] &, {0}, m]]]**

Out[6]= {0, 1, 2, 3, 4, 5, 6, 7, 8, 9, 10, 11, 12, 13, 14, 15}

Systematically check this up to m = 10:

In[7]:= **Table[**
        Sort[Nest[Join[#, Length[#] + Reverse[#]] &, {0}, m]] == Range[0, 2^m − 1], {m, 10}]

Out[7]= {True, True, True, True, True, True, True, True, True, True}

Sometimes it's not sufficient just to see the final result of a piece of code; you need to see what's going on inside as well. You can insert the function Echo anywhere to print intermediate results or values from your code.

Echo prints values, but does not interfere with the result:

In[8]:= **Table[Echo[n] ^ 2, {n, 3}]**

» 1

» 2

» 3

Out[8]= {1, 4, 9}

If you're running a long computation, you can monitor its progress using Monitor.

Continuously show (with a frame) the value of n reached so far:

In[9]:= **Monitor[Table[PrimeQ[2 ^ 2 ^ n + 1], {n, 15}], Framed[n]]**

> 11 12 13 14 15

Out[9]= {True, True, True, True, False, False, False, False, False, False, False, False, False, False, False}

Echo and Monitor just display things. If you want to actually capture intermediate results, you can do it using Sow and Reap.

Reap gives the final result together with a list of everything that was sown by Sow:

In[10]:= **Reap[Total[Table[Sow[n], {n, 5}]]]**

Out[10]= {15, {{1, 2, 3, 4, 5}}}

This sows successive values of Length[#], and reaps the results:

In[11]:= **Last[Reap[Nest[Join[#, Sow[Length[#]] + Reverse[#]] &, {0}, 10]]]**

Out[11]= {{1, 2, 4, 8, 16, 32, 64, 128, 256, 512}}

Vocabulary

With[{x = *value*}, *expr*]	compute *expr* with *x* replaced by *value*
Echo[*expr*]	display and return the value of *expr*
Monitor[*expr*, *obj*]	continually display *obj* during a computation
Sow[*expr*]	sow the value of *expr* for subsequent reaping
Reap[*expr*]	collect values sowed while *expr* is being computed

---

Exercises

47.1 Correct the program Counts[StringTake[#, 2] & /@ WordList[]] for counting possible first two letters in words.

47.2 Use Sow and Reap to find intermediate values of #1 in Fold[10 #1 + #2 &, {1, 2, 3, 4, 5}].

47.3 Use Sow and Reap to get a list of all cases where #/2 is used in Nest[If[EvenQ[#], #/2, 3 # + 1] &, 1000, 20].

Q&A

Can I cause a problem by just trying to run a piece of code?

Not unless your code is for example set up to delete something. The Wolfram Language has protections against "obviously wrong" infinite loops and so on. If something is taking too long, you can always abort it. If you're really concerned about resources, use TimeConstrained and MemoryConstrained.

Is there a most common type of bug in Wolfram Language code?

Not really. The design of the language makes all sorts of bugs that are common in other programming languages rare. For example, "off by one" errors are common in languages where you're always explicitly manipulating loop variables, but are rare when you're using Wolfram Language "whole-list" functions like Table.

If I can't figure out what's going on, is it worth just trying random things?

If you think you're close, it's often not crazy to try making small random changes to code to see what happens. Since in the Wolfram Language simpler code is usually more likely to be correct, it's not uncommon to hit the code you want by a small amount of random searching.

Is there a way to do interactive step-by-step debugging in the Wolfram Language?

Yes (at least with a native desktop interface)—though it's rarely used. Given the structure of the Wolfram Language, systematically capturing and analyzing intermediate results is almost always a better approach.

How can I tell what's wrong when a piece of graphics is "pinked"?

Hover over it and you'll see the underlying symbolic expression. Or press the + to print messages.

What is the code that makes the fractal-like graphics doing?

It's making a *Gray code*—an ordering of integers so that only one binary digit changes at each step.

Tech Notes

- For large-scale software development, the Wolfram Language has a built-in framework for creating and running systematic tests, with functions like VerificationTest and TestReport.
- A major goal of good language design is to encourage people to write correct code.

More to Explore

Guide to Debugging in the Wolfram Language (wolfr.am/eiwl-47-more)

What We Haven't Discussed

There's a lot more to the Wolfram Language than we've been able to cover in this book. Here's a sampling of just a few of the many topics and areas that we've missed.

User Interface Construction

Set up a tabbed interface:

In[1]:= **TabView[Table[ListPlot[Range[20] ^ n], {n, 5}]]**

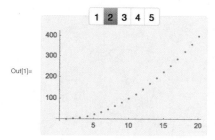

Out[1]=

User interfaces are just another type of symbolic expression; make a grid of sliders:

In[2]:= **Grid[Table[Slider[], 4, 3]]**

Out[2]=

Function Visualization

Plot a function:

In[3]:= **Plot[Sin[x] + Sin[Sqrt[2] x], {x, 0, 20}]**

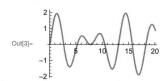

Out[3]=

3D contour plot:

In[4]:= **ContourPlot3D[x^3 + y^2 − z^2, {x, −2, 2}, {y, −2, 2}, {z, −2, 2}]**

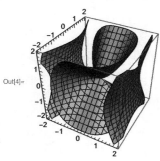

Out[4]=

Mathematical Computation

Do symbolic computations, with x as an algebraic variable:

In[5]:= **Factor[x^10−1]**

Out[5]= $\left(-1+x\right)\left(1+x\right)\left(1-x+x^2-x^3+x^4\right)\left(1+x+x^2+x^3+x^4\right)$

Get symbolic solutions to equations:

In[6]:= **Solve[x^3−2 x+1 == 0, x]**

Out[6]= $\left\{\{x\to 1\},\left\{x\to\frac{1}{2}\left(-1-\sqrt{5}\right)\right\},\left\{x\to\frac{1}{2}\left(-1+\sqrt{5}\right)\right\}\right\}$

Do calculus symbolically:

In[7]:= **Integrate[Sqrt[x+Sqrt[x]], x]**

Out[7]= $\frac{1}{12}\sqrt{\sqrt{x}+x}\left(-3+2\sqrt{x}+8x\right)+\frac{1}{8}\text{Log}\left[1+2\sqrt{x}+2\sqrt{\sqrt{x}+x}\right]$

Display results in traditional mathematical form:

In[8]:= **Integrate[AiryAi[x], x] // TraditionalForm**

Out[8]//TraditionalForm=

$$-\frac{x\left(\sqrt[3]{3}\ x\,\Gamma\!\left(\frac{2}{3}\right)^2\,{}_1F_2\!\left(\frac{2}{3};\frac{4}{3},\frac{5}{3};\frac{x^3}{9}\right)-3\,\Gamma\!\left(\frac{1}{3}\right)\Gamma\!\left(\frac{5}{3}\right){}_1F_2\!\left(\frac{1}{3};\frac{2}{3},\frac{4}{3};\frac{x^3}{9}\right)\right)}{9\times 3^{2/3}\,\Gamma\!\left(\frac{2}{3}\right)\Gamma\!\left(\frac{4}{3}\right)\Gamma\!\left(\frac{5}{3}\right)}$$

Use 2D notation for input:

In[9]:= $\displaystyle\sum_{i=0}^{n}\frac{\textbf{Binomial[n, i] i!}}{\textbf{(n+1+i)!}}$

Out[9]= $\dfrac{\sqrt{\pi}}{2\left(\frac{1}{2}(1+2 n)\right)!}$

Numerics

Minimize a function inside a spherical ball:

In[10]:= **NMinimize[{x^4+y^4−z/(x+1), y > 0}, {x, y, z} ∈ Ball[ ]]**

Out[10]= {−7.34516, {x → −0.971029, y → 0.0139884, z → 0.238555}}

Solve a differential equation to get an approximate function:

In[11]:= **NDSolve[{y''[x] + Sin[y[x]] y[x] == 0, y[0] == 1, y'[0] == 0}, y, {x, 0, 30}]**

Out[11]=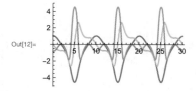

Make a plot using the approximate function:

In[12]:= **Plot[Evaluate[{y[x], y'[x], y''[x]} /. %], {x, 0, 30}]**

Out[12]=

Geometry

The area of a disk (filled circle) of radius r:

In[13]:= **Area[Disk[{0, 0}, r]]**

Out[13]= πr^2

Make a shape by "shrinkwrapping" around 100 random points in 3D:

In[14]:= **ConvexHullMesh[RandomReal[1, {100, 3}]]**

Out[14]=

Algorithms

Find the shortest tour of the capitals of Europe (*traveling salesman problem*):

In[15]:= **With[{c = ▤ europe capital cities coordinates },**
    GeoListPlot[c[[Last@FindShortestTour[c]]], Joined → True]]

Out[15]=

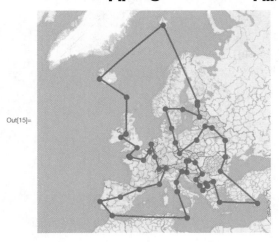

Factor a big number:

In[16]:= **FactorInteger[2^255 − 1]**

Out[16]= {{7, 1}, {31, 1}, {103, 1}, {151, 1}, {2143, 1}, {11 119, 1}, {106 591, 1}, {131 071, 1},
    {949 111, 1}, {9 520 972 806 333 758 431, 1}, {5 702 451 577 639 775 545 838 643 151, 1}}

Logic

Make a truth table:

In[17]:= **BooleanTable[p || q && (p || ! q), {p}, {q}] // Grid**

Out[17]=
True   True
False   False

Find a minimal representation of a Boolean function:

In[18]:= **BooleanMinimize[BooleanCountingFunction[{2, 3}, {a, b, c, d}]] // TraditionalForm**

Out[18]//TraditionalForm= $(a \wedge b \wedge \neg d) \vee (a \wedge \neg b \wedge c) \vee (a \wedge \neg c \wedge d) \vee (\neg a \wedge b \wedge d) \vee (b \wedge c \wedge \neg d) \vee (\neg b \wedge c \wedge d)$

The Computational Universe

Run my favorite example of a very simple program with very complex behavior:

In[19]:= **ArrayPlot[CellularAutomaton[30, {{1}, 0}, 200]]**

Out[19]=

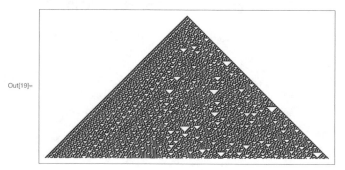

RulePlot shows the underlying rule:

In[20]:= **RulePlot[CellularAutomaton[30]]**

Out[20]=

Building APIs

Deploy a simple web API that finds the distance from a specified location:

In[21]:= **CloudDeploy[APIFunction[{"loc" → "Location"}, GeoDistance[⌗loc, Here] &]]**

Out[21]= CloudObject[https://www.wolframcloud.com/objects/0850dc98−e7d7−4fa6−884b−642ce545d3c3]

Create embeddable code for an external Java program to call the API:

In[22]:= **EmbedCode[%, "Java"]**

Out[22]=

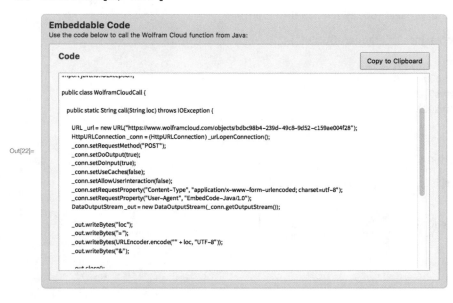

Document Generation

Documents are symbolic expressions, like everything else:

In[23]:= **DocumentNotebook[**
    {Style["A Circle", "Section"], Style["How to make a circle"], Graphics[Circle[ ]]}]

Out[23]=

Evaluation Control

Hold a computation unevaluated:

In[24]:= **Hold[2 + 2 == 4]**

Out[24]= Hold[2 + 2 == 4]

Release the hold:

In[25]:= **ReleaseHold[%]**

Out[25]= True

Systems-Level Operations

Run an external process (not allowed in the cloud!):

In[26]:= **RunProcess["ps", "StandardOutput"]**

Out[26]=
```
 PID TTY        TIME CMD
   374 ttys000   0:00.03 –tcsh
 40192 ttys000   0:00.66 ssh pi
 60521 ttys001   0:00.03 –tcsh
```

Encrypt anything:

In[27]:= **Encrypt["sEcreTkey", "Read this if you can!"]**

Out[27]= EncryptedObject[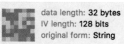]

Parallel Computation

I'm running on a 12-core machine:

In[28]:= **\$ProcessorCount**

Out[28]= 12

Sequentially test a sequence of (big) numbers for primality, and find the total time taken:

In[29]:= **Table[PrimeQ[2 ^ Prime[n] – 1], {n, 500}] // Counts // AbsoluteTiming**

Out[29]= {4.15402, <| True → 18, False → 482 |>}

Doing the same thing in parallel takes considerably less time:

In[30]:= **ParallelTable[PrimeQ[2 ^ Prime[n] – 1], {n, 500}] // Counts // AbsoluteTiming**

Out[30]= {0.572106, <| True → 18, False → 482 |>}

Afterword: Being a Programmer

If you've understood what's in this book, and can do its exercises, then you can now consider yourself a Wolfram Language programmer! There'll always be more you can learn, but you're ready to start using what you know to do real programming.

What can you do? An amazing amount! In fact, there'll probably be something you want to program every day. With a traditional computer language it'd take too long to actually do it, though. But with the Wolfram Language—with all its built-in knowledge and automation—anyone who knows the language can write very useful programs even in a matter of minutes.

And this means you'll routinely be able to write programs for all sorts of things. Things you want to understand, things you want to create, things you want to do for other people. Sometimes you'll dash off a program, run it once and never use it again. But much more often you'll end up using your program many times—and maybe progressively making it more and more sophisticated over time.

For everyday programming, it's normally best to write Wolfram Language programs directly in Wolfram Notebooks, that let you—like in this book—mix results and textual explanations along with code. After a while, you'll probably end up with lots of Wolfram Notebooks, that do lots of different things.

Quite often you'll just run your programs in those notebooks. But you'll also often want to deploy the programs to create websites, apps or whatever. And one of the great things about the Wolfram Language is that this is easy to do.

There's nothing to say that with a few well-chosen lines of Wolfram Language you might not be able to create something like a website that many people will want to use. But more often you'll find there are all sorts of extra details you want to cover, and you'll end up writing a significantly longer program to handle all of them.

In many ways, there's nothing different about a longer Wolfram Language program. Even if there are millions of lines of code (as, for example, in Wolfram|Alpha), they locally all look pretty much like the code in this book; just a lot more of it.

In any programming project, however, there are some new issues that come up when programs get larger. You need to be sure to maintain systematic tests (which in the Wolfram Language you can do using VerificationTest). You need to organize code into properly separated packages. And particularly if multiple programmers are involved, you need version control, code reviews and other management structures.

But beyond that, you need good overall design and architecture. How will users—and programmers—understand your system? What structures will you use to represent whatever you're dealing with? How will different parts of your code interact? These are the kinds of things people in charge of building large software systems need to think about, and it can take considerable skill and experience to get them right.

But what if you're just getting started? What does it take to create the kinds of programs you need to do things? The first step in creating a program for something is to see how to think about the thing in computational terms.

It might be something where computers have long been used. It might be something that's only now conceivable for computers as a result of the Wolfram Language. Whatever it is, try to imagine a Wolfram Language function for doing it.

What input would the function get? What output would it generate? What might the function be called? Don't at first think about how you'd write the code. Just think about what the function should do. And only after you've understood that, start writing the code.

Look in this book and on the Wolfram Language website for examples that are similar to what you're trying to do. If you're lucky, you'll get everything you need. But maybe there'll be some part that it's just not clear how to achieve. And if that happens, it's often good to imagine how you'd explain what's needed to someone with infinite technical capability. Often just doing that will lead you to identify at least some definite tasks—which you can then start formulating in the Wolfram Language.

A great feature of the Wolfram Language is that it's always easy to do experiments with. You can try all sorts of things, and see what works. It's always worthwhile to be as systematic in your explorations as you can. And to recognize that in the Wolfram Language it's usually less about writing lots of code than about understanding how best to think about what you want in computational terms.

It's extremely satisfying to take an idea and turn it into a working program. It's also a powerful and valuable thing to be able to do. And with the Wolfram Language there are now remarkable opportunities to build programs far beyond anything possible before—and to make advances in many areas. And with what you've learned in this book, you should now be in a position to be part of that.

Answers to Exercises

Note: Almost all the exercises have many possible correct answers; what's listed here are merely sample correct answers.

1 | Starting Out: Elementary Arithmetic

1.1   `1 + 2 + 3`

1.2   `1 + 2 + 3 + 4 + 5`

1.3   `1 * 2 * 3 * 4 * 5`

1.4   `5^2`

1.5   `3^4`

1.6   `10^12`

1.7   `3^(7 * 8)`

1.8   `(4 − 2) * (3 + 4)`

1.9   `29 000 * 73`

2 | Introducing Functions

2.1   `Plus[7, 6, 5]`

2.2   `Times[2, Plus[3, 4]]`

2.3   `Max[6 * 8, 5 * 9]`

2.4   `RandomInteger[1000]`

2.5   `10 + RandomInteger[10]`

3 | First Look at Lists

3.1   `Range[4]`

3.2   `Range[100]`

3.3   `Reverse[Range[4]]`

3.4   `Reverse[Range[50]]`

3.5   `Join[Range[4], Reverse[Range[4]]]`

3.6   `ListPlot[Join[Range[100], Reverse[Range[99]]]]`

3.7   `Range[RandomInteger[10]]`

3.8   `Range[10]`

3.9   `Range[5]`

3.10 `Join[Range[10], Range[10], Range[5]]`

3.11 `Join[Range[20], Reverse[Range[20]]]`

4 | Displaying Lists

4.1   `BarChart[{1, 1, 2, 3, 5}]`

4.2   `PieChart[Range[10]]`

4.3   `BarChart[Reverse[Range[20]]]`

4.4   `Column[Range[5]]`

4.5   `NumberLinePlot[{1, 4, 9, 16, 25}]`

4.6   `PieChart[Table[1, 10]]`

4.7   `Column[{PieChart[{1}], PieChart[{1, 1}], PieChart[{1, 1, 1}]}]`

5 | Operations on Lists

5.1   `Reverse[Range[10]^2]`

5.2   `Total[Range[10]^2]`

5.3   `ListPlot[Range[10]^2]`

5.4   `Sort[Join[Range[4], Range[4]]]`

5.5   `9 + Range[11]`

5.6   `Sort[Join[Range[5]^2, Range[5]^3]]`

5.7   `Length[IntegerDigits[2^128]]`

5.8   `First[IntegerDigits[2^32]]`

5.9   `Take[IntegerDigits[2^100], 10]`

5.10 `Max[IntegerDigits[2^20]]`

5.11 `Count[IntegerDigits[2^1000], 0]`

5.12 `Part[Sort[IntegerDigits[2^20]], 2]`

5.13 `ListLinePlot[IntegerDigits[2^128]]`

5.14 `Take[Drop[Range[100], 10], 10]`

6 | Making Tables

6.1   `Table[1000, 5]`

6.2   `Table[n^3, {n, 10, 20}]`

6.3   `NumberLinePlot[Table[n^2, {n, 20}]]`

6.4   `Range[2, 20, 2]`

6.5   `Table[n, {n, 10}]`

6.6   `BarChart[Table[n^2, {n, 10}]]`

6.7   `Table[IntegerDigits[n^2], {n, 10}]`

6.8   `ListLinePlot[Table[Length[IntegerDigits[n^2]], {n, 100}]]`

6.9   `Table[First[IntegerDigits[n^2]], {n, 20}]`

6.10 `ListLinePlot[Table[First[IntegerDigits[n^2]], {n, 100}]]`

7 | Colors and Styles

7.1   `{Red, Yellow, Green}`

7.2   `Column[{Red, Yellow, Green}]`

7.3   `ColorNegate[Orange]`

7.4   `Table[Hue[h], {h, 0, 1, 0.02}]`

7.5   `Table[RGBColor[1, g, 1], {g, 0, 1, 0.05}]`

7.6   `Blend[{Pink, Yellow}]`

7.7   `Table[Blend[{Yellow, Hue[x]}], {x, 0, 1, .05}]`

7.8   `Table[Style[n, Hue[n]], {n, 0, 1, .1}]`

7.9   `Style[Purple, 100]`

7.10 `Table[Style[Red, x], {x, 10, 100, 10}]`

7.11 `Style[999, Red, 100]`

7.12 `Table[Style[n^2, n^2], {n, 10}]`

7.13 `Table[Part[{Red, Yellow, Green}, RandomInteger[2] + 1], 100]`

7.14 `Table[Style[Part[IntegerDigits[2^1000], n], 3 * Part[IntegerDigits[2^1000], n]], {n, 50}]`

8 | Basic Graphics Objects

8.1   `Graphics[RegularPolygon[3]]`

8.2   `Graphics[Style[Circle[], Red]]`

8.3   `Graphics[Style[RegularPolygon[8], Red]]`

8.4   `Table[Graphics[Style[Disk[], Hue[h]]], {h, 0, 1, 0.1}]`

8.5 Column[{Graphics[Style[RegularPolygon[3], Red]], Graphics[Style[RegularPolygon[3], Green]]}]

8.6 Table[Graphics[Style[RegularPolygon[n], Pink]], {n, 5, 10}]

8.7 Graphics3D[Style[Cylinder[], Purple]]

8.8 Graphics[Reverse[Table[Style[RegularPolygon[n], RandomColor[]], {n, 3, 8}]]]

9 | Interactive Manipulation

9.1 Manipulate[Range[n], {n, 0, 100}]

9.2 Manipulate[ListPlot[Range[n]], {n, 5, 50, 1}]

9.3 Manipulate[Column[Table[x, n]], {n, 1, 10, 1}]

9.4 Manipulate[Graphics[Style[Disk[], Hue[h]]], {h, 0, 1}]

9.5 Manipulate[Graphics[Style[Disk[], RGBColor[red, green, blue]]], {red, 0, 1}, {green, 0, 1}, {blue, 0, 1}]

9.6 Manipulate[IntegerDigits[n], {n, 1000, 9999, 1}]

9.7 Manipulate[Table[Hue[h], {h, 0, 1, 1 / n}], {n, 5, 50, 1}]

9.8 Manipulate[Table[Graphics[Style[RegularPolygon[6], Hue[h]]], n], {n, 1, 10, 1}, {h, 0, 1}]

9.9 Manipulate[Graphics[Style[RegularPolygon[n], color]], {n, 5, 20, 1}, {color, {Red, Yellow, Blue}}]

9.10 Manipulate[PieChart[Table[1, n]], {n, 1, 10, 1}]

9.11 Manipulate[BarChart[IntegerDigits[n]], {n, 100, 999, 1}]

9.12 Manipulate[Table[RandomColor[], n], {n, 1, 50, 1}]

9.13 Manipulate[Column[Table[a^m, {m, n}]], {n, 1, 10, 1}, {a, 1, 25, 1}]

9.14 Manipulate[NumberLinePlot[Table[x^n, {x, 10}]], {n, 0, 5}]

9.15 Manipulate[Graphics3D[Style[Sphere[], RGBColor[n, 1 − n, 0]]], {n, 0, 1}]

10 | Images

10.1 ColorNegate[EdgeDetect[🖼]]

10.2 Manipulate[Blur[🖼, r], {r, 0, 20}]

10.3 Table[EdgeDetect[Blur[🖼, n]], {n, 10}]

10.4 ImageCollage[{🖼, Blur[🖼], EdgeDetect[🖼], Binarize[🖼]}]

10.5 ImageAdd[🖼, Binarize[🖼]]

10.6 Manipulate[EdgeDetect[Blur[🖼, r]], {r, 0, 20}]

10.7 EdgeDetect[Graphics3D[Sphere[]]]

10.8 Manipulate[Blur[Graphics[Style[RegularPolygon[5], Purple]], r], {r, 0, 20}]

10.9 ImageCollage[Table[Graphics[Style[Disk[], RandomColor[]]], 9]]

10.10 ImageCollage[Table[Graphics3D[Style[Sphere[], Hue[h]]], {h, 0, 1, 0.2}]]

10.11 Table[Blur[Graphics[Disk[]], n], {n, 0, 30, 5}]

10.12 ImageAdd[Graphics[Disk[]], 🖼]

10.13 ImageAdd[Graphics[Style[RegularPolygon[8], Red]], 🖼]

10.14 ImageAdd[🖼, ColorNegate[EdgeDetect[🖼]]]

11 | Strings and Text

11.1 StringJoin["Hello", "Hello"]

11.2 ToUpperCase[StringJoin[Alphabet[]]]

11.3 StringReverse[StringJoin[Alphabet[]]]

11.4 StringJoin[Table["AGCT", 100]]

11.5 StringTake[StringJoin[Alphabet[]], 6]

11.6 Column[Table[StringTake["this is about strings", n], {n, StringLength["this is about strings"]}]]

11.7 BarChart[StringLength[TextWords["A long time ago, in a galaxy far, far away"]]]

11.8 StringLength[WikipediaData["computer"]]

11.9 Length[TextWords[WikipediaData["computer"]]]

11.10 First[TextSentences[WikipediaData["strings"]]]

11.11 StringJoin[StringTake[TextSentences[WikipediaData["computers"]], 1]]

11.12 Max[StringLength[WordList[]]]

11.13 Count[StringTake[WordList[], 1], "q"]

11.14 ListLinePlot[Take[StringLength[WordList[]], 1000]]

11.15 WordCloud[Characters[StringJoin[WordList[]]]]

11.16 WordCloud[StringTake[StringReverse[WordList[]], 1]]

11.17 RomanNumeral[1959]

11.18 Max[StringLength[RomanNumeral[Range[2020]]]]

11.19 WordCloud[Table[StringTake[RomanNumeral[n], 1], {n, 100}]]

11.20 Length[Alphabet["Russian"]]

11.21 ToUpperCase[Alphabet["Greek"]]

11.22 BarChart[LetterNumber[Characters["wolfram"]]]

11.23 StringJoin[FromLetterNumber[Table[RandomInteger[25] + 1, 1000]]]

11.24 Table[StringJoin[FromLetterNumber[Table[RandomInteger[25] + 1, 5]]], 100]

11.25 Transliterate["wolfram", "Greek"]

11.26 Transliterate[Alphabet["Arabic"]]

11.27 ColorNegate[Rasterize[Style["A", 200]]]

11.28 Manipulate[Style[FromLetterNumber[n], 100], {n, 1, Length[Alphabet[]], 1}]

11.29 Manipulate[ColorNegate[EdgeDetect[Rasterize[Style[c, 100]]]], {c, Alphabet[]}]

11.30 Manipulate[Blur[Rasterize[Style["A", 200]], r], {r, 0, 50}]

12 | Sound

12.1 Sound[{SoundNote[0], SoundNote[4], SoundNote[7]}]

12.2 Sound[SoundNote["A", 2, "Cello"]]

12.3 Sound[Table[SoundNote[n, 0.05], {n, 0, 48}]]

12.4 Sound[Reverse[Table[SoundNote[n], {n, 0, 12}]]]

12.5 Sound[Table[SoundNote[12 ∗ n], {n, 0, 4}]]

12.6 Sound[Table[SoundNote[RandomInteger[12], .2, "Trumpet"], 10]]

12.7 Sound[Table[SoundNote[RandomInteger[12], RandomInteger[10] / 10], 10]]

12.8 Sound[Table[SoundNote[Part[IntegerDigits[2^31], n], .1], {n, Length[IntegerDigits[2^31]]}]]

12.9 Sound[Table[SoundNote[Part[Characters["CABBAGE"], n], .3, "Guitar"], {n, 1, 7}]]

12.10 Sound[Table[SoundNote[Part[LetterNumber[Characters["wolfram"]], n], .1], {n, StringLength["wolfram"]}]]

13 | Arrays, or Lists of Lists

13.1 Grid[Table[i * j, {i, 12}, {j, 12}]]

13.2 Grid[Table[RomanNumeral[i * j], {i, 5}, {j, 5}]]

13.3 Grid[Table[RandomColor[], 10, 10]]

13.4 Grid[Table[Style[RandomInteger[10], RandomColor[]], 10, 10]]

13.5 Grid[Table[StringJoin[FromLetterNumber[{i, j}]], {i, 26}, {j, 26}]]

13.6 Grid[{{PieChart[{1, 4, 3, 5, 2}], NumberLinePlot[{1, 4, 3, 5, 2}]}, {ListLinePlot[{1, 4, 3, 5, 2}], BarChart[{1, 4, 3, 5, 2}]}}]

13.7 ArrayPlot[Table[Hue[i * j], {i, 0, 1, .05}, {j, 0, 1, .05}]]

13.8 ArrayPlot[Table[Hue[x / y], {x, 50}, {y, 50}]]

13.9 ArrayPlot[Table[StringLength[RomanNumeral[i * j]], {i, 100}, {j, 100}]]

14 | Coordinates and Graphics

14.1 Graphics[Table[Circle[{0, 0}, r], {r, 5}]]

14.2 Graphics[Table[Style[Circle[{0, 0}, r], RandomColor[]], {r, 10}]]

14.3 Graphics[Table[Circle[{x, y}], {x, 10}, {y, 10}]]

14.4 Graphics[Table[Point[{x, y}], {x, 10}, {y, 10}]]

14.5 Manipulate[Graphics[Table[Circle[{0, 0}, r], {r, n}]], {n, 1, 20, 1}]

14.6 Graphics3D[Table[Style[Sphere[Table[RandomInteger[10], 3]], RandomColor[]], 50]]

14.7 Graphics3D[Table[Style[Sphere[{x, y, z}, 1 / 2], RGBColor[{x / 10, y / 10, z / 10}]], {x, 10}, {y, 10}, {z, 10}]]

14.8 Manipulate[Graphics[Table[Circle[{t x, 0}, x], {x, 10}]], {t, −2, 2}]

14.9 Graphics[Table[RegularPolygon[{x, y}, 1 / 2, 6], {x, 5}, {y, 5}]]

14.10 Graphics3D[Line[Table[RandomInteger[50], 50, 3]]]

16 | Real−World Data

Note: =[ ] represents natural language input 🔲

16.1 = [flag of switzerland]

16.2 = [elephant]["Image"]

16.3 EntityValue[= [planets], "Mass"]

16.4 BarChart[EntityValue[= [planets], "Mass"]]

16.5 ImageCollage[EntityValue[= [planets], "Image"]]

16.6 EdgeDetect[= [China]["Flag"]]

16.7 = [Empire State Building]["Height"]

16.8 = [Empire State Building]["Height"] / = [Great Pyramid]["Height"]

16.9 = [Mount Everest]["Elevation"] / = [Empire State Building]["Height"]

16.10 DominantColors[= [starry night]["Image"]]

16.11 DominantColors[ImageCollage[EntityValue[= [countries in Europe], "FlagImage"]]]

16.12 PieChart[= [countries in Europe]["GDP"]]

16.13 ImageAdd[= [koala]["Image"], = [australia]["Flag"]]

17 | Units

Note: =[ ] represents natural language input 🔲

17.1 UnitConvert[= [4.5 lbs], "Kilograms"]

17.2 UnitConvert[= [60.25 mph], = [km / hr]]

17.3 UnitConvert[= [height of the Eiffel tower], "Miles"]

17.4 = [height of Mount Everest] / = [height of the Eiffel tower]

17.5 = [mass of Earth] / = [mass of moon]

17.6 CurrencyConvert[= [2500 Japanese yen], = [US dollars]]

17.7 UnitConvert[= [35 ounces + 1 / 4 ton + 45 lbs + 9 stone], = [kilograms]]

17.8 UnitConvert[= [planets]["DistanceFromEarth"], "LightMinutes"]

17.9 Rotate["hello", 180 °]

17.10 Table[Rotate[Style["A", 100], n Degree], {n, 0, 360, 30}]

17.11 Manipulate[Rotate[= [cat]["Image"], θ], {θ, 0 °, 180 °}]

17.12 Graphics[Line[AnglePath[Table[n Degree, {n, 0, 180}]]]]

17.13 Manipulate[Graphics[Line[AnglePath[Table[x, 100]]]], {x, 0, 360 °}]

17.14 Graphics[Line[AnglePath[30 ° * IntegerDigits[2^10 000]]]]

18 | Geocomputation

Note: =[ ] represents natural language input 🔲

18.1 GeoDistance[= [new york], = [london]]

18.2 GeoDistance[= [new york], = [london]] / GeoDistance[= [new york], = [san francisco]]

18.3 UnitConvert[GeoDistance[= [sydney], = [moscow]], = [km]]

18.4 GeoGraphics[= [united states]]

18.5 GeoListPlot[{ = [brazil], = [russia], = [india], = [china]}]

18.6 GeoGraphics[GeoPath[{ = [new york], = [beijing]}]]

18.7 GeoGraphics[GeoDisk[= [Great Pyramid], = [10 miles]]]

18.8 GeoGraphics[GeoDisk[= [new york], GeoDistance[= [new york city], = [san francisco]]]]

18.9 GeoNearest["Country", GeoPosition["NorthPole"], 5]

18.10 EntityValue[GeoNearest["Country", GeoPosition[{45, 0}], 3], "Flag"]

18.11 GeoListPlot[GeoNearest["Volcano", = [rome], 25]]

18.12 GeoPosition[= [new york]][[1, 1]] − GeoPosition[= [los angeles]][[1, 1]]

19 | Dates and Times

Note: =[ ] represents natural language input 🔲

19.1 Now − = [january 1, 1900]

19.2 DayName[= [January 1, 2000]]

19.3 Today − = [100 000 days]

19.4 LocalTime[= [delhi]]

19.5 Sunset[Here, Today] − Sunrise[Here, Today]

19.6 MoonPhase[Now, "Icon"]

19.7 Table[MoonPhase[Today + n = [days]], {n, 10}]

19.8 Table[MoonPhase[Today + n = [days], "Icon"], {n, 10}]

19.9 Sunrise[= [new york city], Today] – Sunrise[
     = [london], Today]

19.10 AirTemperatureData[= [eiffel tower],
      = [noon yesterday]]

19.11 DateListPlot[AirTemperatureData[= [eiffel tower],
      {Now – = [1 week], Now}]]

19.12 AirTemperatureData[= [los angeles]] –
      AirTemperatureData[= [new york]]

19.13 DateListPlot[WordFrequencyData["groovy",
      "TimeSeries"]]

20 | Options

Note: =[ ] represents natural language input 🔲

20.1 ListPlot[Range[10], PlotTheme → "Web"]

20.2 ListPlot[Range[10], Filling → Axis]

20.3 ListPlot[Range[10], Background → Yellow]

20.4 GeoListPlot[= [australia], GeoRange → All]

20.5 GeoListPlot[= [madagascar],
      GeoRange → = [indian ocean]]

20.6 GeoGraphics[= [south america],
      GeoBackground → "ReliefMap"]

20.7 GeoListPlot[{ = [france], = [finland], = [greece]},
      GeoRange → = [Europe], GeoLabels → Automatic]

20.8 Grid[Table[Style[i * j, White], {i, 12}, {j, 12}],
      Background → Black]

20.9 Table[Graphics[Disk[],
      ImageSize → RandomInteger[40]], 100]

20.10 Table[Graphics[RegularPolygon[5], ImageSize → 30,
      AspectRatio → n], {n, 1, 10}]

20.11 Manipulate[Graphics[Circle[], ImageSize → s],
      {s, 5, 500}]

20.12 Grid[Table[RandomColor[], 10, 10], Frame → All]

20.13 ListLinePlot[Table[StringLength[
      RomanNumeral[n]], {n, 100}], PlotRange → Max[
      Table[StringLength[RomanNumeral[n]], {n, 1000}]]]

21 | Graphs and Networks

21.1 Graph[{1 → 2, 2 → 3, 3 → 1}]

21.2 Graph[Flatten[Table[i → j, {i, 4}, {j, 4}]]]

21.3 Table[UndirectedGraph[Flatten[
      Table[i → j, {i, n}, {j, n}]]], {n, 2, 10}]

21.4 Flatten[Table[{1, 2}, 3]]

21.5 ListLinePlot[Flatten[Table[IntegerDigits[n], {n, 100}]]]

21.6 Graph[Table[i → i + 1, {i, 50}]]

21.7 Graph[Flatten[Table[i → Max[i, j], {i, 4}, {j, 4}]]]

21.8 Graph[Flatten[Table[i → j – i, {i, 5}, {j, 5}]]]

21.9 Graph[Table[i → RandomInteger[{1, 100}], {i, 100}]]

21.10 Graph[Flatten[Table[{i → RandomInteger[{1, 100}],
      i → RandomInteger[{1, 100}]}, {i, 100}]]]

21.11 Grid[Table[FindShortestPath[
      Graph[{1 → 2, 2 → 3, 3 → 4, 4 → 1, 3 → 1, 2 → 2}],
      i, j], {i, 4}, {j, 4}]]

22 | Machine Learning

Note: =[ ] represents natural language input 🔲

22.1 LanguageIdentify["ajatella"]

22.2 ImageIdentify[= [image of a tiger]]

22.3 Table[ImageIdentify[
      Blur[= [image of a tiger], r]], {r, 5}]

22.4 Classify["Sentiment", "I'm so happy to be here"]

22.5 Nearest[WordList[], "happy", 10]

22.6 Nearest[RandomInteger[1000, 20], 100, 3]

22.7 Nearest[Table[RandomColor[], 10], Red, 5]

22.8 First[Nearest[Table[n^2, {n, 100}], 2000]]

22.9 Nearest[= [european flags], = [flag of brazil], 3]

22.10 NearestNeighborGraph[Table[Hue[h], {h, 0, 1, .05}],
      2, VertexLabels → All]

22.11 NearestNeighborGraph[Table[
      RandomInteger[100], 40], 2, VertexLabels → All]

22.12 FindClusters[= [flags of Asia]]

22.13 NearestNeighborGraph[Table[Rasterize[Style[
      FromLetterNumber[n], 20]], {n, 26}], 2,
      VertexLabels → All]

22.14 Table[TextRecognize[Blur[Rasterize[
      Style["hello", 50]], n]], {n, 10}]

22.15 Dendrogram[Table[Rasterize[
      FromLetterNumber[n]], {n, 10}]]

22.16 FeatureSpacePlot[Table[Rasterize[
      ToUpperCase[FromLetterNumber[n]]], {n, 26}]]

23 | More about Numbers

23.1 N[Sqrt[2], 500]

23.2 RandomReal[1, 10]

23.3 ListPlot[Table[RandomReal[1, 2], 200]]

23.4 Graphics[Line[AnglePath[RandomReal[2 Pi, 1000]]]]

23.5 Table[Mod[n^2, 10], {n, 0, 30}]

23.6 ListLinePlot[Table[Mod[n^n, 10], {n, 100}]]

23.7 Table[Round[Pi^n], {n, 10}]

23.8 Graph[Table[n → Mod[n^2, 100], {n, 0, 99}]]

23.9 Graphics[Table[Style[Circle[RandomReal[10, 2],
      RandomReal[2]], RandomColor[]], 50]]

23.10 ListPlot[Table[Prime[n] / (n Log[n]), {n, 2, 1000}]]

23.11 ListLinePlot[Table[Prime[n + 1] – Prime[n], {n, 100}]]

23.12 Sound[Table[SoundNote["C", RandomReal[0.5]], 20]]

23.13 ArrayPlot[Table[Mod[i, j], {i, 50}, {j, 50}]]

23.14 Table[ArrayPlot[Table[
      Mod[x^y, n], {x, 50}, {y, 50}]], {n, 2, 10}]

24 | More Forms of Visualization

Note: =[ ] represents natural language input 🔲

24.1 ListLinePlot[Table[n^p, {p, 2, 4}, {n, 10}]]

24.2 ListLinePlot[Table[Prime[n], {n, 20}], Filling → Axis,
      Mesh → True, MeshStyle → Red]

24.3 ListPlot3D[GeoElevationData[GeoDisk[= [mount fuji] ,
       = [20 miles]]]]

24.4 ReliefPlot[GeoElevationData[GeoDisk[= [mount fuji] ,
       = [100 miles]]]]

24.5 ListPlot3D[Table[Mod[i, j], {i, 100}, {j, 100}]]

24.6 Histogram[Table[Prime[n + 1] – Prime[n], {n, 10 000}]]

24.7 Histogram[Table[First[IntegerDigits[n^2]], {n, 10 000}]]

24.8 Histogram[Table[StringLength[
      RomanNumeral[n]], {n, 1000}]]

24.9 Histogram[StringLength[TextSentences[
      WikipediaData["computers"]]]]

24.10   Table[Histogram[Table[Total[
           RandomReal[100, n]], 10 000]], {n, 5}]

24.11   ListPlot3D[1 − ImageData[Binarize[
           Rasterize[Style["W", 200]]]]]

25 | Ways to Apply Functions

Note: =[ ] represents natural language input 🔘

25.1   f /@ Range[5]

25.2   f /@ g /@ Range[10]

25.3   x // d // c // b // a

25.4   Framed /@ Alphabet[]

25.5   ColorNegate /@ EntityValue[= [planets], "Image"]

25.6   GeoGraphics /@ EntityList[= [countries in G5]]

25.7   ImageCollage[Binarize /@ = [flags of europe]]

25.8   Column /@ DominantColors /@ EntityValue[
           = [planets], "Image"]

25.9   Total[LetterNumber /@ Characters["wolfram"]]

26 | Pure Anonymous Functions

Note: =[ ] represents natural language input 🔘

26.1   #^2 & /@ Range[20]

26.2   Blend[{#, Red}] & /@ {Yellow, Green, Blue}

26.3   Framed[Column[{ToUpperCase[#], #}]] & /@ Alphabet[]

26.4   Framed[Style[#, RandomColor[]],
           Background → RandomColor[]] & /@ Alphabet[]

26.5   Grid[{#, EntityValue[#, "Flag"]} & /@ EntityList[
           = [G5 countries]], Frame → All]

26.6   WordCloud[
           WikipediaData[#]] & /@ {"apple", "peach", "pear"}

26.7   Histogram[StringLength[TextWords[WikipediaData[#]]]
           ] & /@ {"apple", "peach", "pear"}

26.8   GeoListPlot[{#}, GeoRange → = [central america]] & /@
           EntityList[= [central america]]

27 | Applying Functions Repeatedly

27.1   NestList[Blur, Rasterize[Style["X", 30]], 10]

27.2   NestList[Framed[#,
           Background → RandomColor[]] &, x, 10]

27.3   NestList[Rotate[Framed[#],
           RandomReal[{0, 360 °}]] &, Style["A", 50], 5]

27.4   ListLinePlot[NestList[4 # (1 − #) &, 0.2, 100]]

27.5   Nest[1 + 1 / # &, 1, 30] // N

27.6   NestList[3 ∗ # &, 1, 10]

27.7   NestList[(# + 2 / #) / 2 &, 1.0, 5] − Sqrt[2]

27.8   Graphics[Line[NestList[# + RandomReal[{−1, 1}, 2] &,
           {0, 0}, 1000]]]

27.9   ArrayPlot[NestList[Mod[
           Join[{0}, #] + Join[#, {0}], 2] &, {1}, 50]]

27.10   NestList[{# + 1, 2 #} &, 0, 10]

27.11   NestGraph[#["BorderingCountries"] &, = [US], 4,
           VertexLabels → All]

28 | Tests and Conditionals

28.1   123^321 > 456^123

28.2   Select[Range[100], Total[IntegerDigits[#]] < 5 &]

28.3   If[PrimeQ[#], Style[#, Red], #] & /@ Range[20]

28.4   Select[WordList[], StringTake[#, 1] == StringTake[
           StringReverse[#], 1] == "p" &]

28.5   Select[Array[Prime, 100], Last[IntegerDigits[#]] < 3 &]

28.6   Select[RomanNumeral[Range[100]], ! MemberQ[
           Characters[#], "I"] &]

28.7   Select[RomanNumeral[Range[1000]],
           # == StringReverse[#] &]

28.8   Select[Table[IntegerName[n], {n, 100}], First[
           Characters[#]] == Last[Characters[#]] &]

28.9   Select[TextWords[WikipediaData["words"]],
           StringLength[#] > 15 &]

28.10   NestList[If[EvenQ[#], # / 2, 3 # + 1] &, 1000, 200]

28.11   WordCloud[Select[TextWords[
           WikipediaData["computers"]],
           StringLength[#] == 5 &]]

28.12   Select[WordList[], StringLength[#] ≥ 3
           && # ≠ StringReverse[#] && StringTake[#, 3] ==
           StringTake[StringReverse[#], 3] &]

28.13   Select[Select[WordList[], StringLength[#] == 10 &],
           Total[LetterNumber /@ Characters[#]] == 100 &]

29 | More about Pure Functions

29.1   Array[Prime, 100]

29.2   Array[Prime[# + 1] − Prime[#] &, 99]

29.3   Grid[Array[Plus, {10, 10}]]

29.4   FoldList[Times, 1, Range[10]]

29.5   FoldList[Times, 1, Array[Prime, 10]]

29.6   FoldList[ImageAdd, Table[Graphics[Style[
           RegularPolygon[n], Opacity[.2]]], {n, 3, 8}]]

30 | Rearranging Lists

Note: =[ ] represents natural language input 🔘

30.1   Thread[Alphabet[] → Range[Length[Alphabet[]]]]

30.2   Grid[Partition[Alphabet[], 6]]

30.3   Grid[Partition[IntegerDigits[2^1000], 50], Frame → All]

30.4   Grid[Partition[Characters[StringTake[
           WikipediaData["computers"], 400]], 20],
           Frame → All]

30.5   ListLinePlot[Flatten[IntegerDigits /@ Range[0, 200]]]

30.6   ArrayPlot /@ NestList[ArrayFlatten[{{#, #, #},
           {#, 0, #}, {#, #, #}}] &, {{1}}, 4]

30.7   Select[Flatten[Table[{x, y, Sqrt[x^2 + y^2]},
           {x, 20}, {y, 20}], 1], IntegerQ[Last[#]] &]

30.8   Table[Max[Length /@ Split[IntegerDigits[2^n]]],
           {n, 100}]

30.9   GatherBy[Array[IntegerName, 100],
           StringTake[#, 1] &]

30.10   SortBy[Take[WordList[], 50], StringTake[
           StringReverse[#], 1] &]

30.11   SortBy[Table[n^2, {n, 20}], First[IntegerDigits[#]] &]

30.12   SortBy[Range[20], StringLength[IntegerName[#]] &]

30.13   GatherBy[RandomSample[WordList[], 20],
           StringLength]

30.14   Complement[Alphabet["Ukrainian"],
           Alphabet["Russian"]]

30.15   Intersection[Range[100]^2, Range[100]^3]

30.16   Intersection[EntityList[= [NATO]], EntityList[= [G8]]]

30.17 Grid[Transpose[Permutations[Range[4]]]]

30.18 Union[StringJoin /@ Permutations[
        Characters["hello"]]]

30.19 ArrayPlot[Tuples[{0, 1}, 5]]

30.20 Table[StringJoin[RandomChoice[Alphabet[], 5]], 10]

30.21 Tuples[{1, 2}, 3]

31 | Parts of Lists

31.1 Take[IntegerDigits[2^1000], −5]

31.2 Alphabet[][[10 ;; 20]]

31.3 Part[Alphabet[], Range[2, Length[Alphabet[]], 2]]

31.4 ListLinePlot[Table[IntegerDigits[12^n][[−2]],
        {n, 100}]]

31.5 TakeSmallest[Join[Table[n^2, {n, 20}],
        Table[n^3, {n, 20}]], 10]

31.6 Flatten[Position[TextWords[
        WikipediaData["computers"]], "software"]]

31.7 Histogram[Flatten[Position[Characters[⌗], "e"] & /@
        WordList[]]]

31.8 ReplacePart[Range[100]^3,
        Thread[Table[n^2, {n, 10}] → Red]]

31.9 If[First[IntegerDigits[⌗]] < 5, Nothing, ⌗] & /@
        Array[Prime, 100]

31.10 Grid[NestList[ReplacePart[⌗, RandomInteger[
        {1, Length[⌗]}] → Nothing] &, Range[10], 9]]

31.11 TakeLargestBy[WordList[], StringLength, 10]

31.12 TakeLargestBy[Array[IntegerName, 100],
        StringLength, 5]

31.13 TakeLargestBy[Array[IntegerName, 100],
        Count[Characters[⌗], "e"] &, 5]

32 | Patterns

32.1 Cases[IntegerDigits[Range[1000]], {1, ___, 9}]

32.2 Cases[IntegerDigits[Range[1000]], {x_, x_, x_}]

32.3 Cases[IntegerDigits[Range[1000]^2], {9, ___, 0 | 1}]

32.4 IntegerDigits[Range[100]] /. {0 → Gray, 9 → Orange}

32.5 IntegerDigits[2^1000] /. 0 → Red

32.6 Characters["The Wolfram Language"] /.
        "a" | "e" | "i" | "o" | "u" → Nothing

32.7 Cases[IntegerDigits[2^1000], 0 | 1]

32.8 Cases[IntegerDigits[Range[100, 999]], {x_, _, x_}]

33 | Expressions and Their Structure

33.1 Head[ListPlot[Range[5]]]

33.2 Times @@ Range[100]

33.3 f @@@ Tuples[{a, b}, 2]

33.4 TreeForm /@ NestList[⌗^⌗ &, x, 4]

33.5 Union[Cases[Flatten[Table[i^2 / (j^2 + 1),
        {i, 20}, {j, 20}]], _Integer]]

33.6 Graph[Rule @@@ Partition[Table[Mod[n^2 + n, 100],
        {n, 100}], 2, 1]]

33.7 Graph[Rule @@@ Partition[TextWords[WikipediaData[
        "computers"], 200], 2, 1], VertexLabels → All]

33.8 f @@@ {{1, 2}, {7, 2}, {5, 4}}

34 | Associations

34.1 Values[KeySort[Counts[IntegerDigits[3^100]]]]

34.2 BarChart[KeySort[Counts[IntegerDigits[2^1000]]],
        ChartLabels → Automatic]

34.3 BarChart[Counts[StringTake[WordList[], 1]],
        ChartLabels → Automatic]

34.4 TakeLargest[Counts[StringTake[WordList[], 1]], 5]

34.5 ⌗q / ⌗u &@LetterCounts[
        WikipediaData["computers"]] // N

34.6 Keys[TakeLargest[Counts[TextWords[ExampleData[
        {"Text", "AliceInWonderland"}]]], 10]]

35 | Natural Language Understanding

Note: =[ ] represents natural language input ▦

35.1 Interpreter["Location"]["eiffel tower"]

35.2 Interpreter["University"]["U of T"]

35.3 Interpreter["Chemical"][{"C2H4", "C2H6", "C3H8"}]

35.4 Interpreter["Date"]["20140108"]

35.5 Cases[Interpreter["University"][StringJoin["U of ",
        ⌗] & /@ ToUpperCase[Alphabet[]]], _Entity]

35.6 Cases[Interpreter["Movie"][CommonName /@
        = [US state capitals]], _Entity]

35.7 Cases[Interpreter["City"][StringJoin /@
        Permutations[{"l", "i", "m", "a"}]], _Entity]

35.8 WordCloud[TextCases[WikipediaData["gunpowder"],
        "Country"]]

35.9 TextCases["She sells seashells by the sea shore.",
        "Noun"]

35.10 Length[TextCases[StringTake[WikipediaData[
        "computers"], 1000], ⌗]] & /@
        {"Noun", "Verb", "Adjective"}

35.11 TextStructure[First[TextSentences[
        WikipediaData["computers"]]]]

35.12 Keys[TakeLargest[Counts[TextCases[
        ExampleData[{"Text", "AliceInWonderland"}],
        "Noun"]], 10]]

35.13 CommunityGraphPlot[First[TextStructure[
        First[TextSentences[WikipediaData["language"]]],
        "ConstituentGraphs"]]]

35.14 Length[WordList[⌗]] & /@
        {"Noun", "Verb", "Adjective", "Adverb"}

35.15 Flatten[Table[WordTranslation[IntegerName[n],
        "French"], {n, 2, 10}]]

36 | Creating Websites and Apps

36.1 CloudDeploy[GeoGraphics[]]

36.2 CloudDeploy[Delayed[GeoGraphics[]]]

36.3 CloudDeploy[Delayed[Style[
        RandomInteger[1000], 100]]]

36.4 CloudDeploy[FormFunction[{"x" → "Number"},
        ⌗x^⌗x &]]

36.5 CloudDeploy[FormFunction[{"x" → "Number",
        "y" → "Number"}, ⌗x^⌗y &]]

36.6 CloudDeploy[FormFunction[{"topic" → "String"},
        WordCloud[WikipediaData[⌗topic]] &]]

36.7 CloudDeploy[FormPage[{"string" → "String"},
        Style[StringReverse[⌗string], 50] &]]

36.8   CloudDeploy[FormPage[{"n" → "Integer"}, Graphics[
          Style[RegularPolygon[#n], RandomColor[]]] &]]

36.9   CloudDeploy[FormPage[{"location" → "Location",
          "n" → "Integer"}, GeoListPlot[
          GeoNearest["Volcano", #location, #n]] &]]

37 | Layout and Display

Note: =[ ] represents natural language input 🔲

37.1   Style[#, Background → If[EvenQ[#], Yellow,
          LightGray]] & /@ Range[100]

37.2   If[PrimeQ[#], Framed[#], #] & /@ Range[100]

37.3   If[PrimeQ[#], Labeled[Framed[#], Style[Mod[#, 4],
          LightGray]], #] & /@ Range[100]

37.4   GraphicsGrid[Table[Graphics[Style[Disk[],
          RandomColor[]]], 3, 6]]

37.5   PieChart[Labeled[#["GDP"], #] & /@
          EntityList[= [G5 countries]]]

37.6   PieChart[Legended[#["Population"], #] & /@
          EntityList[= [G5 countries]]]

37.7   GraphicsGrid[Partition[Table[PieChart[
          Counts[IntegerDigits[2^n]]], {n, 25}], 5]]

37.8   GraphicsRow[WordCloud[DeleteStopwords[
          WikipediaData[#]]] & /@ EntityList[
          = [G5 countries]]]

38 | Assigning Names to Things

Note: =[ ] represents natural language input 🔲

38.1   Module[{x = Range[10]}, x^2 + x]

38.2   Module[{x = RandomInteger[100, 10] },
          Column[{ x, Sort[x], Max[x], Total[x] }]]

38.3   Module[{g = [picture of a giraffe]}, ImageCollage[
          {g, Blur[g], EdgeDetect[g], ColorNegate[g]}]]

38.4   Module[{r = Range[10]}, ListLinePlot[
          Join[r, Reverse[r], r, Reverse[r]]]]

38.5   Module[{x = Range[10]}, {x + 1, x − 1, Reverse[x]}]

38.6   NestList[Mod[17 # + 2, 11] &, 10, 20]

38.7   Table[StringJoin[Module[{v = Characters["aeiou"], c},
          c = Complement[Alphabet[], v];
          RandomChoice /@ {c, v, c, v, c}]], 10]

39 | Immediate and Delayed Values

39.1   {x, x + 1, x + 2, x^2} /. x → RandomInteger[100]

39.2   {x, x + 1, x + 2, x^2} /. x :→ RandomInteger[100]

40 | Defining Your Own Functions

40.1   f[x_] := x^2

40.2   poly[n_Integer] := Graphics[Style[
          RegularPolygon[n], Orange]]

40.3   f[{a_, b_}] := {b, a}

40.4   f[x_, y_] := (x ∗ y) / (x + y)

40.5   f[{a_, b_}] := {a + b, a − b, a / b}

40.6   evenodd[n_Integer] := If[EvenQ[n], Black, White];
          evenodd[0] = Red

40.7   f[1, x_, y_] := x + y; f[2, x_, y_] := x ∗ y;
          f[3, x_, y_] := x^y

40.8   f[0] = f[1] = 1; f[n_Integer] := f[n − 1] + f[n − 2]

40.9   animal[s_String] := Interpreter["Animal"][s]["Image"]

40.10   nearwords[s_String, n_Integer] := Nearest[
          WordList[], s, n]

41 | More about Patterns

41.1   Cases[Table[IntegerDigits[n^2], {n, 100}],
          {___, x_, x_, ___}]

41.2   StringJoin /@ Cases[Array[
          Characters[RomanNumeral[#]] &, 100],
          {___, "L", ___, "I", ___, "X", ___}]

41.3   f[x : {_Integer ..}] := x == Reverse[x]

41.4   Cases[Partition[TextWords[
          WikipediaData["alliteration"]], 2, 1], {a_, b_} /;
          StringTake[a, 1] == StringTake[b, 1]]

41.5   Grid[FixedPointList[(# /. {x___, b_, a_, y___} /; b >
          a → {x, a, b, y}) &, {4, 5, 1, 3, 2}]]

41.6   ArrayPlot[Transpose[FixedPointList[(
          # /. {x___, b_, a_, y___} /; b > a → {x, a, b, y}) &,
          RandomSample[Range[50]]]]]

41.7   FixedPointList[(# + 2 / #) / 2 &, 1.0]

41.8   FixedPointList[# /. {a_, b_} /; b ≠ 0 → {b, Mod[a, b]} &,
          {12 345, 54 321}]

41.9   FixedPointList[# /. {s[x_][y_][z_] → x[z][y[z]],
          k[x_][y_] → x} &, s[s][k][s[s[s]][s]][s]]

41.10   IntegerDigits[100!] /. {x___, 0 ..} → {x}

41.11   Length /@ NestList[# /. {{1, _, x___} → {x, 0, 1},
          {0, _, x___} → {x, 1, 0, 0}} &, {1, 0}, 200]

41.12   ListLinePlot[Length /@ NestList[# /. {
          {0, _, x___} → {x, 2, 1}, {1, _, x___} → {x, 0},
          {2, _, x___} → {x, 0, 2, 1, 2}} &, {0, 0}, 200]]

42 | String Patterns and Templates

Note: =[ ] represents natural language input 🔲

42.1   StringReplace["1 2 3 4", " " → "---"]

42.2   Sort[StringCases[WikipediaData["computers"],
          DigitCharacter ~~ DigitCharacter ~~
          DigitCharacter ~~ DigitCharacter]]

42.3   StringCases[WikipediaData["computers"],
          Shortest["===" ~~ x__ ~~ "==="] → x]

42.4   Grid[Table[StringTemplate["`1`+`2`=`3`"][i, j, i + j],
          {i, 9}, {j, 9}]]

42.5   Select[Table[IntegerName[n], {n, 50}],
          StringMatchQ[#, ___ ~~ "i" ~~ ___ ~~ "e" ~~ ___] &]

42.6   StringReplace[
          First[TextSentences[WikipediaData["computers"]]],
          x : (Whitespace ~~ LetterCharacter ~~
          LetterCharacter ~~ Whitespace) :→ ToUpperCase[x]]

42.7   BarChart[KeySort[Counts[StringTake[
          TextString /@ EntityList[= [countries]], 1]]],
          ChartLabels → Automatic]

42.8   Table[StringTemplate["`1`^`2`=`3`"][i, j, i^j],
          {i, 5}, {j, 5}] // Grid

44 | Importing and Exporting

Note: =[ ] represents natural language input 🔲

44.1   Import["http://google.com", "Images"]

44.2   ImageCollage[Graphics[Style[Disk[], #]] & /@
          (Union @@ DominantColors /@
          Import["http://google.com", "Images"])]

44.3   WordCloud[Import["http://bbc.co.uk"]]

44.4   ImageCollage[Import["http://www.nps.gov",
          "Images"]]

44.5   Select[Import["https://en.wikipedia.org/wiki/Ostrich",
          "Images"], ImageInstanceQ[#, = [bird]] &]

44.6   WordCloud[TextCases[Import["http://www.nato.int/"],
          "Country"]]

44.7   Length[Import["https://en.wikipedia.org/",
       "Hyperlinks"]]

44.8   SendMail[GeoGraphics[Here]]

44.9   SendMail[MoonPhase[Now, "Icon"]]

45 | Datasets

Note: =[ ] represents natural language input ▣⃝

45.1   WordCloud[Normal[planets[All, "Moons", Length]]]

45.2   BarChart[planets[All, "Moons", Length],
       ChartLabels → Automatic]

45.3   planets[SortBy[Length[#Moons] &], "Mass"]

45.4   planets[All, "Moons", Max, "Mass"]

45.5   planets[All, "Moons", Total, "Mass"][Sort]

45.6   planets[All, "Moons", Median, "Mass"]

45.7   planets[All, "Moons", Select[#Mass >
       = [0.0001 earth mass] &] /* Keys]

45.8   WordCloud[Association[# –> StringLength[
       WikipediaData[#]] & /@ EntityList[
       = [central america]]]]

45.9   ResourceData["Fireballs and Bolides"][Max,
       "Altitude"]

45.10 ResourceData["Fireballs and Bolides"][
       TakeLargest[5], "Altitude"]

45.11 Histogram[Differences[Normal[ResourceData[
       "Fireballs and Bolides"][All, "PeakBrightness"]]]]

45.12 GeoListPlot[ResourceData["Fireballs and Bolides"][
       1 ;; 10, "NearestCity"], GeoLabels → True]

45.13 GeoListPlot[ResourceData["Fireballs and Bolides"][
       TakeLargestBy[#Altitude &, 10], "NearestCity"],
       GeoLabels → True]

46 | Writing Good Code

46.1   Total[Table[i * (i + 1), {i, 1000}]]

46.2   Nest[1 / (1 + #) &, x, 10]

46.3   Flatten[Array[List, {10, 10}]]

46.4   ListLinePlot[Table[First[Timing[n^n]], {n, 10 000}]]

46.5   ListLinePlot[Table[First[Timing[Sort[
       RandomSample[Range[n]]]]], {n, 200}]]

47 | Debugging Your Code

47.1   Counts[If[StringLength[#] > 1, StringTake[#, 2],
       Nothing] & /@ WordList[]]

47.2   First[Last[Reap[Fold[10 Sow[#1] + #2 &,
       {1, 2, 3, 4, 5}]]]]

47.3   Last[Reap[Nest[If[EvenQ[#], Sow[#] / 2, 3 # + 1] &,
       1000, 20]]] // First

Index